Early praise for
OpenGL ES 2.0 for Android

Kevin's book is stuffed full of useful code and explanations, to the point of being inspirational. The math/matrix stuff is the best I have ever read on the topic. If you already know Java well and want to break into 3D graphics, this book is perfect.

➤ **John Horton**
HadronWebDesign.com and author of the Android math league app Math Legends

Cuts out the academic fluff and teaches you what you need to become productive quickly. I wish I had access to such a clear, concise, and humorous book when I first learned OpenGL.

➤ **Mark F. Guerra**
Developer, GLWallpaperService library for OpenGL

An amazing introduction to Android graphics programming, covering all the topics that give headaches to OpenGL beginners with such extensive detail that you'll be perfectly prepared to implement your own ideas.

➤ **Carsten Haubold**
Maintainer, NeHe OpenGL tutorials

I wish I had this book when I first started programming Android games. It's well written and up-to-date.

➤ **Owen Alanzo Hogarth**
President, Team Blubee, Inc.

I am greatly impressed by this book and would gladly recommend it to any programming enthusiast or anyone who's ever dreamed of making a game.

➤ **Tibor Simic**

OpenGL ES 2 for Android

A Quick-Start Guide

Kevin Brothaler

The Pragmatic Bookshelf

Dallas, Texas • Raleigh, North Carolina

Many of the designations used by manufacturers and sellers to distinguish their products are claimed as trademarks. Where those designations appear in this book, and The Pragmatic Programmers, LLC was aware of a trademark claim, the designations have been printed in initial capital letters or in all capitals. The Pragmatic Starter Kit, The Pragmatic Programmer, Pragmatic Programming, Pragmatic Bookshelf, PragProg and the linking *g* device are trademarks of The Pragmatic Programmers, LLC.

Every precaution was taken in the preparation of this book. However, the publisher assumes no responsibility for errors or omissions, or for damages that may result from the use of information (including program listings) contained herein.

Our Pragmatic courses, workshops, and other products can help you and your team create better software and have more fun. For more information, as well as the latest Pragmatic titles, please visit us at *http://pragprog.com*.

The Android robot is reproduced from work created and shared by Google and is used according to terms described in the Creative Commons 3.0 Attribution License (*http://creativecommons.org/licenses/by/3.0/us/legalcode*.

The unit circle image in Figure 43, from *http://en.wikipedia.org/wiki/File:Unit_circle.svg*, is used according to the terms described in the Creative Commons Attribution-ShareAlike license, located at *http://creativecommons.org/licenses/by-sa/3.0/legalcode*.

Day skybox and night skybox courtesy of Jockum Skoglund, also known as hipshot, hipshot@zfight.com,*http://www.zfight.com*.

The image of the trace capture button is created and shared by the Android Open Source Project and is used according to terms described in the Creative Commons 2.5 Attribution License.

Printed in the United States of America.
ISBN-13: 978-1-937785-34-5
Printed on acid-free paper.
Book version: P1.0—June 2013

To Anne and my Oma

You have brought so much joy and wonder into my life. Thank you for making it all possible.

Contents

Foreword

Games are visual experiences. As game developers, we want to create environments and characters that pull players into our games, be it through stunningly realistic 3D scenery or quirky, out-of-this-world experiences. We are longing for millions to play our games and experience our worlds, making their lives a tiny bit more fun. Android and its ecosystem provide us with an audience. OpenGL ES gives us the technological means to realize the games of our dreams.

OpenGL ES is the de facto standard in mobile graphics programming. It's the lean and mean brother of desktop OpenGL, removing a lot of the cruft kept for backward compatibility. OpenGL ES comes in three major versions: version 1.0, which gave us an inflexible fixed-function pipeline; version 2.0, which introduced a programmable pipeline with all the bells and whistles we can ask for; and finally, the very young and not-yet-widely-available version 3.0, which adds new features on top of the 2.0 standard.

While OpenGL ES has been in use for almost a decade, hands-on material for beginners is hard to come by, especially for version 2.0, which introduced shaders, an esoteric topic for newcomers. In addition to device- and platform-specific issues, this lack of material sets the entry barrier rather high.

This is where Kevin's book comes in. He cuts through all the boilerplate talk and takes you on a pragmatic tour of OpenGL ES 2.0. Not only does Kevin cover the fundamental concepts behind 3D graphics, but he also documents all the Android-specific pitfalls you run into. Even experienced developers will find a few nuggets here. To paraphrase: "It's dangerous to go it alone, so read this book!"

Mario Zechner
Creator of libgdx,[1] author of *Beginning Android Games [Zec12]*

---

1. https://code.google.com/p/libgdx/

Acknowledgments

I am so grateful to the wonderful team over at The Pragmatic Programmers for giving me the chance to write this book and for doing such a great job in helping me bring it to completion. When I first started out, I wasn't quite sure what to expect, but they did an excellent job of teaching me the ropes. I owe a special debt of gratitude to my editor, Susannah Pfalzer, for guiding me so expertly through the process, and to Aron Hsiao for skillfully coaching a new and bewildered author to the Pragmatic writing style.

I am also thankful for all of my technical reviewers and for everyone else who provided invaluable feedback, including (in no particular order) Mario Zechner, Owen Alanzo Hogarth, Sam Rose, Mike Riley, Aaron Kalair, Rene van der Lende, John Horton, Ed Burnette, Mark Guerra, Maik Schmidt, Kevin Gisi, Brian Schau, Marius Marinescu, Stephen Wolff, Haress Das, Bill Yee, Chad Dumler-Montplaisir, Tibor Simic, Michael Hunter, Jonathan Mischo, and Stefan Turalski, as well as everyone who reported errata or sent in their feedback. Your feedback and advice helped to greatly improve the book, and your encouragement is much appreciated.

I couldn't have done it without the support of the greater community and the generosity of those willing to share their knowledge, including my wonderful readers over at Learn OpenGL ES, the guys at the Khronos Group, NeHe Productions, the Android team, John Carmack, and all of the other giants whom I may have missed and who are too numerous to mention. I stand on their shoulders, and this work wouldn't be possible without them.

Perhaps my greatest debt of gratitude goes to the two women in my life who have kept me grounded all this time: my Oma, for showing me that a little bit of toughness can go a long way, and Anne, my fiancée, for letting me spend so many hours tucked away in my home office and for being so encouraging from beginning to end.

Finally, thank you, dear reader, for deciding to pick up this book and give it a read. May it prove valuable to you and serve you well in the journey ahead.

Welcome to OpenGL ES for Android!

Android has just gone through an incredible period of growth, with more than 750 million devices in the hands of consumers around the world and more than 1 million activations per day.[1] Along with Apple, Android also has a centralized market available on every Android phone and tablet, called Google Play. With this market installed on every Android device, there's never been a better opportunity for anyone who's ever had a dream to publish his or her own game or live wallpaper.

On Android, as well as on Apple's iOS and many other mobile platforms, developers create 2D and 3D graphics through a cross-platform application programming interface called *OpenGL*. OpenGL has been used on the desktop for a while now, and the mobile platforms use a special embedded version known as *OpenGL ES*. The first version of OpenGL ES brought 3D to mobile, which was very popular with developers because it was easy to learn and because it had a well-defined feature set. However, this feature set was also limited, and it wasn't able to keep up with the latest and greatest features from the most powerful smartphones and tablets.

Enter OpenGL ES 2.0. Most of the old APIs were completely removed and replaced with new *programmable* APIs, which makes it much easier to add special effects and take advantage of what the latest devices have to offer. These devices can now produce graphics that rival consoles from just a few years ago! However, to take advantage of this power, we need to learn the new APIs that come with 2.0. In August 2012, the Khronos Group finalized the specification for the next version, OpenGL ES 3.0, which is fully compatible with 2.0, extending it with a few advanced features.

So, what can be done with OpenGL on Android? We can create amazing live wallpapers and have them downloaded by millions of users. We can create a compelling 3D game that has vivid and breathtaking graphics. With the

---

1.	http://googleblog.blogspot.ca/2013/03/update-from-ceo.html

declining cost of hardware and the increasingly massive reach of online stores, it's a great time to begin!

What Will We Cover?

Here's a quick look at what we're going to discuss:

- In the first part of the book, you'll learn how to create a simple game of air hockey, including touch, texturing, and basic physics. This project will teach you how to successfully initialize OpenGL and send data to the screen, as well as how to use basic vector and matrix math to create a 3D world. You'll also learn many details that are specific to Android, such as how to marshal data between the Dalvik virtual machine and the native environment and how to safely pass data between the main thread and the rendering thread.

- In the second part of the book, you'll build upon what you learned in the first part. You'll use some advanced techniques, such as lighting and terrain rendering, and then you'll learn how to create a live wallpaper that can run on your Android's home screen.

Who Should Read This book?

If you're interested in learning how to develop more advanced graphics on Android, then this is the book for you. This book assumes that you have some programming experience, including experience with Java and Android.

Java

If you've worked with other managed languages before, such as C#, then moving to Java will be straightforward. If you're more experienced with native languages, then one of the main differences that you'll need to keep in mind is that Java on Android is a garbage-collected language that runs in a virtual machine, which has both benefits and costs.

The following books will help bring your Java up to speed:

- *The Java Programming Language [AGH05]* by Ken Arnold, James Gosling, and David Holmes

- *Effective Java [Blo08]* by Joshua Bloch

- *Thinking in Java [Eck06]* by Bruce Eckel

Android

Once you're comfortable with Java, developing for Android just requires some experience with the appropriate libraries and methods. To cover all of the basics, I recommend reading *Hello, Android [Bur10]* by Ed Burnette. You can also follow the first two lessons of Google's Android training online:

- Building Your First App[2]
- Managing the Activity Lifecycle[3]

While it's possible to go through most of this book with the emulator, having an Android device on hand will make life much easier. We'll go into more detail about that soon, in Section 1.1, *Installing the Tools*, on page 1.

This should be enough to get you through this book. We'll cover all of the basics from first principles, so you don't need prior experience in 3D graphics programming, and while we'll cover some math in this book, if you've taken trigonometry and linear algebra in the past, then you're well prepared! If not, no fear: everything will be explained in detail as we go along.

How to Read This Book

Each chapter builds on the chapter before it, so this book is best read in sequence. However, all of the code samples are available online (see Section 5, *Online Resources*, on page xviii), so if you want to check out a specific chapter, you can always follow along by downloading the completed project from the previous chapter and continuing on from there. This can also help out if you ever get lost or want to start from a fresh base.

Conventions

We'll use *OpenGL* to refer to OpenGL ES 2.0, the modern version of OpenGL for mobile and the Web.

In most parts of the book, we'll be working with the GLES20 class, which is part of the Android Software Development Kit (SDK). Since most of our OpenGL constants and methods will be in this class, I'll generally omit the class name and just mention the constant or method directly. We'll use static imports (see Section 1.5, *Using Static Imports*, on page 14) to omit the class name in the code as well.

---

2. http://developer.android.com/training/basics/firstapp/index.html
3. http://developer.android.com/training/basics/activity-lifecycle/index.html

Online Resources

All of the resources for this book can be found at http://pragprog.com/book/kbogla, where you can find code samples and accompanying images and textures. If you have purchased the ebook, then you can also click on the hyperlink above each code extract to download that extract directly. You can also join in the discussions at the book's website and help improve the book by submitting your feedback and errata.

Please feel free to also visit *Learn OpenGL ES*, an OpenGL ES tutorial blog that I maintain.[4]

The following is a list of some great online resources maintained by the Khronos Group:[5]

- OpenGL ES 2.0 API Quick Reference Card[6]
- OpenGL ES 2.0 Reference Pages[7]
- OpenGL ES Shading Language (GLSL ES) Reference Pages[8]
- The OpenGL® ES Shading Language[9]
- OpenGL® ES Common Profile Specification Version 2.0.25 (Full Specification)[10]

I recommend printing out the reference card and keeping it handy, so you can quickly refer to it when needed. Android uses the EGL (a native platform interface) to help set up the display, so you may also find the Khronos EGL API Registry to be useful.[11]

Let's Get Started!

There are more people with powerful cell phones and tablets than ever before, and the market continues to grow. Android's software tools make it easy to develop an application for Android, and Google's Play Store makes it easy for us to share our applications with the world. Let's head over to Chapter 1, *Getting Started*, on page 1, and get things started!

---

4. http://www.learnopengles.com/
5. http://www.khronos.org/
6. http://www.khronos.org/opengles/sdk/docs/reference_cards/OpenGL-ES-2_0-Reference-card.pdf
7. http://www.khronos.org/opengles/sdk/docs/man/
8. http://www.khronos.org/opengles/sdk/docs/manglsl/
9. http://www.khronos.org/registry/gles/specs/2.0/GLSL_ES_Specification_1.0.17.pdf
10. http://www.khronos.org/registry/gles/specs/2.0/es_full_spec_2.0.25.pdf
11. http://www.khronos.org/registry/egl/

CHAPTER 1

Getting Started

In this chapter, we're going to dive straight into creating our very first OpenGL application for Android. As we progress through the chapters in this book, each chapter will start off with an overview, and then we'll go over the "game plan"—our plan of attack for that chapter. Here's our game plan to get things started:

- First we'll install and configure our development environment.

- We'll then create our very first OpenGL application, which will initialize OpenGL and handle Android's activity life cycle. We'll talk more about the life cycle soon.

This will give us the base we need to draw stuff onto the screen.

Ready? Let's go!

1.1 Installing the Tools

Here's a basic list of things we'll need to develop OpenGL for Android:

- A personal computer running Windows, OS X, or Linux
- A Java Development Kit (JDK)
- The Android Software Development Kit (SDK)
- An integrated development environment (IDE)
- A phone, tablet, or emulator supporting OpenGL ES 2.0

The first thing you'll need is a personal computer suitable for development; any recent computer running Windows, OS X or Linux should do. On that computer, you'll need to install a JDK, which you can download from Oracle's website.[1] Google currently specifies JDK 6 for Android development, but later

---

1. www.oracle.com/technetwork/java/javase/downloads/index.html

JDKs should work by default. On the off chance that they don't, you'll just need to double-check that your compiler compliance level is set to 1.6.

You'll also need to install the Android SDK bundle, which you can download from the Android developer site.[2] This bundle contains everything that you'll need for Android development, including an emulator with OpenGL ES 2.0 support and an IDE. Once you have the JDK installed, go ahead and unzip the Android SDK bundle to the folder of your choice.

The Android SDK bundle comes with Eclipse, a popular IDE that's officially supported by Google with the Android development tools (ADT). We'll be using Eclipse for the rest of this book, but if you prefer to use something different, another great choice is IntelliJ's IDEA Community Edition. Google also recently announced Android Studio, a spinoff of IntelliJ with new tools and features specially focused on Android development.[3,4]

Configuring a New Emulator

Now that the tools are installed, let's use the Android Virtual Device (AVD) Manager to create a new virtual device:

1. Go to the folder where the Android SDK is installed. If you're on Windows, run SDK Manager.exe to open the Android SDK Manager. On other platforms, run sdk/tools/android.

2. Select Tools→Manage AVDs to open up the Android Virtual Device Manager.

3. Select New to bring up the 'Create new Android Virtual Device (AVD)' dialog.

4. Select Galaxy Nexus as the device.

5. Check the checkbox next to Use Host GPU (graphics processing unit).

6. Give the virtual device a name and leave the rest of the settings on their defaults. The window should look similar to the following figure.

7. Select OK to create the new emulator image (Figure 1, *Creating a new Android virtual device*, on page 3).

You may now close the AVD and SDK managers.

---

2. http://developer.android.com/sdk/index.html
3. http://www.jetbrains.com/idea/
4. http://developer.android.com/sdk/installing/studio.html

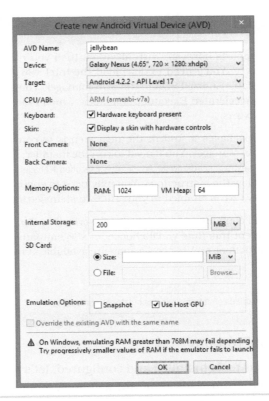

Figure 1—Creating a new Android virtual device

Using the Emulator

You can start an emulator instance by using the AVD manager, or you can let your IDE take care of things automatically; the Android development tools for Eclipse will launch an emulator if there isn't one already running. It's a good idea to keep one emulator instance running so that you don't have to wait for it to start each time.

Obtaining a Device Supporting OpenGL ES 2.0.

You can work with the emulator, but it's much better to have an actual device, because emulators do not accurately reflect real-world performance and results, and it can also be very slow, even on high-end hardware. The Nexus 7 is a great and inexpensive choice, and it can be purchased online at Google Play.[5]

---

5.   https://play.google.com/store/devices

Using an x86 Emulator

If your computer supports hardware virtualization, then you may also want to give the x86 emulator a try. You'll need to download the Intel x86 Atom System Image under the latest available Android SDK in the SDK manager. You'll also need to install the Intel Hardware Accelerated Execution Manager, which is located all the way at the bottom, under Extras.

Once you have the packages installed, the next step is to configure the Hardware Accelerated Execution Manager. You'll need to run the installer, which will be in your SDK directory under extras/intel/Hardware_Accelerated_Execution_Manager. Run the executable in that folder and follow the instructions. You may need to ensure that 'Intel Virtualization Technology (VT-x)' is enabled in your BIOS system settings.

Now you just need to configure an emulator as described in *Configuring a New Emulator*, on page 2, except this time you'll choose an x86 emulator instead of an ARM emulator. More instructions on VM acceleration are available at the Android developer website.[a]

---

a.   http://developer.android.com/tools/devices/emulator.html#accel-vm

1.2   Creating Our First Program

Now that we have our tools installed and configured, let's go ahead and create our first OpenGL program. This program will be very simple: all it will do is initialize OpenGL and clear the screen continuously. That's the minimum we need to have an OpenGL program that actually does something.

If you want to follow along in the code, all of the source code and accompanying data for this book can be downloaded from this book's home page.[6]

Creating a New Project

Go ahead and create a new project by following these steps:

1. Select File→New→Android Application Project. When the dialog comes up, enter the following details:

    Application Name:
    Enter 'First Open GL Project'.

    Package Name:
    The package name is a unique identifier for our project. The convention is to enter a Java-style package name, so let's enter 'com.firstopengl-project.android' as the name.

---

6.   http://pragprog.com/book/kbogla

\|/   **Joe asks:**

Why Do We Need to Continually Clear the Screen?

Clearing the screen seems wasteful if we're already drawing over the entire screen on each frame, so why do we need to do it?

Back in the days when everything was rendered in software, it usually *was* wasteful to clear the screen. Developers would optimize by assuming that everything would get painted over, so there would be no need to wipe away stuff from the previous frame. They did this to save processing time that would otherwise have been wasted. This sometimes led to the famous "hall of mirrors" effect, as seen in games such as Doom: the resulting visual effect was like being in the middle of a hall of mirrors, with old content repeated over and over.[a]

This optimization is no longer useful today. The latest GPUs work differently, and they use special rendering techniques that can actually work faster if the screen is cleared. By telling the GPU to clear the screen, we save time that would have been wasted on copying over the previous frame. Because of the way that GPUs work today, clearing the screen also helps to avoid problems like flickering or stuff not getting drawn. Preserving old content can lead to unexpected and undesirable results.

You can learn more by reading the following links:

- http://developer.amd.com/gpu_assets/gdc2008_ribble_maurice_TileBasedGpus.pdf
- http://www.beyond3d.com/content/articles/38/

-----

a.   http://en.wikipedia.org/wiki/Noclip_mode

Minimum SDK:

> Select 'API 10: Android 2.3.3 (Gingerbread)'. This is the minimum version with full OpenGL ES 2.0 support.

2. Use defaults for the rest; the form should now look similar to Figure 2, *Creating a new Android project in Eclipse*, on page 6.

3. Select Next. Uncheck 'Create custom launcher icon' and make sure that 'Create Activity' is checked. You can choose to place the project in a different location if you prefer.

4. Select Next again to reach the Create Activity screen. Make sure 'Blank Activity' is selected and then click Next again to reach the New Blank Activity configuration screen. Set the activity name to 'FirstOpenGLProject-Activity'. Your screen should look similar to Figure 3, *Creating a new Android project: configuring the activity*, on page 7.

5. Hit Finish to go ahead and build the project.

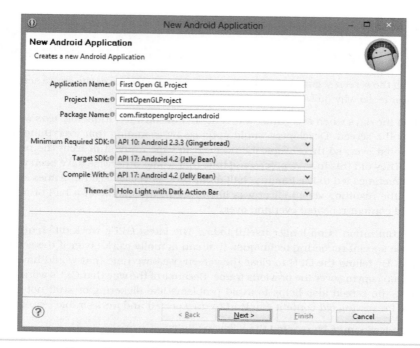

Figure 2—Creating a new Android project in Eclipse

After hitting Finish, Eclipse will crunch for a while, and then your new project will be ready.

1.3 Initializing OpenGL

Our next step is to go ahead and initialize OpenGL by using a special class called GLSurfaceView. GLSurfaceView takes care of the grittier aspects of OpenGL initialization, such as configuring the display and rendering on a background thread. This rendering is done on a special area of the display, called a *surface*; this is also sometimes referred to as a *viewport*.

The GLSurfaceView class also makes it easy to handle the standard Android activity life cycle. In Android, activities can be created and destroyed, and they are also paused and resumed when the user switches to another activity and later returns. In accordance with this life cycle, we need to release OpenGL's resources when our activity is paused. GLSurfaceView provides helper methods to take care of this for us.

You can learn more about the activity life cycle in *Hello, Android [Bur10]*, by Ed Burnette.

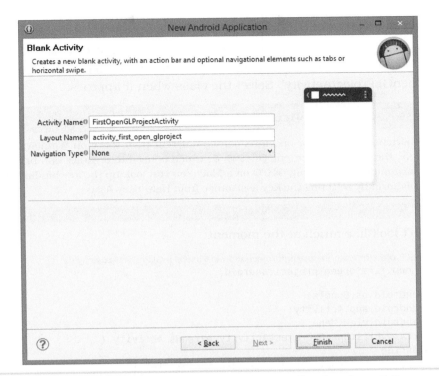

Figure 3—Creating a new Android project: configuring the activity

TextureViews

Behind the scenes, a GLSurfaceView actually creates its own window and punches a "hole" in the view hierarchy to allow the underlying OpenGL surface to be displayed. For many uses, this is good enough; however, since the GLSurfaceView is part of a separate window, it doesn't animate or transform as well as a regular view.

Starting with Android 4.0 Ice Cream Sandwich, Android provides a TextureView that can be used to render OpenGL without having a separate window or hole punching, which means that the view can be manipulated, animated, and transformed as well as any regular Android view. Since there's no OpenGL initialization built into the TextureView class, one way of using a TextureView is by performing your own OpenGL initialization and running that on top of a TextureView; another is to grab the source code of GLSurfaceView and adapt it onto a TextureView.[a]

---

a.   For more information, take a look at https://groups.google.com/d/msg/android-developers/U5RXFGpAHPE/IqHeIeGXhr0J and http://stackoverflow.com/q/12061419.

Creating an Instance of GLSurfaceView

Let's open up our auto-generated activity class, FirstOpenGLProjectActivity. Press Ctrl-Shift-T to bring up the Open Type dialog, and then start typing in 'FirstOpenGLProjectActivity'. Select the class when it appears.

Eclipse Keyboard Shortcuts

The shortcuts on a Mac or on Linux can be different than those on Windows. For example, the keyboard shortcut Ctrl-Shift-O, which is used to organize and bring in new Java imports, is actually ⌘⇧O on a Mac. You can look up the key bindings for your platform by selecting the key assistance from Help→Key Assist.

It doesn't look like much at the moment:

FirstOpenGLProject/src/com/firstopenglproject/android/FirstOpenGLProjectActivity.java

```java
package com.firstopenglproject.android;

import android.os.Bundle;
import android.app.Activity;
import android.view.Menu;
public class FirstOpenGLProjectActivity extends Activity {
    @Override
    public void onCreate(Bundle savedInstanceState) {
        super.onCreate(savedInstanceState);
        setContentView(R.layout.activity_first_open_glproject);
    }
    @Override
    public boolean onCreateOptionsMenu(Menu menu) {
        getMenuInflater().inflate(R.menu.activity_first_open_glproject, menu);
        return true;
    }
}
```

We'll add a GLSurfaceView to the activity so we can initialize OpenGL. Add two new member variables to the top of the class as follows:

FirstOpenGLProject/src/com/firstopenglproject/android/FirstOpenGLProjectActivity.java

```java
public class FirstOpenGLProjectActivity extends Activity {
    private GLSurfaceView glSurfaceView;
    private boolean rendererSet = false;
```

We need to import GLSurfaceView, so press Ctrl-Shift-O to organize imports and bring in the new class; we should do this any time we add in a new reference to a class that needs to be imported. We'll use rendererSet to remember if our GLSurfaceView is in a valid state or not. Let's remove the call to setContentView() and add the following code to initialize our glSurfaceView:

FirstOpenGLProject/src/com/firstopenglproject/android/FirstOpenGLProjectActivity.java
```
@Override
public void onCreate(Bundle savedInstanceState) {
    super.onCreate(savedInstanceState);
    glSurfaceView = new GLSurfaceView(this);
```

Checking If the System Supports OpenGL ES 2.0

Since we'll only be writing code for 2.0, the next thing we'll want to do is check if the system actually supports OpenGL ES 2.0. Let's do that by adding the following lines to onCreate():

FirstOpenGLProject/src/com/firstopenglproject/android/FirstOpenGLProjectActivity.java
```
final ActivityManager activityManager =
    (ActivityManager) getSystemService(Context.ACTIVITY_SERVICE);

final ConfigurationInfo configurationInfo =
    activityManager.getDeviceConfigurationInfo();

final boolean supportsEs2 = configurationInfo.reqGlEsVersion >= 0x20000;
```

First, we get a reference to Android's ActivityManager. We use this to get the device configuration info, and then we access reqGlEsVersion to check the device's OpenGL ES version. If this is 0x20000 or greater, then we can use OpenGL ES 2.0.

This check doesn't actually work on the emulator due to a bug with the GPU emulation; so to make our code work there as well, let's modify the check as follows:

FirstOpenGLProject/src/com/firstopenglproject/android/FirstOpenGLProjectActivity.java
```
final boolean supportsEs2 =
    configurationInfo.reqGlEsVersion >= 0x20000
        || (Build.VERSION.SDK_INT >= Build.VERSION_CODES.ICE_CREAM_SANDWICH_MR1
        && (Build.FINGERPRINT.startsWith("generic")
        || Build.FINGERPRINT.startsWith("unknown")
        || Build.MODEL.contains("google_sdk")
        || Build.MODEL.contains("Emulator")
        || Build.MODEL.contains("Android SDK built for x86")));
```

This code tests if the current device is an emulator build, and if it is, we assume that it supports OpenGL ES 2.0. For this to actually work, we need to be sure that we're running on an emulator image that has been configured for OpenGL ES 2.0, as described in *Configuring a New Emulator*, on page 2.

Configuring the Surface for OpenGL ES 2.0

The next step is to configure our rendering surface. Let's add the following lines of code:

```
if (supportsEs2) {
    // Request an OpenGL ES 2.0 compatible context.
    glSurfaceView.setEGLContextClientVersion(2);

    // Assign our renderer.
    glSurfaceView.setRenderer(new FirstOpenGLProjectRenderer());
    rendererSet = true;
} else {
    Toast.makeText(this, "This device does not support OpenGL ES 2.0.",
        Toast.LENGTH_LONG).show();
    return;
}
```

If the device has support for OpenGL ES 2.0, then we configure our surface view to use OpenGL ES 2.0 by calling setEGLContextClientVersion(2). We then call setRenderer() to pass in a new instance of a custom Renderer class, which we'll soon create, and we remember that the renderer was set by setting rendererSet to true. This renderer will be called by the GLSurfaceView when the surface is created or changed, as well as when it's time to draw a new frame.

What if a device doesn't support OpenGL ES 2.0? It's possible to add a fallback renderer that supports OpenGL ES 1.0, but this situation is so rare these days that it may not be worth the effort. According to the Android Developer Dashboard,[7] only around 9 percent of devices are GL 1.1 only, and this number should keep shrinking as time goes on. In *Updating the Android Manifest and Excluding from Unsupported Devices*, on page 280, we'll learn how to hide a published application on the market from devices that don't support OpenGL ES 2.0.

We need to add one more call to add our GLSurfaceView to the activity and display it on the screen. Replace the old call to setContentView() with the following code at the end of onCreate():

FirstOpenGLProject/src/com/firstopenglproject/android/FirstOpenGLProjectActivity.java
```
setContentView(glSurfaceView);
```

Handling Android's Activity Life Cycle Events

We still need to handle Android's activity life cycle events; otherwise we're going to crash if the user switches to another application. Let's add the following methods to round out our activity class:

FirstOpenGLProject/src/com/firstopenglproject/android/FirstOpenGLProjectActivity.java
```
@Override
protected void onPause() {
    super.onPause();
```

---

7. http://developer.android.com/resources/dashboard/opengl.html

```
    if (rendererSet) {
        glSurfaceView.onPause();
    }
}

@Override
protected void onResume() {
    super.onResume();

    if (rendererSet) {
        glSurfaceView.onResume();
    }
}
```

It's very important to have these methods there so that our surface view can properly pause and resume the background rendering thread as well as release and renew the OpenGL context. If it doesn't, our application may crash and get killed by Android. We also make sure that a renderer was actually set, or calling these methods will also cause the app to crash.

1.4 Creating a Renderer Class

Now we're going to define a Renderer so that we can start clearing the screen. Let's take a quick overview of the methods defined by the Renderer interface:

onSurfaceCreated(GL10 glUnused, EGLConfig config)
  GLSurfaceView calls this when the surface is created. This happens the first time our application is run, and it may also be called when the device wakes up or when the user switches back to our activity. In practice, this means that this method may be called multiple times while our application is running.

onSurfaceChanged(GL10 glUnused, int width, int height)
  GLSurfaceView calls this after the surface is created and whenever the size has changed. A size change can occur when switching from portrait to landscape and vice versa.

onDrawFrame(GL10 glUnused)
  GLSurfaceView calls this when it's time to draw a frame. We *must* draw something, even if it's only to clear the screen. The rendering buffer will be swapped and displayed on the screen after this method returns, so if we don't draw anything, we'll probably get a bad flickering effect.

What's going on with those unused arguments of type GL10? This is a vestige of the OpenGL ES 1.0 API. We would use this parameter if we were writing an OpenGL ES 1.0 renderer, but for OpenGL ES 2.0, we call static methods on the GLES20 class instead.

Rendering in a Background Thread

The renderer methods will be called on a separate thread by the GLSurfaceView. The GLSurfaceView will render continuously by default, usually at the display's refresh rate, but we can also configure the surface view to render only on request by calling GLSurfaceView.setRenderMode(), with GLSurfaceView.RENDERMODE_WHEN_DIRTY as the argument.

Since Android's GLSurfaceView does rendering in a background thread, we must be careful to call OpenGL only within the rendering thread, and Android UI calls only within Android's main thread. We can call queueEvent() on our instance of GLSurfaceView to post a Runnable on the background rendering thread. From within the rendering thread, we can call runOnUIThread() on our activity to post events on the main thread.

Creating a New Renderer

Let's go ahead and create a new class in the same package. Let's call it FirstOpenGLProjectRenderer and have it implement Renderer. To create the new class, right-click com.firstopenglproject.android in the Package Explorer and then select New→Class. When the New Java Class window pops up, enter 'FirstOpenGL-ProjectRenderer' as the name and select Finish.

We'll start off with the following header and add our first method, which is onSurfaceCreated():

FirstOpenGLProject/src/com/firstopenglproject/android/FirstOpenGLProjectRenderer.java

```
package com.firstopenglproject.android;

import static android.opengl.GLES20.GL_COLOR_BUFFER_BIT;
import static android.opengl.GLES20.glClear;
import static android.opengl.GLES20.glClearColor;
import static android.opengl.GLES20.glViewport;

import javax.microedition.khronos.egl.EGLConfig;
import javax.microedition.khronos.opengles.GL10;

import android.opengl.GLSurfaceView.Renderer;

public class FirstOpenGLProjectRenderer implements Renderer {
    @Override
    public void onSurfaceCreated(GL10 glUnused, EGLConfig config) {
        glClearColor(1.0f, 0.0f, 0.0f, 0.0f);
    }
```

First we set the clear color in onSurfaceCreated() with a call to glClearColor(1.0f, 0.0f, 0.0f, 0.0f). The first three components correspond to red, green, and blue, and the last corresponds to a special component called *alpha*, which is often used for translucency and transparency. By setting the first component to 1 and the rest to 0, we are setting red to full strength and the screen will become red when cleared. We'll discuss this color model in more detail in Section 2.6, *The OpenGL Color Model*, on page 34.

The next step is to set the viewport size. Let's add the following code:

FirstOpenGLProject/src/com/firstopenglproject/android/FirstOpenGLProjectRenderer.java
```
@Override
public void onSurfaceChanged(GL10 glUnused, int width, int height) {
    // Set the OpenGL viewport to fill the entire surface.
    glViewport(0, 0, width, height);
}
```

We set the viewport size in onSurfaceChanged() with a call to glViewport(0, 0, width, height). This tells OpenGL the size of the surface it has available for rendering.

We'll finish off the renderer class with the following code:

FirstOpenGLProject/src/com/firstopenglproject/android/FirstOpenGLProjectRenderer.java
```
    @Override
    public void onDrawFrame(GL10 glUnused) {
        // Clear the rendering surface.
        glClear(GL_COLOR_BUFFER_BIT);
    }
}
```

We clear the screen in onDrawFrame() with a call to glClear(GL_COLOR_BUFFER_BIT). This will wipe out all colors on the screen and fill the screen with the color previously defined by our call to glClearColor().

We're now ready to try out our code and see what happens. Go ahead and press Ctrl-F11 to run the program. You should see a blank red screen, as seen in Figure 4, *Our first OpenGL project*, on page 14.

Try changing the clear color and then running the program again to see what happens! You should see the color on the screen match your changes to the code.

If you're using the emulator and it's not working for you, and you've checked that Use Host GPU is checked in the emulator settings, then try adding a call to glSurfaceView.setEGLConfigChooser(8, 8, 8, 8, 16, 0); before the call to glSurfaceView.setRenderer().

Figure 4—Our first OpenGL project

1.5 Using Static Imports

This is the first point where we use the import static directive. We'll be using this a lot in our code, as this directive helps to greatly reduce verbosity by reducing a call like GLES20.glClear(GLES20.GL_COLOR_BUFFER_BIT); to glClear(GL_COLOR_BUFFER_BIT);. This makes a big difference when a significant amount of our code is working with OpenGL and other utilities.

Unfortunately, Eclipse doesn't have great support for static imports. To make things easier, I recommend that you select Window→Preferences and then select Java→Editor→Content Assist→Favorites and add the following types:

- android.opengl.GLES20
- android.opengl.GLUtils
- android.opengl.Matrix

This will help with autocomplete, but unfortunately it won't fix 'Organize Imports'. To fix this, paste the code below to the top of your class:

```
import static android.opengl.GLES20.*;
import static android.opengl.GLUtils.*;
import static android.opengl.Matrix.*;
```

Now when you organize your imports, all of the required static imports will be brought in automatically. Whenever you add in a reference that requires a new import, you can fix it again by just going to the top of the class, replacing the end of one of the static imports with an asterisk (*), and organizing imports again.

1.6 A Review

In this chapter, we learned how to create a new OpenGL project and clear the screen. We installed and configured our development environment, created a new project, initialized OpenGL, responded to Android's activity life cycle, and cleared the screen!

We now have a base that we can build on for all of our future projects. Take a moment to breathe. In the next couple of chapters, we'll continue to build on this base, learn how to program the GPU, and add more features. When you're ready, let's race to the next chapter.

Part I

A Simple Game of Air Hockey

CHAPTER 2

Defining Vertices and Shaders

This chapter introduces our first project: a simple game of air hockey. As we work on this project, we'll learn about some of the major building blocks of OpenGL along the way.

We're going to start off by learning how to build objects by using a set of independent points known as *vertices*, and then we're going to learn how to draw these objects by using *shaders*, small programs that tell OpenGL how to draw an object. These two concepts are extremely important because just about every object is built by joining together vertices into points, lines, and triangles, and these primitives all get drawn by using shaders.

We'll first learn about vertices so that we can build up our air hockey table and position it in the world using OpenGL's coordinate space. We'll then follow up by creating a set of very basic shaders to draw this air hockey table on the screen. In the next chapter, we'll also learn how to draw vertices as points, lines, and triangles on the screen, and as we go through later chapters, we'll learn about colors, smooth shading, texturing, and touch interaction, as well as about parallel and perspective projections.

By the time we're done, our air hockey game will look like Figure 5, *A simple game of air hockey*, on page 20.

2.1 Why Air Hockey?

Air hockey is a simple, popular game often found at bowling alleys and bars. Although simple, it can also be incredibly addictive. Some of the top sellers in Google Play, Android's app market, are based on one variant or another of this enjoyable game.

As we develop our game of air hockey, we'll learn quite a few OpenGL concepts along the way. We'll learn how to define and draw a table to play on, as well

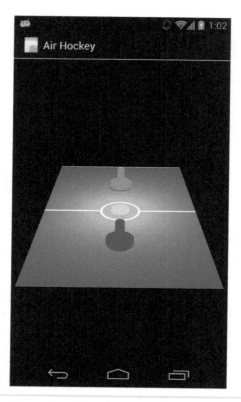

Figure 5—A simple game of air hockey

as how to add detail with colors, shades, and textures. We'll also learn how to respond to the user by acting on touch-screen events.

The Rules of the Game

To play a game of air hockey, we need a long rectangular table with two goals (one on each end), a puck, and two mallets to strike the puck with. Each round starts with the puck placed in the middle of the table. Each player then tries to strike the puck into the opponent's goal while preventing the opponent from doing the same. The first player to reach seven goals wins the game.

As part of our game plan, the first thing that we'll need to do is learn how to define the structure of our air hockey table as well as how to write the code that will draw this table on the screen. As we do this, we'll be building up a framework that we'll be able to use as a base for future chapters. We're going to keep things easy for now and define the table as a single rectangle. We'll also separate each player's side by defining a single dividing line across the middle of the table.

We'll also need to represent the puck and the goalies somehow; we'll define these as individual points. By the end of this chapter, we'll have our structure in place and we'll be ready to add the commands that will actually draw our table to the screen.

2.2 Don't Start from Scratch

Let's get started by reusing our project from Chapter 1, *Getting Started*, on page 1.

1. In Eclipse, select FirstOpenGLProject and make sure that the project is open, and then press Ctrl-C. Now press Ctrl-V to duplicate the project.

2. When prompted, enter 'AirHockey1' as the project name. The location is up to you.

3. Open the new project, and expand the src folder until you find the class files FirstOpenGLProjectActivity.java and FirstOpenGLProjectRenderer.java, which we created in Chapter 1, *Getting Started*, on page 1.

4. We're going to rename our classes. First select FirstOpenGLProjectActivity.java and open up the rename dialog by pressing Alt-Shift-R. Enter 'AirHockey-Activity' (without the .java suffix) as the new name. Eclipse will append the suffix to the file automatically. Select Finish to complete the renaming process.

    If Next highlights instead, press it to go to the Preview window, and then press Finish to complete the renaming process.

5. Repeat the same steps to rename FirstOpenGLProjectRenderer.java to 'AirHock-eyRenderer.java'.

6. Open res/values/strings.xml, and change the value of the string defined by 'app_name' to 'Air Hockey'.

7. Expand src in the tree and select the 'com.firstopenglproject.android' package. Press Alt-Shift-R to rename this to 'com.airhockey.android'.

8. Open AndroidManifest.xml and change the package to 'com.airhockey.android'. Also change android:name for the activity to 'com.airhockey.android.AirHock-eyActivity'.

9. Eclipse may have added import com.firstopenglproject.android.R; to the top of AirHockeyActivity, which may now be underlined as an error. If this happens, just remove that line.

We're now ready to begin with our new project.

2.3 Defining the Structure of Our Air Hockey Table

Before we can draw our table to the screen, we need to tell OpenGL what to draw. The first step in that chain is to define the structure of our table in a form that OpenGL understands. In OpenGL, the structure of everything begins with a vertex.

Introducing Vertices

A vertex is simply a point representing one corner of a geometric object, with various attributes associated with that point. The most important attribute is the position, which represents where this vertex is located in space.

Building Our Table with Vertices

We said we would keep things easy for now, so what's the most basic shape we could use to represent the structure of our air hockey table? We could use a rectangle. Since a rectangle has four corners, we would need four vertices. A rectangle is a two-dimensional object, so each vertex would need a position, with a coordinate for each dimension.

If we were to draw this out on a sheet of graph paper, we might end up with something similar to the following figure:

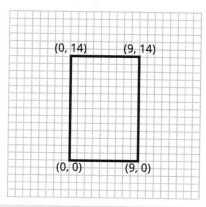

Figure 6—Drawing a table on graph paper

Defining Vertices in Code

Let's go ahead and write some code to store these vertices. We'll represent the vertices as a list of floating point numbers; and since we're working in two dimensions, we'll use two floating point numbers per vertex: one for the *x* position and one for the *y* position.

Since we have two components per vertex, let's first create a constant to contain that fact. Open up AirHockeyRenderer and add the following constant to the top of the class:

AirHockey1/src/com/airhockey/android/AirHockeyRenderer.java
```
private static final int POSITION_COMPONENT_COUNT = 2;
```

Now add the following constructor before onSurfaceCreated():

AirHockey1/src/com/airhockey/android/AirHockeyRenderer.java
```
public AirHockeyRenderer() {
        float[] tableVertices = {
                0f,  0f,
                0f, 14f,
                9f, 14f,
                9f,  0f
        };
}
```

We define our vertex data using a sequential list of floating point numbers so that we can store positions with decimal points. We'll refer to this array as our *vertex attribute array*. We've only stored the position for now, but later on we'll also store the color and other attributes using the same concept seen here.

Points, Lines, and Triangles

Remember when I said that the easiest way to represent our hockey table would be as a rectangle? Well, I'm about to throw a wrench in the works: in OpenGL, we can only draw points, lines, and triangles.

The triangle is the most basic geometric shape around. We see it everywhere in the world, such as in the structural components of a bridge, because it is such a strong shape. It has three sides connected to three vertices. If we took away one vertex, we'd end up with a line, and if we took away one more, we'd have a point.

Points and lines can be used for certain effects, but only triangles can be used to construct an entire scene of complex objects and textures. We build triangles in OpenGL by grouping individual vertices together, and then we tell OpenGL literally how to connect the dots. Everything we want to build needs to be defined in terms of these points, lines, and triangles, and if we want to build more complex shapes, such as an arch, then we need to use enough points to approximate the curve.

So how can we define our air hockey table if we can't use rectangles? Well, it turns out that we can think of the table as two triangles joined together, as seen in the next figure:

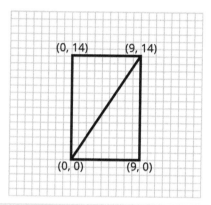

Figure 7—Drawing a table on graph paper: two triangles joined together

Let's change the code to reflect the fact that we'll now use two triangles instead of one rectangle:

AirHockey1/src/com/airhockey/android/AirHockeyRenderer.java

```
float[] tableVerticesWithTriangles = {
        // Triangle 1
        0f,  0f,
        9f, 14f,
        0f, 14f,

        // Triangle 2
        0f,  0f,
        9f,  0f,
        9f, 14f
};
```

Our array now holds six vertices, which will be used to represent two triangles. The first triangle is bounded by the points at (0, 0), (9, 14), and (0, 14). The second triangle shares two of these positions and is bounded by (0, 0), (9, 0), and (9, 14).

Whenever we want to represent an object in OpenGL, we need to think about how we can compose it in terms of points, lines, and triangles.

The Winding Order of a Triangle

You might notice that when we define our triangles we order the vertices in counter-clockwise order; this is known as the *winding order*. When we're consistent in using the same winding order everywhere, we can often optimize performance by using the winding order to figure out if a triangle belongs to the front or to the back of any given object, and then we can ask OpenGL to skip the back triangles since we won't be able to see them anyway.

We'll learn more about this later in *Culling*, on page 249.

Adding the Center Line and Two Mallets

We're almost done defining our vertices. We just need to add a few more vertices for the center line and our two mallets. We want to end up with something like the following figure:

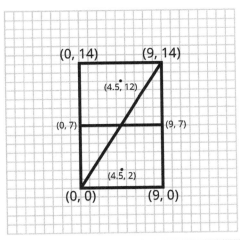

Figure 8—Drawing a table on graph paper: with a line and two mallets

We'll use a line for the center line and a point for each mallet. Add a comma to the end of the array, and then add the following new vertices:

AirHockey1/src/com/airhockey/android/AirHockeyRenderer.java
```
// Line 1
0f,  7f,
9f,  7f,

// Mallets
4.5f,  2f,
4.5f, 12f
```

As you can see, we can also use decimal coordinates since our array is composed of floating point values. In order to keep the Java compiler happy, we need to add a small *f* after the number to inform the compiler that this number should be interpreted as a float and not as a double. Doubles have about double the precision (hence the name), so if we don't add the *f*, Java will see it as a precision-losing conversion and ask us to add an explicit cast.

2.4 Making the Data Accessible to OpenGL

We've finished defining our vertices, but we need to do an extra step before OpenGL can access them. The main problem is that the environment where our code runs and the environment where OpenGL runs don't speak the same language. There are two main concepts that we need to understand:

1. When we compile and run our Java code in the emulator or on a device, it doesn't run directly on the hardware. Instead, it runs through a special environment known as the Dalvik virtual machine. Code running in this virtual machine has no direct access to the native environment other than via special APIs.

2. The Dalvik virtual machine also uses *garbage collection*. This means that when the virtual machine detects that a variable, object, or some other piece of memory is no longer being used, it will go ahead and release that memory so that it can be reused. It might also move things around so that it can use the space more efficiently.

   The native environment does not work the same way, and it will not expect blocks of memory to be moved around and freed automatically.

Android was designed in this way so that developers could develop applications without worrying about the particular CPU or machine architecture and without having to worry about low-level memory management. This usually works well until we need to interface with a native system such as OpenGL. OpenGL runs directly on top of the hardware as a native system library. There's no virtual machine, and there's no garbage collection or memory compaction.

Calling Native Code from Java

The Dalvik approach is one of the major strengths of Android, but if our code is inside a virtual machine, then how can we communicate with OpenGL? Well, there are two tricks. The first trick is to use the Java Native Interface (JNI), and this trick is already done for us by the Android SDK guys. When we call methods in the android.opengl.GLES20 package, the SDK is actually using JNI behind the scenes to call the native system library.

Copying Memory from Java's Memory Heap to the Native Memory Heap

The second trick is to change how we allocate our memory. We have access to a special set of classes in Java that will allocate a block of native memory and copy our data to that memory. This native memory will be accessible to the native environment, and it will not be managed by the garbage collector.

We'll need to transfer the data, as seen in the next figure. Let's add some code at the top of our class, before the constructor:

AirHockey1/src/com/airhockey/android/AirHockeyRenderer.java
```
private static final int BYTES_PER_FLOAT = 4;
private final FloatBuffer vertexData;
```

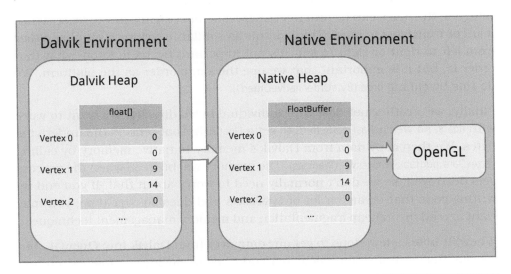

Figure 9—Transferring data from Dalvik to OpenGL

We've added a constant, BYTES_PER_FLOAT, and a FloatBuffer. A float in Java has 32 bits of precision, while a byte has 8 bits of precision. This might seem like an obvious point to make, but there are 4 bytes in every float. We'll need to refer to that in many places down the road. The FloatBuffer will be used to store data in native memory.

Let's add some more code, this time to the end of the constructor's body:

AirHockey1/src/com/airhockey/android/AirHockeyRenderer.java
```
vertexData = ByteBuffer
    .allocateDirect(tableVerticesWithTriangles.length * BYTES_PER_FLOAT)
    .order(ByteOrder.nativeOrder())
    .asFloatBuffer();

vertexData.put(tableVerticesWithTriangles);
```

Let's take a look at each part. First we allocated a block of native memory using ByteBuffer.allocateDirect(); this memory will not be managed by the garbage collector. We need to tell the method how large the block of memory should be in bytes. Since our vertices are stored in an array of floats and there are 4 bytes per float, we pass in tableVerticesWithTriangles.length * BYTES_PER_FLOAT.

The next line tells the byte buffer that it should organize its bytes in native order. When it comes to values that span multiple bytes, such as 32-bit integers, the bytes can be ordered either from most significant to least significant or from least to most. Think of this as similar to writing a number either from left to right or right to left. It's not important for us to know what that order is, but it is important that we use the same order as the platform. We do this by calling order(ByteOrder.nativeOrder()).

Finally, we'd rather not deal with individual bytes directly. We want to work with floats, so we call asFloatBuffer() to get a FloatBuffer that reflects the underlying bytes. We then copy data from Dalvik's memory to native memory by calling vertexData.put(tableVerticesWithTriangles). The memory will be freed when the process gets destroyed, so we don't normally need to worry about that. If you end up writing code that creates a lot of ByteBuffers and does so over time, you may want to read up on heap fragmentation and memory management techniques.[1]

Whew! It takes a few steps to get our data over from Dalvik into OpenGL, but it's vital that we understand how this works before moving on. Just like culture and customs differ from country to country, we also have to be aware of changes when we cross the border into native code.

2.5 Introducing the OpenGL Pipeline

We've now defined the structure of our hockey table, and we've copied the data over to native memory, where OpenGL will be able to access it. Before we can draw our hockey table to the screen, we need to send it through the OpenGL pipeline, and to do this we need to use small subroutines known as *shaders* (see Figure 10, *An overview of the OpenGL pipeline*, on page 30). These

---

1.   http://en.wikipedia.org/wiki/Memory_pool

Joe asks:
What Is Endianness?

Endianness is a way of describing how a hardware architecture orders the bits and bytes that make up a number at a low level. The most common place where we see this in action is with multibyte numbers, where we can either store them in *big-endian order*, with the most significant byte first, or in *little-endian order*, with the least significant byte first.

As an example, let's take the decimal number 10000. If we convert this to binary, we end up with 10011100010000. Now on a big-endian architecture, the bits will be stored in this order:

00100111 00010000

On a small-endian architecture, they'll be stored in this order:

00010000 00100111

Let's take a look at that again, using hex this time. The decimal number 10000 is 2710 in the hex number system. This system is sometimes nice to work with when looking at computer code because every two characters correspond to one 8-bit byte. On a big-endian architecture, we'd store this number as follows:

27 10

On a small-endian architecture, the same number would be stored as follows:

10 27

We don't normally need to worry about endianness. When we use a ByteBuffer, we just need to make sure that it uses the same order as the hardware; otherwise our results will be wildly wrong. You can read more about endianness on Wikipedia.[a]

---

a.   http://en.wikipedia.org/wiki/Endianness

shaders tell the graphics processing unit (GPU) how to draw our data. There are two types of shaders, and we need to define both of them before we can draw anything to the screen.

1. A *vertex shader* generates the final position of each vertex and is run once per vertex. Once the final positions are known, OpenGL will take the visible set of vertices and assemble them into points, lines, and triangles.

2. A *fragment shader* generates the final color of each *fragment* of a point, line, or triangle and is run once per fragment. A fragment is a small, rectangular area of a single color, analogous to a pixel on a computer screen.

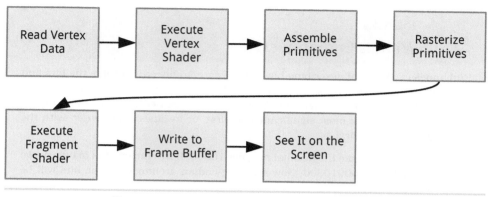

Figure 10—An overview of the OpenGL pipeline

Once the final colors are generated, OpenGL will write them into a block of memory known as the *frame buffer*, and Android will then display this frame buffer on the screen.

For a quick reference on OpenGL and shaders, khronos.org has a great quick reference card, which can be printed out and kept by your side.[2]

Joe asks:

Why Should We Use Shaders?

Before shaders were around, OpenGL used a fixed set of functions that let us control a few limited things, such as how many lights there were in the scene or how much fog to add. This fixed API was easy to use, but it wasn't easy to extend. You had what the APIs gave you, and that was it. If you wanted to add custom effects like cartoon shading, you were pretty much out of luck.

As the underlying hardware improved over time, the guys behind OpenGL realized that the API also had to evolve and keep up with the changes. In OpenGL ES 2.0, they added a programmable API using shaders; and to keep things concise, they took out the fixed API completely, so shaders *must* be used.

We now have shaders to control how each vertex gets drawn to the screen, and we can also control how each fragment of every point, line, and triangle gets drawn. This has opened up a new world of possibilities. We can now do per-pixel lighting and other neat effects, like cartoon-cel shading. We can add any custom effect we dream up, as long as we can express it in the shader language.

---

2.   http://www.khronos.org/opengles/sdk/docs/reference_cards/OpenGL-ES-2_0-Reference-card.pdf

Creating Our First Vertex Shader

Let's create a simple vertex shader that will assign the positions as we've defined them in our code. To do this, we'll first need to create a new file for the shader by following these steps:

1. First we need to create a new folder. Right-click the res folder in your project, select New, select Folder, and name the new folder raw.

2. Now we need to create a new file. Right-click the new folder we've just created, select New, select File, and name the new file simple_vertex_shader.glsl.

Now that the new file for the shader has been created, let's add the following code:

AirHockey1/res/raw/simple_vertex_shader.glsl
```
attribute vec4 a_Position;

void main()
{
    gl_Position = a_Position;
}
```

These shaders are defined using GLSL, OpenGL's shading language. This shading language has a syntax structure that is similar to C. For more information, refer to the quick reference card or to the full specification.[3]

This vertex shader will be called once for every single vertex that we've defined. When it's called, it will receive the current vertex's position in the a_Position attribute, which is defined to be a vec4.

A vec4 is a vector consisting of four components. In the context of a position, we can think of the four components as the position's x, y, z, and w coordinates. x, y, and z correspond to a 3D position, while w is a special coordinate that we'll cover in more detail in Chapter 6, *Entering the Third Dimension*, on page 95. If unspecified, OpenGL's default behavior is to set the first three coordinates of a vector to 0 and the last coordinate to 1.

Remember that we talked about how a vertex can have several attributes, such as a color and a position? The attribute keyword is how we feed these attributes into our shader.

We then define main(), the main entry point to the shader. All it does is copy the position that we've defined to the special output variable gl_Position. Our

---

3. http://www.khronos.org/opengles/sdk/docs/reference_cards/OpenGL-ES-2_0-Reference-card.pdf and http://www.khronos.org/registry/gles/specs/2.0/GLSL_ES_Specification_1.0.17.pdf, respectively.

shader *must* write something to gl_Position. OpenGL will use the value stored in gl_Position as the final position for the current vertex and start assembling vertices into points, lines, and triangles.

Creating Our First Fragment Shader

Now that we've created a vertex shader, we have a subroutine for generating the final position of each vertex. We still need to create a subroutine for generating the final color of each fragment. Before we do that, let's take some time to learn more about what a fragment is and how one is generated.

The Art of Rasterization

Your mobile display is composed of thousands to millions of small, individual components known as pixels. Each of these pixels appears to be capable of displaying a single color out of a range of millions of different colors. However, this is actually a visual trick: most displays can't actually create millions of different colors, so instead each pixel is usually composed of just three individual subcomponents that emit red, green, and blue light, and because each pixel is so small, our eyes blend the red, green, and blue light together to create a huge range of possible colors. Put enough of these individual pixels together and we can show a page of text or the *Mona Lisa*.

OpenGL creates an image that we can map onto the pixels of our mobile display by breaking down each point, line, and triangle into a bunch of small fragments through a process known as rasterization. These fragments are analogous to the pixels on your mobile display, and each one also consists of a single solid color. To represent this color, each fragment has four components: red, green, and blue for color, and *alpha* for transparency. We'll go into more detail about how this color model works in Section 2.6, *The OpenGL Color Model*, on page 34.

In Figure 11, *Rasterization: generating fragments*, on page 33, we can see an example of how OpenGL might rasterize a line onto a set of fragments. The display system usually maps these fragments directly to the pixels on the screen so that one fragment corresponds to one pixel. However, this isn't always true: a super high-res device might want to use bigger fragments so that the GPU has less work to do.

Writing the Code

The main purpose of a fragment shader is to tell the GPU what the final color of each fragment should be. The fragment shader will be called once for every

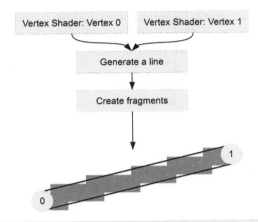

Figure 11—Rasterization: generating fragments

fragment of the primitive, so if a triangle maps onto 10,000 fragments, then the fragment shader will be called 10,000 times.

Let's go ahead and write our fragment shader. Create a new file in your project, /res/raw/simple_fragment_shader.glsl, and add the following code:

AirHockey1/res/raw/simple_fragment_shader.glsl
```
precision mediump float;

uniform vec4 u_Color;

void main()
{
    gl_FragColor = u_Color;
}
```

Precision Qualifiers

The first line at the top of the file defines the default precision for all floating point data types in the fragment shader. This is like choosing between float and double in our Java code.

We can choose between lowp, mediump, and highp, which correspond to low precision, medium precision, and high precision. However, highp is only supported in the fragment shader on some implementations.

Why didn't we have to do this for the vertex shader? The vertex shader can also have its default precision changed, but because accuracy is more important when it comes to a vertex's position, the OpenGL designers decided to set vertex shaders to the highest setting, highp, by default.

As you've probably guessed, higher precision data types are more accurate, but they come at the cost of decreased performance. For our fragment shader, we'll select mediump for maximum compatibility and as a good tradeoff between speed and quality.

Generating the Fragment's Color

The rest of the fragment shader is similar to the vertex shader we defined earlier. This time, we pass in a *uniform* called u_Color. Unlike an attribute that is set on each vertex, a uniform keeps the same value for all vertices until we change it again. Like the attribute we were using for position in the vertex shader, u_Color is also a four-component vector, and in the context of a color, its four components correspond to red, green, blue, and alpha.

We then define main(), the main entry point to the shader. It copies the color that we've defined in our uniform to the special output variable gl_FragColor. Our shader *must* write something to gl_FragColor. OpenGL will use this color as the final color for the current fragment.

2.6 The OpenGL Color Model

OpenGL uses the additive RGB color model, which works with just the three primary colors: red, green, and blue. Many colors can be created by mixing these primary colors together in various proportions. For example, red and green together create yellow, red and blue together create magenta, and blue and green together create cyan. Add red, green, and blue together and you get white (as seen in the following figure).

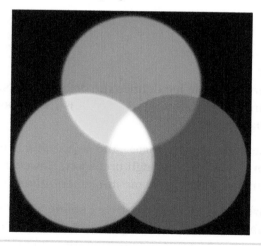

Figure 12—The RGB additive color model

This model works differently than the subtractive paint model you might have learned about in school: in the subtractive paint model, adding blue and yellow makes green, and adding a bunch of colors together creates a dark brown or black. This is because paint does not emit light; it *absorbs* it. The more colors of paint we use, the more light is absorbed and the darker the paint appears.

The additive RGB model follows the properties of light itself: when two beams of light of different colors mix together, we don't get a darker color; we get a brighter color. When we observe a rainbow in the sky after a heavy rainfall, we're actually seeing all of the different colors of the visible light spectrum that can combine to make white.

For the curious, Wikipedia goes into a lot more detail.[4]

Mapping Colors to the Display

OpenGL assumes that these colors all have a linear relationship with each other: a red value of 0.5 should be twice as bright as a red value of 0.25, and a red value of 1 should be twice as bright as a red value of 0.5. These primary colors are clamped to the range [0, 1], with 0 representing the absence of that particular primary color and 1 representing the maximum strength for that color.

This color model maps well to the display hardware used by mobiles and computer displays (however, in *The Nonlinear Nature of Your Display*, on page 269, we'll learn that the mapping isn't quite one to one). These displays almost always use the three primary colors of red, green, and blue (some may include yellow as an additional primary color, for a "purer yellow"), with 0 mapping to an unlit pixel component and 1 mapping to full brightness for that color. With this color model, almost every color that our eyes can see can be rendered in OpenGL and displayed on the screen.

We'll learn more about using colors in Chapter 4, *Adding Color and Shade*, on page 59.

2.7 A Review

We spent most of the chapter just learning how to define our data and the shaders that will move this data along the OpenGL pipeline. Let's take a moment to review the key concepts that we learned in this chapter:

---

4. http://en.wikipedia.org/wiki/RGB_color_model

- We first learned how to define a vertex attribute array and copy this array over to native memory so that OpenGL can access it.

- We then wrote a vertex and a fragment shader. We learned that a shader is just a special type of program that runs on the GPU.

In the next chapter, we'll continue to build on the work in this chapter; by the end of that chapter, we'll be able to see our air hockey table and we'll also be ready to continue with further exercises. We'll start out by learning how to read in and compile the shaders that we've defined. Because vertex and fragment shaders always go together, we'll also learn how to link these shaders together into an OpenGL program.

Once we've compiled and linked our shaders together, we'll be able to put everything together and tell OpenGL to draw the first version of our air hockey table to the screen.

CHAPTER 3

Compiling Shaders and Drawing to the Screen

This chapter will continue the work that we started in the last chapter. As our game plan for this chapter, we'll first load and compile the shaders that we've defined, and then we'll link them together into an OpenGL program. We'll then be able to use this shader program to draw our air hockey table to the screen.

Let's open AirHockey1, the project we started in the previous chapter, and pick up from where we left off.

3.1 Loading Shaders

Now that we've written the code for our shaders, the next step is to load them into memory. To do that, we'll first need to write a method to read in the code from our resources folder.

Loading Text from a Resource

Create a new Java source package in your project, com.airhockey.android.util, and in that package, create a new class called TextResourceReader. Add the following code inside the class:

AirHockey1/src/com/airhockey/android/util/TextResourceReader.java
```
public static String readTextFileFromResource(Context context,
    int resourceId) {
    StringBuilder body = new StringBuilder();

    try {
        InputStream inputStream =
            context.getResources().openRawResource(resourceId);
        InputStreamReader inputStreamReader =
```

```
            new InputStreamReader(inputStream);
    BufferedReader bufferedReader = new BufferedReader(inputStreamReader);

    String nextLine;

    while ((nextLine = bufferedReader.readLine()) != null) {
        body.append(nextLine);
        body.append('\n');
    }
} catch (IOException e) {
    throw new RuntimeException(
        "Could not open resource: " + resourceId, e);
} catch (Resources.NotFoundException nfe) {
    throw new RuntimeException("Resource not found: " + resourceId, nfe);
}

return body.toString();
}
```

We've defined a method to read in text from a resource, readTextFileFromResource(). The way this will work is that we'll call readTextFileFromResource() from our code, and we'll pass in the current Android context and the resource ID. The Android context is required in order to access the resources. For example, to read in the vertex shader, we might call the method as follows: readTextFileFromResource(this.context, R.raw.simple_fragment_shader).

We also check for a couple of standard scenarios we might run into. The resource might not exist, or there might be an error trying to read the resource. In those cases, we trap the errors and throw a wrapped exception with an explanation of what happened. If this code fails and an exception does get thrown, we'll have a better idea of what happened when we take a look at the exception's message and the stack trace.

Don't forget to press Ctrl-Shift-O (⌘⇧O on a Mac) to bring in any missing imports.

Reading in the Shader Code

We're now going to add the calls to actually read in the shader code. Switch to AirHockeyRender.java and add the following code after the call to glClearColor() in onSurfaceCreated():

AirHockey1/src/com/airhockey/android/AirHockeyRenderer.java
```
String vertexShaderSource = TextResourceReader
    .readTextFileFromResource(context, R.raw.simple_vertex_shader);
String fragmentShaderSource = TextResourceReader
    .readTextFileFromResource(context, R.raw.simple_fragment_shader);
```

Don't forget to bring in the import for TextResourceReader. The code won't compile because we don't yet have a reference to an Android context. Add the following to the top of the class:

AirHockey1/src/com/airhockey/android/AirHockeyRenderer.java
```
private final Context context;
```

Change the beginning of the constructor as follows:

AirHockey1/src/com/airhockey/android/AirHockeyRenderer.java
```
public AirHockeyRenderer(Context context) {
    this.context = context;
```

We'll also have to change AirHockeyActivity.java to pass in the Android context. Open AirHockeyActivity.java and change the call to glSurfaceView.setRenderer() as follows:

AirHockey1/src/com/airhockey/android/AirHockeyActivity.java
```
glSurfaceView.setRenderer(new AirHockeyRenderer(this));
rendererSet = true;
```

An Activity is an Android context, so we pass in a reference to this.

Keeping a Log of What's Happening

As we start to write more involved code, it often helps a lot to see a trace of what's happening, just in case we've made a mistake somewhere. With Android, we can use the Log class to log everything to the system log, which we can then view in Eclipse using the LogCat view.

We don't always want to log everything, so let's add a new class called Logger-Config to com.airhockey.android.util with the following code:

AirHockey1/src/com/airhockey/android/util/LoggerConfig.java
```
package com.airhockey.android.util;

public class LoggerConfig {
    public static final boolean ON = true;
}
```

Whenever we want to log something, we'll check to see if this constant is true or false. To turn logging on or off, all we have to do is update the constant and recompile the application.

3.2 Compiling Shaders

Now that we've read in the shader source from our files, the next step is to compile each shader. We'll create a new helper class that is going to create a new OpenGL shader object, compile our shader code, and return the shader object for that shader code. Once we have this boilerplate code in place, we'll be able to reuse it in our future projects.

To begin, create a new class, ShaderHelper, and add the following code inside the class:

AirHockey1/src/com/airhockey/android/util/ShaderHelper.java

```java
private static final String TAG = "ShaderHelper";

public static int compileVertexShader(String shaderCode) {
    return compileShader(GL_VERTEX_SHADER, shaderCode);
}

public static int compileFragmentShader(String shaderCode) {
    return compileShader(GL_FRAGMENT_SHADER, shaderCode);
}

private static int compileShader(int type, String shaderCode) {

}
```

We'll use this as the base for our shader helper. As before, don't forget to bring in the imports. If you are having issues with the static imports, please see Section 1.5, *Using Static Imports*, on page 14; we'll follow this style for the rest of the book.

In the next section, we'll build up compileShader() step by step:

Creating a New Shader Object

The first thing we should do is create a new shader object and check if the creation was successful. Add the following code to compileShader():

AirHockey1/src/com/airhockey/android/util/ShaderHelper.java

```java
final int shaderObjectId = glCreateShader(type);

if (shaderObjectId == 0) {
    if (LoggerConfig.ON) {
        Log.w(TAG, "Could not create new shader.");
    }

    return 0;
}
```

We create a new shader object with a call to glCreateShader() and store the ID of that object in shaderObjectId. The type can be GL_VERTEX_SHADER for a vertex shader, or GL_FRAGMENT_SHADER for a fragment shader. The rest of the code is the same either way.

Take note of how we create the object and check if it's valid; this pattern is used everywhere in OpenGL:

1. We first create an object using a call such as glCreateShader(). This call will return an integer.

2. This integer is the reference to our OpenGL object. Whenever we want to refer to this object in the future, we'll pass the same integer back to OpenGL.

3. A return value of 0 indicates that the object creation failed and is analogous to a return value of null in Java code.

If the object creation failed, we'll return 0 to the calling code. Why do we return 0 instead of throwing an exception? Well, OpenGL doesn't actually throw any exceptions internally. Instead, we'll get a return value of 0 or OpenGL will inform us of the error through glGetError(), a method that lets us ask OpenGL if any of our API calls have resulted in an error. We'll follow the same convention to stay consistent.

To learn more about glGetError() and other ways of debugging your OpenGL code, see Appendix 2, *Debugging*, on page 305.

Uploading and Compiling the Shader Source Code

Let's add the following code to upload our shader source code into the shader object:

AirHockey1/src/com/airhockey/android/util/ShaderHelper.java
```
glShaderSource(shaderObjectId, shaderCode);
```

Once we have a valid shader object, we call glShaderSource(shaderObjectId, shaderCode) to upload the source code. This call tells OpenGL to read in the source code defined in the String shaderCode and associate it with the shader object referred to by shaderObjectId. We can then call glCompileShader(shaderObjectId) to compile the shader:

```
glCompileShader(shaderObjectId);
```

This tells OpenGL to compile the source code that was previously uploaded to shaderObjectId.

Retrieving the Compilation Status

Let's add the following code to check if OpenGL was able to successfully compile the shader:

```
final int[] compileStatus = new int[1];
glGetShaderiv(shaderObjectId, GL_COMPILE_STATUS, compileStatus, 0);
```

To check whether the compile failed or succeeded, we first create a new int array with a length of 1 and call it compileStatus. We then call glGetShaderiv(shaderObjectId, GLES20.GL_COMPILE_STATUS, compileStatus, 0). This tells OpenGL to read the compile status associated with shaderObjectId and write it to the 0th element of compileStatus.

This is another common pattern with OpenGL on Android. To retrieve a value, we often use arrays with a length of 1 and pass the array into an OpenGL call. In the same call, we tell OpenGL to store the result in the array's first element.

Retrieving the Shader Info Log

When we get the compile status, OpenGL will give us a simple yes or no answer. Wouldn't it also be interesting to know what went wrong and where we screwed up? It turns out that we can get a human-readable message by calling glGetShaderInfoLog(shaderObjectId). If OpenGL has anything interesting to say about our shader, it will store the message in the shader's info log.

Let's add the following code to get the shader info log:

AirHockey1/src/com/airhockey/android/util/ShaderHelper.java
```
if (LoggerConfig.ON) {
    // Print the shader info log to the Android log output.
    Log.v(TAG, "Results of compiling source:" + "\n" + shaderCode + "\n:"
        + glGetShaderInfoLog(shaderObjectId));
}
```

We print this log to Android's log output, wrapping everything in an if statement that checks the value of LoggerConfig.ON. We can easily turn off these logs by flipping the constant to *false*.

Verifying the Compilation Status and Returning the Shader Object ID

Now that we've logged the shader info log, we can check to see if the compilation was successful:

AirHockey1/src/com/airhockey/android/util/ShaderHelper.java
```
if (compileStatus[0] == 0) {
    // If it failed, delete the shader object.
    glDeleteShader(shaderObjectId);

    if (LoggerConfig.ON) {
        Log.w(TAG, "Compilation of shader failed.");
    }

    return 0;
}
```

All we need to do is check if the value returned in the step *Retrieving the Compilation Status*, on page 41, is 0 or not. If it's 0, then compilation failed. We no longer need the shader object in that case, so we tell OpenGL to delete it and return 0 to the calling code. If the compilation succeeded, then our shader object is valid and we can use it in our code.

That's it for compiling a shader, so let's return the new shader object ID:

AirHockey1/src/com/airhockey/android/util/ShaderHelper.java
```
return shaderObjectId;
```

Compiling the Shaders from Our Renderer Class

Now it's time to make good use of the code that we've just created. Switch to AirHockeyRenderer.java and add the following code to the end of onSurfaceCreated():

AirHockey1/src/com/airhockey/android/AirHockeyRenderer.java
```
int vertexShader = ShaderHelper.compileVertexShader(vertexShaderSource);
int fragmentShader = ShaderHelper.compileFragmentShader(fragmentShaderSource);
```

Let's review the work we've done in this section. First we created a new class, ShaderHelper, and added a method to create and compile a new shader object. We also created LoggerConfig, a class to help us turn logging on and off at one single point.

If you take a look again at ShaderHelper, you'll see that we actually defined three methods:

compileShader()
> The compileShader(shaderCode) method takes in source code for a shader and the shader's type. The type can be GL_VERTEX_SHADER for a vertex shader, or GL_FRAGMENT_SHADER for a fragment shader. If OpenGL was able to successfully compile the shader, then this method will return the shader object ID to the calling code. Otherwise it will return zero.

compileVertexShader()
> The compileVertexShader(shaderCode) method is a helper method that calls compileShader() with shader type GL_VERTEX_SHADER.

compileFragmentShader()
> The compileVertexShader(shaderCode) method is a helper method that calls compileShader() with shader type GL_FRAGMENT_SHADER.

As you can see, the meat of the code is within compileShader(); all the other two methods do is call it with either GL_VERTEX_SHADER or GL_FRAGMENT_SHADER.

3.3   Linking Shaders Together into an OpenGL Program

Now that we've loaded and compiled a vertex shader and a fragment shader, the next step is to bind them together into a single program.

Understanding OpenGL Programs

An OpenGL program is simply one vertex shader and one fragment shader linked together into a single object. Vertex shaders and fragment shaders always go together. Without a fragment shader, OpenGL wouldn't know how to draw the fragments that make up each point, line, and triangle; and without a vertex shader, OpenGL wouldn't know where to draw these fragments.

We know that the vertex shader calculates the final position of each vertex on the screen. We also know that when OpenGL groups these vertices into points, lines, and triangles and breaks them down into fragments, it will then ask the fragment shader for the final color of each fragment. The vertex and fragment shaders cooperate together to generate the final image on the screen.

Although vertex shaders and fragment shaders always go together, they don't necessarily have to remain monogamous: we can use the same shader in more than one program at a time.

Let's open up ShaderHelper and add the following code to the end of the class:

AirHockey1/src/com/airhockey/android/util/ShaderHelper.java
```
public static int linkProgram(int vertexShaderId, int fragmentShaderId) {

}
```

As we did for compileShader(), we'll also build this method up step by step. Much of the code will be similar in concept to compileShader().

Creating a New Program Object and Attaching Shaders

The first thing we'll do is create a new program object with a call to glCreatePro-gram() and store the ID of that object in programObjectId. Let's add the following code:

```
final int programObjectId = glCreateProgram();

if (programObjectId == 0) {
    if (LoggerConfig.ON) {
        Log.w(TAG, "Could not create new program");
    }

    return 0;
}
```

The semantics are the same as when we created a new shader object earlier: the integer returned is our *reference* to the program object, and we'll get a return value of 0 if the object creation failed.

The next step is to attach our shaders:

```
glAttachShader(programObjectId, vertexShaderId);
glAttachShader(programObjectId, fragmentShaderId);
```

Using glAttachShader(), we attach both our vertex shader and our fragment shader to the program object.

Linking the Program

We're now ready to join our shaders together. We'll do this with a call to glLinkProgram(programObjectId):

```
glLinkProgram(programObjectId);
```

To check whether the link failed or succeeded, we'll follow the same steps as we did for compiling the shader:

```
final int[] linkStatus = new int[1];
glGetProgramiv(programObjectId, GL_LINK_STATUS, linkStatus, 0);
```

We first create a new int array to hold the result. We then call glGetProgramiv(programObjectId, GLES20.GL_LINK_STATUS, linkStatus, 0) to store the result in this array. We'll also check the program info log so that if something went wrong or if OpenGL has anything interesting to say about our program, we'll see it in Android's log output:

```
if (LoggerConfig.ON) {
    // Print the program info log to the Android log output.
    Log.v(TAG, "Results of linking program:\n"
        + glGetProgramInfoLog(programObjectId));
}
```

Verifying the Link Status and Returning the Program Object ID

We now need to check the link status: if it's 0, that means that the link failed and we can't use this program object, so we should delete it and return 0 to the calling code:

```
if (linkStatus[0] == 0) {
    // If it failed, delete the program object.
    glDeleteProgram(programObjectId);
    if (LoggerConfig.ON) {
        Log.w(TAG, "Linking of program failed.");
    }
    return 0;
}
```

Whew! If we made it this far, then our program linked successfully and we can use it in our code. We're now done, so let's return the new program object ID to our calling code:

AirHockey1/src/com/airhockey/android/util/ShaderHelper.java
```
return programObjectId;
```

Adding the Code to Our Renderer Class

Now that we have code to link our shaders together, let's go ahead and call that from our program. First let's add the following member variable to the top of AirHockeyRenderer:

AirHockey1/src/com/airhockey/android/AirHockeyRenderer.java
```
private int program;
```

This integer will store the ID of the linked program. Let's link the shaders together by adding the following call to the end of onSurfaceCreated():

AirHockey1/src/com/airhockey/android/AirHockeyRenderer.java
```
program = ShaderHelper.linkProgram(vertexShader, fragmentShader);
```

Now would probably be a good time to grab a cup of coffee and let your mind rest for a few moments. In the next section, we'll start making the final connections and link our data to OpenGL.

3.4 Making the Final Connections

We spent a good part of the last two chapters laying down a basic foundation for our application: we learned how to define the structure of an object using an array of attributes, and we also learned how to create shaders, load and compile them, and link them together into an OpenGL program.

Now it's time to start building on this foundation and making the final connections. In the next few steps, we're going to put the pieces together, and then we'll be ready to draw the first version of our air hockey table to the screen.

Validate Our OpenGL Program Object

Before we start using an OpenGL program, we should validate it first to see if the program is valid for the current OpenGL state. According to the OpenGL ES 2.0 documentation, it also provides a way for OpenGL to let us know why the current program might be inefficient, failing to run, and so on.[1]

Let's add the following method to ShaderHelper:

---

1.   http://www.khronos.org/opengles/sdk/docs/man/xhtml/glValidateProgram.xml

```java
public static boolean validateProgram(int programObjectId) {
    glValidateProgram(programObjectId);

    final int[] validateStatus = new int[1];
    glGetProgramiv(programObjectId, GL_VALIDATE_STATUS, validateStatus, 0);
    Log.v(TAG, "Results of validating program: " + validateStatus[0]
        + "\nLog:" + glGetProgramInfoLog(programObjectId));

    return validateStatus[0] != 0;
}
```

We call glValidateProgram() to validate the program, and then we check the results with a call to glGetProgramiv(), using GL_VALIDATE_STATUS as the parameter name. If OpenGL had anything interesting to say, it will be in the program log, so we also print out the log with a call to glGetProgramInfoLog().

We should validate our program before we start using it, and we should also validate only when we're developing and debugging our application. Let's add the following to the end of onSurfaceCreated():

```java
if (LoggerConfig.ON) {
    ShaderHelper.validateProgram(program);
}
```

This will call the validation code we defined earlier, but only if logging is turned on. The next thing we should do is enable the OpenGL program that we've worked so hard to create. Add the following code to the end of onSurfaceCreated():

```java
glUseProgram(program);
```

We call glUseProgram() to tell OpenGL to use the program defined here when drawing anything to the screen.

Getting the Location of a Uniform

The next step is to get the location of the uniform that we defined in our shader earlier on. When OpenGL links our shaders into a program, it will actually associate each uniform defined in the vertex shader with a location number. These location numbers are used to send data to the shader, and we'll need the location for u_Color so that we can set the color when we're about to draw.

Let's take a quick look at our fragment shader:

AirHockey1/res/raw/simple_fragment_shader.glsl

```
precision mediump float;

uniform vec4 u_Color;

void main()
{
    gl_FragColor = u_Color;
}
```

In our shader, we've defined a uniform called u_Color, and in main() we assign the value of this uniform to gl_FragColor. We'll use this uniform to set the color of what we're drawing. We have to draw a table, a central dividing line, and two mallets, and we're going to draw them all using different colors.

Let's add the following definitions to the top of AirHockeyRenderer:

AirHockey1/src/com/airhockey/android/AirHockeyRenderer.java

```
private static final String U_COLOR = "u_Color";
private int uColorLocation;
```

We've created a constant for the name of our uniform and a variable to hold its location in the OpenGL program object. Uniform locations don't get specified beforehand, so we'll need to query the location once the program's been successfully linked. A uniform's location is unique to a program object: even if we had the same uniform name in two different programs, that doesn't mean that they'll share the same location.

Add the following to the end of onSurfaceCreated():

AirHockey1/src/com/airhockey/android/AirHockeyRenderer.java

```
uColorLocation = glGetUniformLocation(program, U_COLOR);
```

We call glGetUniformLocation() to get the location of our uniform, and we store that location in uColorLocation. We'll use that when we want to update the value of this uniform later on.

Getting the Location of an Attribute

Like with uniforms, we also need to get the locations of our attributes before we can use them. We can let OpenGL assign these attributes to location numbers automatically, or we can assign the numbers ourselves with a call to glBindAttribLocation() before we link the shaders together. We'll let OpenGL assign the attribute locations automatically, as it makes our code easier to manage.

Let's add the following definitions to the top of AirHockeyRenderer:

AirHockey1/src/com/airhockey/android/AirHockeyRenderer.java
```
private static final String A_POSITION = "a_Position";
private int aPositionLocation;
```

Now we just need to add some code to get the attribute location once the shaders have been linked together. Let's add the following to the end of onSurfaceCreated():

AirHockey1/src/com/airhockey/android/AirHockeyRenderer.java
```
aPositionLocation = glGetAttribLocation(program, A_POSITION);
```

We call glGetAttribLocation() to get the location of our attribute. With this location, we'll be able to tell OpenGL where to find the data for this attribute.

Associating an Array of Vertex Data with an Attribute

The next step is to tell OpenGL where to find data for our attribute a_Position. Add the following code to the end of onSurfaceCreated():

AirHockey1/src/com/airhockey/android/AirHockeyRenderer.java
```
vertexData.position(0);
glVertexAttribPointer(aPositionLocation, POSITION_COMPONENT_COUNT, GL_FLOAT,
    false, 0, vertexData);
```

Back when we started this chapter, we created an array of floating point values to represent the positions of the vertices that make up our air hockey table. We created a buffer in native memory, called vertexData, and copied these positions over to this buffer.

Before we tell OpenGL to read data from this buffer, we need to make sure that it'll read our data starting at the beginning and not at the middle or the end. Each buffer has an internal pointer that can be moved by calling position(int), and when OpenGL reads from our buffer, it will start reading at this position. To ensure that it starts reading at the very beginning, we call position(0) to set the position to the beginning of our data.

We then call glVertexAttribPointer() to tell OpenGL that it can find the data for a_Position in the buffer vertexData. This is a very important function, so let's take a closer look at what we're passing in for each argument (Table 1, *glVertexAttribPointer parameters*, on page 49):

glVertexAttribPointer(int index, int size, int type, boolean normalized, int stride, Buffer ptr)

int index	This is the attribute location, and we pass in aPositionLocation to refer to the location that we retrieved earlier in *Getting the Location of an Attribute*, on page 48.

int size	This is the data count per attribute, or how many components are associated with each vertex for this attribute. Back in Section 2.3, *Defining the Structure of Our Air Hockey Table*, on page 22, we decided to use two floating point values per vertex: an *x* coordinate and a *y* coordinate to represent the position. This means that we have two components, and we had previously created the constant POSITION_COMPONENT_COUNT to contain that fact, so we pass that constant in here.
	Note that we're only passing two components per vertex, but in the shader, a_Position is defined as a vec4, which has four components. If a component is not specified, OpenGL will set the first three components to 0 and the last component to 1 by default.
int type	This is the type of data. We defined our data as a list of floating point values, so we pass in GL_FLOAT.
boolean normalized	This only applies if we use integer data, so we can safely ignore it for now.
int stride	The fifth argument, the *stride*, applies when we store more than one attribute in a single array. We only have one attribute in this chapter, so we can ignore this and pass in 0 for now. We'll talk about the stride in more detail in Section 4.4, *Rendering with the New Color Attribute*, on page 71.
Buffer ptr	This tells OpenGL where to read the data. Don't forget that it will start reading from the buffer's current position, so if we hadn't called vertexData.position(0), it would probably try to read past the end of the buffer and crash our application.

Table 1—glVertexAttribPointer() parameters

Passing incorrect arguments to glVertexAttribPointer() can lead to strange results and can even cause the program to crash. These kinds of crashes can be hard to trace, so I can't overstate how important it is to make sure that we get these arguments right.

After calling glVertexAttribPointer(), OpenGL now knows where to read the data for the attribute a_Position.

Enabling the Vertex Array

Now that we've linked our data to the attribute, we need to enable the attribute with a call to glEnableVertexAttribArray() before we can start drawing. Add the following code after the call to glVertexAttribPointer():

AirHockey1/src/com/airhockey/android/AirHockeyRenderer.java
```
glEnableVertexAttribArray(aPositionLocation);
```

With this final call, OpenGL now knows where to find all the data it needs.

In this section, we retrieved the locations of the uniform u_Color and the attribute a_Position. Each variable has a location, and OpenGL works with these locations rather than with the name of the variable directly. We then called glVertexAttribPointer() to tell OpenGL that it can find the data for the attribute a_Position from vertexData.

3.5 Drawing to the Screen

With the final connections in place, we're now ready to start drawing to the screen! We'll draw the table first, and then we'll draw the dividing line and the mallets.

Drawing the Table

Let's add the following code after the call to glClear(), at the end of onDrawFrame():

AirHockey1/src/com/airhockey/android/AirHockeyRenderer.java
```
glUniform4f(uColorLocation, 1.0f, 1.0f, 1.0f, 1.0f);
glDrawArrays(GL_TRIANGLES, 0, 6);
```

First we update the value of u_Color in our shader code by calling glUniform4f(). Unlike attributes, uniforms don't have default components, so if a uniform is defined as a vec4 in our shader, we need to provide all four components. We want to start out by drawing a white table, so we set red, green, and blue to 1.0f for full brightness. The alpha value doesn't matter, but we still need to specify it since a color has four components.

Once we've specified the color, we then draw our table with a call to glDrawArrays(GLES20.GL_TRIANGLES, 0, 6). The first argument tells OpenGL that we want to draw triangles. To draw triangles, we need to pass in at least three vertices per triangle. The second argument tells OpenGL to read in vertices starting at the beginning of our vertex array, and the third argument tells OpenGL to read in six vertices. Since there are three vertices per triangle, this call will end up drawing two triangles.

Let's take a quick look at our vertex array as we defined it back at the beginning of this chapter:

AirHockey1/src/com/airhockey/android/AirHockeyRenderer.java
```
float[] tableVerticesWithTriangles = {
        // Triangle 1
        0f,  0f,
        9f, 14f,
        0f, 14f,

        // Triangle 2
        0f,  0f,
        9f,  0f,
        9f, 14f,

        // Line 1
        0f,  7f,
        9f,  7f,

        // Mallets
        4.5f,  2f,
        4.5f, 12f
};
```

Remember that when we called glVertexAttribPointer(), we told OpenGL that each vertex's position consists of two floating point components. Our call to glDrawArrays() asks OpenGL to draw triangles using the first six vertices, so OpenGL will draw them using these positions:

```
// Triangle 1
0f,  0f,
9f, 14f,
0f, 14f,

// Triangle 2
0f,  0f,
9f,  0f,
9f, 14f,
```

The first triangle drawn will be bounded by the points (0, 0), (9, 14), and (0, 14), and the second will be bounded by (0, 0), (9, 0), and (9, 14).

Drawing the Dividing Line

The next step is to draw the center dividing line across the middle of the table. Add the following code to the end of onDrawFrame():

```
glUniform4f(uColorLocation, 1.0f, 0.0f, 0.0f, 1.0f);
glDrawArrays(GL_LINES, 6, 2);
```

We set the color to red by passing in 1.0f to the first component (red) and 0.0f to green and blue. This time we also ask OpenGL to draw lines. We start six vertices after the first vertex and ask OpenGL to draw lines by reading in two vertices. Just like with Java arrays, we're using zero-based numbering here: 0, 1, 2, 3, 4, 5, 6 means that the number 6 corresponds to six vertices after the first vertex, or the seventh vertex. Since there are two vertices per line, we'll end up drawing one line using these positions:

AirHockey1/src/com/airhockey/android/AirHockeyRenderer.java
```
// Line 1
0f,  7f,
9f,  7f,
```

OpenGL will draw a line from (0, 7) to (9, 7).

Drawing the Mallets as Points

The last thing to do now is to draw the two mallets. Add the following code to the end of onDrawFrame():

AirHockey1/src/com/airhockey/android/AirHockeyRenderer.java
```
// Draw the first mallet blue.
glUniform4f(uColorLocation, 0.0f, 0.0f, 1.0f, 1.0f);
glDrawArrays(GL_POINTS, 8, 1);

// Draw the second mallet red.
glUniform4f(uColorLocation, 1.0f, 0.0f, 0.0f, 1.0f);
glDrawArrays(GL_POINTS, 9, 1);
```

We ask OpenGL to draw points by passing in GL_POINTS to glDrawArrays(). For the first mallet, we set the color to blue, start at offset 8, and draw one point using one vertex. For the second mallet, we set the color to red, start at offset 9, and draw one point using one vertex. We'll draw the points using these positions:

AirHockey1/src/com/airhockey/android/AirHockeyRenderer.java
```
// Mallets
4.5f,  2f,
4.5f, 12f
```

OpenGL will draw the first point at (4.5, 2) and the second at (4.5, 12).

What Do We Have So Far?

Let's run the application and see what comes out on the screen. Press Ctrl-F11 to run the application, and observe what appears on your device or in the emulator. Your screen should look similar to the following figure. If you have any issues, try cleaning the project in Eclipse first by selecting Project→Clean.

Figure 13—Drawing to the screen: initial attempt

Well, something doesn't look quite right there! The background is still that garish red color we were using back in Chapter 1, *Getting Started*, on page 1, for one, and why do we only see the corner of our air hockey table? Before we talk about that, let's fix the clear color. Find the call to glClearColor() at the beginning of onSurfaceCreated(), and update it to the following:

AirHockey1/src/com/airhockey/android/AirHockeyRenderer.java
```
glClearColor(0.0f, 0.0f, 0.0f, 0.0f);
```

This will tell OpenGL to clear the screen to black when we call glClear() instead of red. Now that we've at least fixed that garish red color, we need to look at why we can only see the corner of our air hockey table.

How Does OpenGL Map Coordinates to the Screen?

One of the big questions that we haven't yet tackled is this: How does OpenGL take the coordinates that we've given it and map those to actual physical coordinates on the screen?

The answer to this question is complicated, and we'll learn more about it as we progress through the chapters. For now, all we need to know is that OpenGL will map the screen to the range [-1, 1] for both the *x* and the *y* coordinates. This means that the left edge of the screen will correspond to -1 on the *x*-axis, while the right edge of the screen will correspond to +1. The bottom edge of the screen will correspond to -1 on the *y*-axis, while the top edge of the screen will correspond to +1.

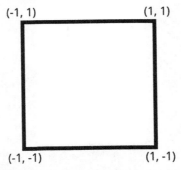

This range stays the same regardless of the shape or size of the screen, and everything that we draw needs to fit within this range if we want it to show up on the screen. Let's go back to the constructor and update the coordinates defined in tableVerticesWithTriangles as follows:

AirHockey1/src/com/airhockey/android/AirHockeyRenderer.java
```java
float[] tableVerticesWithTriangles = {
    // Triangle 1
    -0.5f, -0.5f,
     0.5f,  0.5f,
    -0.5f,  0.5f,

    // Triangle 2
    -0.5f, -0.5f,
     0.5f, -0.5f,
     0.5f,  0.5f,

    // Line 1
    -0.5f, 0f,
     0.5f, 0f,

    // Mallets
    0f, -0.25f,
    0f,  0.25f
};
```

Let's run the app again. We should now see something similar to the following figure:

Figure 14—Drawing to the screen: second attempt

That looks much better, but where are our mallets? It turns out that for points, OpenGL needs us to specify how large each point should appear on the screen, and we haven't done that yet.

Specifying the Size of Points

Let's update our code so we can tell OpenGL how large the points should appear on the screen. We can do this by adding the following line to simple_vertex_shader.glsl, after the assignment to gl_Position:

AirHockey1/res/raw/simple_vertex_shader.glsl
```
gl_PointSize = 10.0;
```

By writing to another special output variable, gl_PointSize, we tell OpenGL that the size of the points should be 10. Ten of what, you might ask? Well, when OpenGL breaks the point down into fragments, it will generate fragments in a square that is centered around gl_Position, and the length of each side of this square will be equal to gl_PointSize. The larger gl_PointSize is, the larger the point drawn on the screen.

Let's run the app one more time. We should now see the mallets as shown in the following figure, each rendered as a single point.

Figure 15—Drawing to the screen: including the mallets

We're finally there! Take a break, sit back, and reflect on everything that you've learned in this chapter. This was a big lesson to get through, but we made it and managed to get something displayed on the screen.

When you're ready, let's review what we've learned and do a couple of follow-up exercises.

3.6   A Review

We had to write a lot of boilerplate code before we could finally display the first version of our air hockey table, but the good thing is that we'll be able to reuse this code for our future projects. Let's take a moment to review what we learned in the chapter:

- How to create and compile a shader

- That vertex shaders and fragment shaders always go together—we also learned how to link them together into an OpenGL program object.

- How to associate our vertex attribute array with an attribute variable inside a vertex shader

We were then finally able to put everything together so that we could display something on the screen.

Now might be a good time to review any parts of the chapter that might have seemed unclear at the time, now that we've connected all of the dots. You can access the code at this book's home page.[2]

3.7 Exercises

Try drawing a puck in the center of the table. For something a bit more challenging, see if you can add a border around the table. How would you do it? As a hint, see if you can draw *two* rectangles, each with a different color.

Once you've completed these exercises, let's move on to the next chapter and learn how to make things be more colorful.

---

2. http://pragprog.com/book/kbogla

CHAPTER 4

Adding Color and Shade

In the real world, objects have varying color and shade. If we look at a wall inside of our home, we can observe that it's painted a single color. At the same time, some parts of the wall will seem darker or brighter, depending on how these parts of the wall are oriented to the surrounding light. Our brains use these slight differences in shade as one of the main visual cues to help make sense of what we see; artists have been using these cues to fool our brains to no end since the beginning of time. In this chapter, we're going to learn from the artists and use *varying* color and shade to make our table look less flat and more realistic.

In the previous chapter, it was quite a bit of work to get our air hockey table drawn to the screen, including two mallets and a dividing line down the middle of the table. There was a lot of preparatory work, including writing code to load and compile shaders and to link them together into an OpenGL program object.

The nice thing with OpenGL ES 2.0 is that a lot of the overhead comes at the very beginning, and it's going to get better from here on out. Although there will be more code to come, we'll be able to reuse all of this base code in each subsequent chapter. In fact, adding varying color and shade to our scene will be much easier now that we have a basic framework in place.

Here's our game plan for this chapter:

- First we'll learn how to define a color at each point as a vertex attribute instead of using a single color for an entire object.

- We'll then learn how to smoothly blend these colors between the different vertices that make up an object.

Let's start off by copying the project from Chapter 2, *Defining Vertices and Shaders*, on page 19, over into a new project:

1. In Eclipse, select our project from the last chapter, AirHockey1, and press Ctrl-C. Now, press Ctrl-V to duplicate the project.

2. When prompted, enter 'AirHockey2' as the project name. As in the previous chapter, the location is up to you.

3. We can continue with the same application package name and class names as before.

4.1 Smooth Shading

In Chapter 2, *Defining Vertices and Shaders*, on page 19, we learned how to draw objects with a single color in a uniform, as seen in the following image:

We already know that that we're limited to drawing points, lines, and triangles, and we build everything up from that. Since we're limited to those three primitives, how can we represent a complex scene with many different colors and shades?

One way we could do it is by using a million small triangles, each with a different color. If we use enough triangles, we can fool the viewer into seeing a nice, complex scene with a rich variation of colors. While this could technically work, the performance and memory overhead would also be horrible.

Instead of drawing a bunch of flat triangles, what if there was a way to blend different colors across the same triangle? If we had a different color at each point of a triangle and blended these colors across the surface of the triangle, we would end up with a smoothly shaded triangle, such as the following one:

Smooth Shading Is Done Between Vertices

OpenGL gives us a way to smoothly blend the colors at each vertex across a line or across the surface of a triangle. We'll use this type of shading to make our table appear brighter in the middle and dimmer toward the edges, as if there were a light hovering over the middle of the table. Before we can do that, though, we'll need to update the structure of our table. Right now we're drawing the table using two triangles, as seen in the following image:

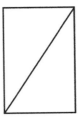

How could we make this appear brighter in the middle? There's no point in the middle, so there's nothing to blend toward or away from. We'll need to add a point in the middle so that we can blend colors between the middle of the table and the edges. Our table structure will then look as follows:

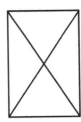

The first thing we'll need to do is update our table to match this new structure.

4.2 Introducing Triangle Fans

With a new point in the middle of the table, we'll end up with four triangles instead of two. We'll center the new point at (0, 0). Let's open up AirHockeyRenderer in the new project that we created at the beginning of this chapter and update the triangles as follows:

AirHockey2/src/com/airhockey/android/AirHockeyRenderer.java
```
// Triangle Fan
    0,    0,
-0.5f, -0.5f,
 0.5f, -0.5f,
 0.5f,  0.5f,
-0.5f,  0.5f,
-0.5f, -0.5f,
```

The first question you might be asking is, "Why did we only define six points? Don't we need to define three vertices per triangle?" While it's true that we need three vertices per triangle, we can sometimes reuse the same vertex in more than one triangle. Let's take a look at our new structure again, with each unique point numbered:

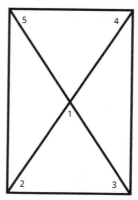

Each edge vertex is used in two triangles, and the center vertex is used in all four triangles! It would quickly become tiresome if we had to type out the same coordinates again and again, so instead we tell OpenGL to reuse these vertices. We can do that by drawing these vertices as a *triangle fan*. A triangle fan looks something like the following image:

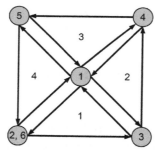

A triangle fan begins with a center vertex, using the next two vertices to create the first triangle. Each subsequent vertex will create another triangle, fanning around the original center point. To complete the fan, we just repeat the second point at the end.

We'll need to update our draw call so that OpenGL knows that this data represents a triangle fan. In onDrawFrame(), update the call to the first glDrawArrays() as follows:

AirHockey2/src/com/airhockey/android/AirHockeyRenderer.java
```
glDrawArrays(GL_TRIANGLE_FAN, 0, 6);
```

This will ask OpenGL to draw a triangle fan using the six new points that we've defined. Let's give the application a quick run, just to see that everything still looks as we expect. It should look like the following figure:

Figure 16—Air hockey, before adding shading

Now that we've redefined the table with a center point, let's learn how we can add a color to each vertex as a second attribute.

4.3 Adding a New Color Attribute

Now that we've updated our table structure by adding an additional point in the center of the table, we can now add a color attribute to each point. Let's update the entire array of data as follows:

```
AirHockey2/src/com/airhockey/android/AirHockeyRenderer.java
float[] tableVerticesWithTriangles = {
    // Order of coordinates: X, Y, R, G, B

    // Triangle Fan
      0f,    0f,   1f,   1f,   1f,
```

```
   -0.5f, -0.5f, 0.7f, 0.7f, 0.7f,
    0.5f, -0.5f, 0.7f, 0.7f, 0.7f,
    0.5f,  0.5f, 0.7f, 0.7f, 0.7f,
   -0.5f,  0.5f, 0.7f, 0.7f, 0.7f,
   -0.5f, -0.5f, 0.7f, 0.7f, 0.7f,

   // Line 1
   -0.5f, 0f, 1f, 0f, 0f,
    0.5f, 0f, 1f, 0f, 0f,

   // Mallets
   0f, -0.25f, 0f, 0f, 1f,
   0f,  0.25f, 1f, 0f, 0f
};
```

As you can see, we've added three additional numbers to each vertex. These
numbers represent red, green, and blue, and together they will form the color
for that particular vertex.

Converting Colors Using Android's Color Class

When we use floating-point attributes, we need to specify each color component in a
range from 0 to 1, with 1 being the maximum value for that color component. Figuring
out the right numbers for a certain color might not be obvious, but by using Android's
Color class, we can easily come up with the right values. For example, here's what we
do to get the OpenGL color values for green:

```
float red = Color.red(Color.GREEN) / 255f;
float green = Color.green(Color.GREEN) / 255f;
float blue = Color.blue(Color.GREEN) / 255f;
```

We can also do this with web colors:

```
int parsedColor = Color.parseColor("#0099CC");

float red = Color.red(parsedColor) / 255f;
float green = Color.green(parsedColor) / 255f;
float blue = Color.blue(parsedColor) / 255f;
```

The values returned by Color.red(), Color.green(), and Color.blue() range from 0 to 255, so
to convert these into OpenGL colors, we just divide each component by 255.

Adding the Color Attribute to the Shaders

The next step will be to remove the color uniform from the shader and replace
it with an attribute. We'll then update the Java code to reflect the new shader
code.

Open simple_vertex_shader.glsl and update it as follows:

AirHockey2/res/raw/simple_vertex_shader.glsl

```
attribute vec4 a_Position;
attribute vec4 a_Color;

varying vec4 v_Color;

void main()
{
    v_Color = a_Color;

    gl_Position = a_Position;
    gl_PointSize = 10.0;
}
```

We added a new attribute, a_Color, and we also added a new varying called v_Color. "What on earth is a *varying*?" you might ask. Remember that we said we wanted our colors to *vary* across the surface of a triangle? Well, this is done by using a special variable type known as a varying. To better understand what a varying does, let's go back and review how OpenGL combines vertices together to create objects, as seen in Figure 11, *Rasterization: generating fragments*, on page 33.

As we learned in Section 2.5, *Introducing the OpenGL Pipeline*, on page 28, when OpenGL builds a line, it takes the two vertices that make up that line and generates fragments for it. When OpenGL builds a triangle, it does the same thing by using three vertices to build a triangle. The fragment shader will then be run for every fragment generated.

A varying is a special type of variable that *blends* the values given to it and sends these values to the fragment shader. Using the line above as an example, if a_Color was red at vertex 0 and green at vertex 1, then by assigning a_Color to v_Color, we're telling OpenGL that we want each fragment to receive a blended color. Near vertex 0, the blended color will be mostly red, and as the fragments get closer to vertex 1, the color will start to become green.

Before we go into more detail on how this blending is done, let's add the varying to the fragment shader as well. Open simple_fragment_shader.glsl and update it as follows:

AirHockey2/res/raw/simple_fragment_shader.glsl

```
precision mediump float;
varying vec4 v_Color;

void main()
{
    gl_FragColor = v_Color;
}
```

We've replaced the uniform that was there before with our varying, v_Color. If the fragment belongs to a line, then OpenGL will use the two vertices that make up that line to calculate the blended color. If the fragment belongs to a triangle, then OpenGL will use the three vertices that make up that triangle to calculate the blended color.

Now that we've updated our shaders, we'll also need to update our Java code so that we pass in the new color attribute to a_Color in the vertex shader. Before we do that, let's take some time to learn more about how OpenGL can smoothly blend colors from one point to another.

How Does a Varying Get Blended at Each Fragment?

We just learned that we can use a varying to produce a blended color at each fragment of a line or triangle. We can blend more than just colors; we can send any value to a varying, and OpenGL will take the two values belonging to a line, or the three belonging to a triangle, and smoothly blend these values across the primitive, with a different value for each fragment. This blending is done using linear interpolation. To learn how this works, let's first start with the example of a line.

Linear Interpolation Along a Line

Let's say that we had a line with a red vertex and a green vertex, and we wanted to blend the colors from one to the other. The blended colors would look something like this:

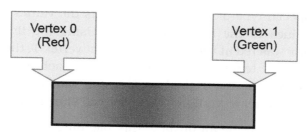

At the left side of the line, the color of each fragment is mostly red. As we move toward the right, the fragments become less red, and in the middle, they are somewhere in between red and green. As we get closer to the green vertex, the fragments become more and more green.

We can see that each color scales linearly along the length of the line. Since the left vertex of the line is red and the right vertex is green, the left end of the line should be 100 percent red, the middle should be 50 percent red, and the right should be 0 percent red:

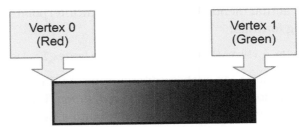

The same thing happens with green. Since the left vertex is red and the right vertex is green, the left end of the line will be 0 percent green, the middle will be 50 percent green, and the right will be 100 percent green:

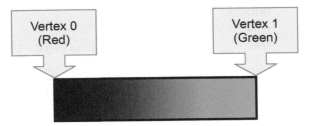

Once we add the two together, we end up with a blended line:

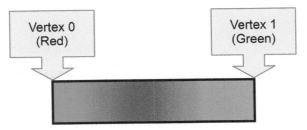

This is linear interpolation in a nutshell. The strength of each color depends on the distance of each fragment from the vertex containing that color.

To calculate this, we can take the value at vertex 0 and the value at vertex 1, and then we calculate the *distance ratio* for the current fragment. The distance ratio is simply a ratio between 0 and 100 percent, with 0 percent being the left vertex and 100 percent being the right vertex. As we move from left to right, the distance ratio will increase linearly from 0 to 100 percent. Here's an example of a few distance ratios:

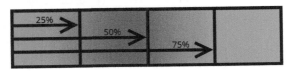

To calculate the actual blended value using linear interpolation, we can then use the following formula:

blended_value = (vertex_0_value * (100% - distance_ratio)) + (vertex_1_value * distance_ratio)

This calculation is done for each component, so if we're dealing with color values, this calculation will be done for the red, green, blue, and alpha components separately, with the results combined into a new color value.

Let's try this out with our line example. Let the vertex_0_value equal red, with an RGB value of (1, 0, 0), and the vertex_1_value equal green, with an RGB value of (0, 1, 0). Let's calculate the final color for a few positions on the line:

Position	Distance ratio	Equation
Far left	0%	(vertex_0_value * (1 - distance_ratio)) + (vertex_1_value * distance_ratio) =
		((1, 0, 0) * (100% – 0%)) + ((0, 1, 0) * 0%) =
		((1, 0, 0) * 100%) =
		(1, 0, 0) (red)
One-quarter along the line	25%	(vertex_0_value * (1 - distance_ratio)) + (vertex_1_value * distance_ratio) =
		((1, 0, 0) * (100% – 25%)) + ((0, 1, 0) * 25%) =
		((1, 0, 0) * 75%) + ((0, 1, 0) * 25%) =
		(0.75, 0, 0) + (0, 0.25, 0) =
		(0.75, 0.25, 0) (mostly red)
Middle of the line	50%	(vertex_0_value * (1 - distance_ratio)) + (vertex_1_value * distance_ratio) =
		((1, 0, 0) * (100% – 50%)) + ((0, 1, 0) * 50%) =
		((1, 0, 0) * 50%) + ((0, 1, 0) * 50%) =
		(0.5, 0, 0) + (0, 0.5, 0) =
		(0.5, 0.5, 0) (half red, half green)
Three-quarters along the line	75%	(vertex_0_value * (1 - distance_ratio)) + (vertex_1_value * distance_ratio) =
		((1, 0, 0) * (100% – 75%)) + ((0, 1, 0) * 75%) =

Position	Distance ratio	Equation
Far right	100%	((1, 0, 0) * 25%) + ((0, 1, 0) * 75%) =
		(0.25, 0, 0) + (0, 0.75, 0) =
		(0.25, 0.75, 0) (mostly green)
		(vertex_0_value * (1 - distance_ratio)) + (vertex_1_value * distance_ratio) =
		((1, 0, 0) * (100% - 100%)) + ((0, 1, 0) * 100%) =
		((1, 0, 0) * 0%) + ((0, 1, 0) * 100%) =
		(0, 1, 0) (green)

Table 2—Linear interpolation equation examples

Notice that at all times the weights of both colors add up to 100 percent. If red is at 100 percent, green is at 0 percent. If red is 50 percent, green is 50 percent.

Using a varying, we can blend any two colors together. We're also not limited to colors: we can interpolate other attributes as well.

Now that we know how linear interpolation works with a line, let's read on to see how this works with a triangle.

Blending Across the Surface of a Triangle

Figuring out how linear interpolation works wasn't so bad when we were dealing with just two points; we learned that each color scales from 100 percent to 0 percent from that color's vertex to the other vertex on the line, and that both scaled colors are added together to give the final color.

Linear interpolation across a triangle works with the same idea, but there are now three points and three colors to deal with. Let's look at a visual example:

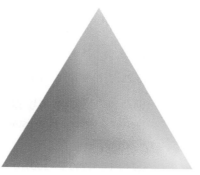

This triangle has three colors associated with it: the top vertex is cyan, the left vertex is magenta, and the right is yellow. Let's break the triangle down into the colors derived from each vertex:

Just like with the line, each color is strongest near its vertex and fades away toward the other vertices. We also use ratios to determine the relative weights of each color, except this time we use ratios of areas instead of lengths:

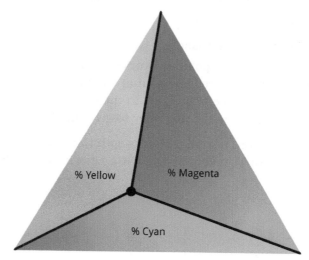

At any given point inside the triangle, three inner triangles can be created by drawing a line from that point to each vertex. The ratios of the areas of these inner triangles determine the weight of each color at that point. For example, the strength of yellow at that point is determined by the area of the inner triangle that is opposite of the yellow vertex. The closer the point gets to the yellow vertex, the larger that triangle gets, and the more yellow the fragment at that point will be.

Just like with the line, these weights always equal 100 percent. We can use the following formula to calculate the color at any point inside the triangle:

blended_value = (vertex_0_value * vertex_0_weight) + (vertex_1_value * vertex_1_weight) + (vertex_2_value * (100% – vertex_0_weight – vertex_1_weight))

Given that we understand how this works with a line, we don't need to go into specific examples here. The idea is the same, but we have three points instead of two.

4.4 Rendering with the New Color Attribute

Now that we've added a color attribute to our data and we've updated the vertex and fragment shaders to use this attribute, the next steps are to remove the old code that passed in the color via a uniform and to tell OpenGL to read in colors as a vertex attribute.

Updating Constants

Let's add the following constants to the top of AirHockeyRenderer:

AirHockey2/src/com/airhockey/android/AirHockeyRenderer.java
```
private static final String A_COLOR = "a_Color";
private static final int COLOR_COMPONENT_COUNT = 3;
private static final int STRIDE =
    (POSITION_COMPONENT_COUNT + COLOR_COMPONENT_COUNT) * BYTES_PER_FLOAT;
```

We'll also need a new member variable:

AirHockey2/src/com/airhockey/android/AirHockeyRenderer.java
```
private int aColorLocation;
```

We can now remove the old constants and variables associated with u_Color.

Did you notice that we added a special constant, called STRIDE? As we now have both a position and a color attribute in the same data array, OpenGL can no longer assume that the next position follows immediately after the previous position. Once OpenGL has read the position for a vertex, it will have to skip over the color for the current vertex if it wants to read the position for the next vertex. We'll use the stride to tell OpenGL how many bytes are between each position so that it knows how far it has to skip.

In Figure 17, *A single vertex array with multiple attributes*, on page 73, we can see a visual example of how our vertex array is currently storing the data.

The stride tells OpenGL the interval between each position or each color. Instead of using a stride, we could use multiple vertex arrays for each attribute, as seen in Figure 18, *Multiple vertex arrays, each with a single attribute*, on page 73. While packing everything into a single array is usually more efficient, using multiple arrays might make more sense if we need to update all of the colors or all of the positions on a regular basis.

Updating onSurfaceCreated()

The next step will be to update onSurfaceCreated() to reflect the new color attribute. We first need to get the location of our new attribute, so let's remove the code associated with u_Color and add the following code:

AirHockey2/src/com/airhockey/android/AirHockeyRenderer.java
```
aColorLocation = glGetAttribLocation(program, A_COLOR);
```

We should also update the call to glVertexAttribPointer() to add in the stride:

AirHockey2/src/com/airhockey/android/AirHockeyRenderer.java
```
glVertexAttribPointer(aPositionLocation, POSITION_COMPONENT_COUNT, GL_FLOAT,
    false, STRIDE, vertexData);
```

Now we can add in the code to tell OpenGL to associate our vertex data with a_Color in the shader. Add the following code to the end of onSurfaceCreated():

AirHockey2/src/com/airhockey/android/AirHockeyRenderer.java
```
vertexData.position(POSITION_COMPONENT_COUNT);
glVertexAttribPointer(aColorLocation, COLOR_COMPONENT_COUNT, GL_FLOAT,
    false, STRIDE, vertexData);

glEnableVertexAttribArray(aColorLocation);
```

This is an important bit of code, so let's take the time to understand each line carefully:

1. First we set the position of vertexData to POSITION_COMPONENT_COUNT, which is set to 2. Why do we do this? Well, when OpenGL starts reading in the color attributes, we want it to start at the first *color* attribute, not the first position attribute.

   We need to skip over the first position ourselves by taking the position component size into account, so we set the position to POSITION_COMPONENT_COUNT so that the buffer's position is set to the position of the very first color attribute. Had we set the position to 0 instead, OpenGL would be reading in the position as the color.

2. We then call glVertexAttribPointer() to associate our color data with a_Color in our shaders. The stride tells OpenGL how many bytes are between each

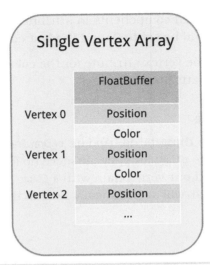

Figure 17—A single vertex array with multiple attributes

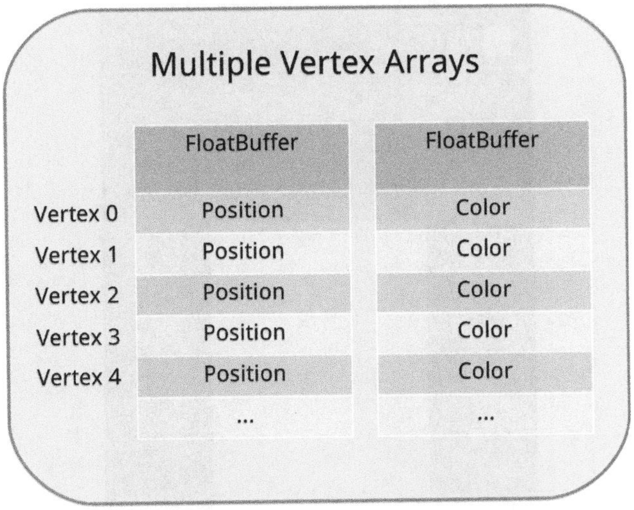

Figure 18—Multiple vertex arrays, each with a single attribute

color, so that when it reads in the colors for all of the vertices, it knows how many bytes it needs to skip to read the color for the next vertex. It's very important that the stride be specified in terms of bytes.

Even though a color in OpenGL has four components (red, green, blue, and alpha), we don't have to specify all of them. Unlike uniforms, OpenGL will replace unspecified components in attributes with defaults: the first three components will be set to 0, and the last component set to 1.

3. Finally, we enable the vertex attribute for the color attribute, just like we did for the position attribute.

Updating onDrawFrame

We have just one more thing to do: update onDrawFrame(). All we have to do here is delete the calls to glUniform4f(), because we no longer need them. Since we've already associated our vertex data with a_Color, all we need to do is call glDrawArrays(), and OpenGL will automatically read in the color attributes from our vertex data.

Putting It All Together

Let's run our program and see what we get; it should look like the following figure:

Figure 19—Brightening the center with linear interpolation

Our air hockey table looks nicer than before, and we can definitely see that the table is now brighter in the center than on the edges. However, we can also make out the shape of each triangle. The reason for this is because the direction of the linear interpolation follows the triangle, so while things look smooth within that triangle, we can sometimes still see where one triangle ends and another begins.

To reduce or eliminate this effect, we can use more triangles or we can use a lighting algorithm and calculate the color values on a per-fragment basis. We'll learn more about lighting algorithms in Chapter 13, *Lighting Up the World*, on page 253.

4.5 A Review

Adding color to each vertex wasn't so bad now that we have a basic framework in place. To do this, we added a new attribute to our vertex data and vertex shader, and we also told OpenGL how to read this data by using a stride. We then learned how to interpolate this data across the surface of a triangle by using a varying.

One important point to remember is that when we pass in our attribute data, we need to make sure to also pass in the right values for the component counts and the stride. If we get these wrong, we could end up with anything from a garbled screen to a crash.

4.6 Exercises

See if you can add some color interpolation to the line cutting across the middle of the screen. For a more challenging exercise, how would you change the triangles that make up the air hockey table so that the edges are less visible? Hint: You can try adding more triangles to the fan.

Once you've completed these exercises, we'll start to learn about vectors and matrices and learn how we can fix a pesky problem that appears when we rotate from portrait to landscape.

CHAPTER 5

Adjusting to the Screen's Aspect Ratio

You might not have noticed it yet, but we currently have an aspect ratio problem with our air hockey table. To see what's happening, open the latest project from the previous chapter and go ahead and run the app on your device or in the emulator. Once it's running, rotate your device from portrait to landscape (if using the emulator, press CTRL-F12).

The app should look like the next figure in portrait mode, and the subsequent figure in landscape mode:

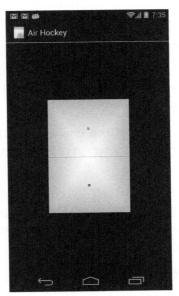

Figure 20—Air hockey in portrait

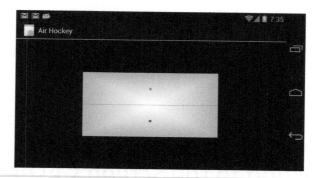

Figure 21—Air hockey in landscape

Our table is squashed in landscape mode! The reason why this is happening is because we've been passing our coordinates into OpenGL directly, without compensating for the aspect ratio of the screen. Every 2D and 3D application shares one big problem: how does it decide what to display on the screen, and how do they adjust for the screen dimensions? This problem also has a common solution: in OpenGL, we can use a projection to map a part of our world onto the screen, and we can map it in such a way that it looks correct across different screen sizes and orientations. With the wide variety of devices out there, it's important to be able to adjust to all of them.

In this chapter, we're going to learn why our table appears squashed and how we can use a projection to fix the problem. Here's our game plan:

- First we'll review some basic linear algebra and learn how to multiply a matrix and a vector together.

- Then we'll learn how to define and use a projection with a matrix, which will let us compensate for the screen's orientation so that our table doesn't appear squashed.

As in the last chapter, let's start off by copying the project from the last chapter over into a new project. Let's call this new project 'AirHockeyOrtho'. If you need a quick refresher, please follow the sequence in Section 2.2, *Don't Start from Scratch*, on page 21.

5.1 We Have an Aspect Ratio Problem

We're now pretty familiar with the fact that everything we render in OpenGL gets mapped to a range of [-1, 1] on both the *x*- and *y*-axes; this is also true of the *z*-axis. Coordinates in this range are known as *normalized device coordinates* and are independent of the actual size or shape of the screen.

Unfortunately, because they are independent of the actual screen dimensions, we can run into problems if we use them directly, such as a squashed table in landscape mode.

Let's say that our actual device resolution is 1280 x 720 in pixels, which is a common resolution on new Android devices. Let's also pretend for a moment that we're using the whole display for OpenGL, as it will make this discussion easier.

If our device is in portrait mode, then [-1, 1] will range over 1280 pixels of height but only 720 pixels of width. Our image would appear flattened along the *x*-axis. The same problem happens along the *y*-axis if we're in landscape mode.

Normalized device coordinates assume that the coordinate space is a square, as seen in the following image:

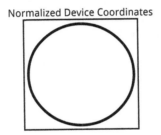
Normalized Device Coordinates

However, since the actual viewport might not be a square, the image will get stretched in one direction and squashed in the other. An image defined in normalized device coordinates would be squashed horizontally when seen on a portrait device:

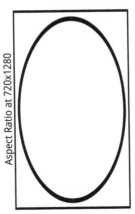
Aspect Ratio at 720x1280

The same image would be squashed the other way when in landscape mode:

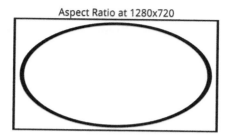

Aspect Ratio at 1280x720

Adjusting to the Aspect Ratio

We need to adjust the coordinate space so that it takes the screen shape into account, and one way that we can do this is to keep the smaller range fixed to [-1, 1] and adjust the larger range in proportion to the screen dimensions.

For example, in portrait, the width is 720 while the height is 1280, so we can keep the width range at [-1, 1] and adjust the height range to [-1280/720, 1280/720] or [-1.78, 1.78]. We can also do the same thing in landscape mode, with the width range set to [-1.78, 1.78] and the height range set to [-1, 1].

By adjusting the coordinate space that we have, we will end up changing the space that we have available:

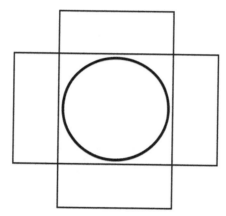

This way, objects will look the same in both portrait and landscape modes.

5.2 Working with a Virtual Coordinate Space

To adjust the coordinate space so that we can take screen orientation into account, we need to stop working directly in normalized device coordinates and start working in a virtual coordinate space. We then need to find some way of converting coordinates from our virtual space back into normalized device coordinates so that OpenGL can render them correctly. This conversion should take the screen orientation into account so that our air hockey table will look correct in both portrait and landscape modes.

What we want to do is called an *orthographic projection*. With an orthographic projection, everything always appears the same size, no matter how close or far away it is. To better understand what this type of projection does, imagine that we had a set of train tracks in our scene. This is what the tracks might look like from directly overhead:

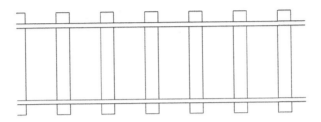

There's also a special type of orthographic projection known as an *isometric projection*, which is an orthographic projection shown from a side angle. This type of projection can be used to recreate a classic 3D angle, as seen in some city simulations and strategy games.

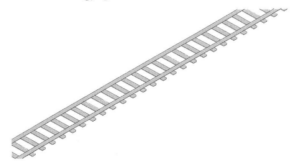

From Virtual Coordinates Back to Normalized Device Coordinates

When we use an orthographic projection to transform from virtual coordinates back into normalized device coordinates, we're actually defining a region inside of our 3D world. Everything inside that region will get displayed on the screen, and everything outside of that region will be clipped. In the following image, we can see a simple scene with an enclosing cube (Figure 22, *Scene in an Orthographic Cube*, on page 82).

When we use an orthographic projection matrix to map this cube onto the screen, we'll see Figure 23, *An Orthographic Projection*, on page 82.

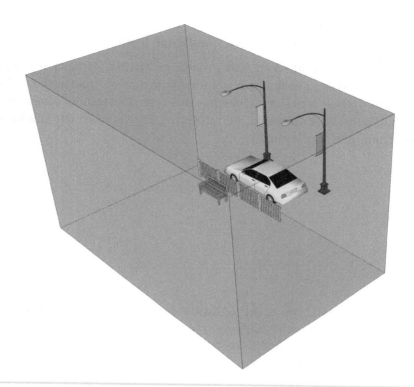

Figure 22—Scene in an Orthographic Cube

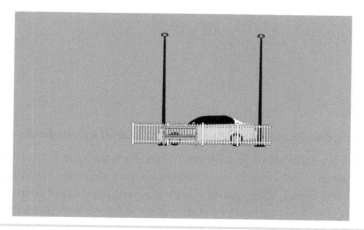

Figure 23—An Orthographic Projection

With an orthographic projection matrix, we can change the size of this cube so that we can see more or less of our scene on the screen. We can also change the shape of this cube to compensate for the screen's aspect ratio.

Before we start using an orthographic projection, we'll need to review some basic linear algebra.

5.3 Linear Algebra 101

So much of OpenGL works with vectors and matrices, and one of the most important uses of a matrix is in setting up orthographic and perspective projections. One of the reasons for this is that at the heart of things, using a matrix to do a projection just involves a bunch of "adds" and "multiplies" over a set of data in sequence, and modern GPUs are very, very fast at that sort of thing.

Let's go back in time to when you were in high school or college and review the basics of linear algebra. If you don't remember, have bad memories, or never took the class, there's no need to worry; we'll walk through the basic math together. Once we understand the basic math, we'll then learn how we can use a matrix to do an orthographic projection.

Vectors

A vector is a one-dimensional array of elements. In OpenGL, a position is usually a four-element vector, as is a color. Most of the vectors we work with will generally have four elements. In the following example, we can see a position vector with an x, a y, a z, and a w component.

$$\begin{bmatrix} x \\ y \\ z \\ w \end{bmatrix}.$$

We'll explain the w component in more detail in Chapter 6, *Entering the Third Dimension*, on page 95.

Matrices

A matrix is a two-dimensional array of elements. In OpenGL, we generally use matrices to project vectors using an orthographic or perspective projection, and we can also use them to do rotations, translations, and scaling of an object. We do this by multiplying the matrix with each vector that we want to transform.

The following is an example of a matrix. The labeling will make sense once we look at how to multiply a matrix and a vector together.

$$\begin{bmatrix} x_x & x_y & x_z & x_w \\ y_x & y_y & y_z & y_w \\ z_x & z_y & z_z & z_w \\ w_x & w_y & w_z & w_w \end{bmatrix}$$

Matrix-Vector Multiplication

To multiply a vector with a matrix, we put the matrix on the left side and the vector on the right side. We then start with the first row of the matrix and multiply the first component of that row with the first component of the vector, the second component of that row with the second component of the vector, and so on. We then add all of the results for that row together to create the first component of the result.

The following is an example of a complete matrix-vector multiply:

$$\begin{bmatrix} x_x & x_y & x_z & x_w \\ y_x & y_y & y_z & y_w \\ z_x & z_y & z_z & z_w \\ w_x & w_y & w_z & w_w \end{bmatrix} \begin{bmatrix} x \\ y \\ z \\ w \end{bmatrix} = \begin{bmatrix} x_x x & + & x_y y & + & x_z z & + & x_w w \\ y_x x & + & y_y y & + & y_z z & + & y_w w \\ z_x x & + & z_y y & + & z_z z & + & z_w w \\ w_x x & + & w_y y & + & w_z z & + & w_w w \end{bmatrix}$$

For the first row, we multiply x_x and x, x_y and y, x_z and z, x_w and w, and then add all four results together to create the x component of the result.

The labeling of the matrix should hopefully make more sense now that we've seen it in action. All four components of the first row of the matrix will affect the resulting x, all four components of the second row will affect the resulting y, and so on. Within each row of the matrix, the first component gets multiplied with the x of the vector, the second component gets multiplied with the y, and so on.

The Identity Matrix

Let's look at an example with some actual numbers. We'll start off with a very basic matrix, called the identity matrix. An identity matrix looks like the following:

$$\begin{bmatrix} 1 & 0 & 0 & 0 \\ 0 & 1 & 0 & 0 \\ 0 & 0 & 1 & 0 \\ 0 & 0 & 0 & 1 \end{bmatrix}$$

The reason this is called an identity matrix is because we can multiply this matrix with any vector and we'll always get back the same vector, just like we get back the same number if we multiply any number by 1.

Here's an example of multiplying an identity matrix with a vector containing 1, 2, 3, and 4:

$$\begin{bmatrix} 1 & 0 & 0 & 0 \\ 0 & 1 & 0 & 0 \\ 0 & 0 & 1 & 0 \\ 0 & 0 & 0 & 1 \end{bmatrix} \begin{bmatrix} 1 \\ 2 \\ 3 \\ 4 \end{bmatrix} = \begin{bmatrix} 1\times1 & + & 0\times2 & + & 0\times3 & + & 0\times4 \\ 0\times1 & + & 1\times2 & + & 0\times3 & + & 0\times4 \\ 0\times1 & + & 0\times2 & + & 1\times3 & + & 0\times4 \\ 0\times1 & + & 0\times2 & + & 0\times3 & + & 1\times4 \end{bmatrix}$$

For the first row, we multiply the first component of the vector by 1 and ignore the other components by multiplying them by 0. For the second row, we do the same thing, except we preserve the second component of the vector. The net result of all of this is that the answer will be identical to the original vector.

Let's simplify those multiplies and add the results together. This is what we'll get:

$$\begin{bmatrix} 1 \\ 2 \\ 3 \\ 4 \end{bmatrix}$$

Translations Using a Matrix

Now that we understand the identity matrix, let's look at a very simple type of matrix that gets used quite often in OpenGL: the translation matrix. With this type of matrix, we can move one of our objects along a distance that we specify. This matrix looks just like an identity matrix, with three additional elements specified on the right-hand side:

$$\begin{bmatrix} 1 & 0 & 0 & x_{translation} \\ 0 & 1 & 0 & y_{translation} \\ 0 & 0 & 1 & z_{translation} \\ 0 & 0 & 0 & 1 \end{bmatrix}$$

Let's look at an example with a position of (2, 2), with a default z of 0 and a default w of 1. We want to translate the vector by 3 along the x-axis and 3 along the y-axis, so we'll put 3 for $x_{translation}$ and 3 for $y_{translation}$.

Here's the result:

$$\begin{bmatrix} 1 & 0 & 0 & 3 \\ 0 & 1 & 0 & 3 \\ 0 & 0 & 1 & 0 \\ 0 & 0 & 0 & 1 \end{bmatrix} \begin{bmatrix} 2 \\ 2 \\ 0 \\ 1 \end{bmatrix} = \begin{bmatrix} 1 \times 2 & + & 0 \times 2 & + & 0 \times 0 & + & 3 \times 1 \\ 0 \times 2 & + & 1 \times 2 & + & 0 \times 0 & + & 3 \times 1 \\ 0 \times 2 & + & 0 \times 2 & + & 1 \times 0 & + & 0 \times 1 \\ 0 \times 2 & + & 0 \times 2 & + & 0 \times 0 & + & 1 \times 1 \end{bmatrix}$$

After we simplify the multiplies, we're left with this:

$$\begin{bmatrix} 2 & + & 0 & + & 0 & + & 3 \\ 0 & + & 2 & + & 0 & + & 3 \\ 0 & + & 0 & + & 0 & + & 0 \\ 0 & + & 0 & + & 0 & + & 1 \end{bmatrix}$$

Adding the results together gives us the final answer:

$$\begin{bmatrix} 5 \\ 5 \\ 0 \\ 1 \end{bmatrix}$$

The position is now at (5, 5), which is what we expected.

The reason this works is that we built this matrix from an identity matrix, so the first thing that will happen is that the original vector will be copied over. Since the translation components are multiplied by w, and we normally specify a position's w component as 1 (remember that if we don't specify the w component, OpenGL sets it to 1 by default), the translation components just get added to the result.

The effect of w is important to take note of here. In the next chapter, we'll learn about perspective projections, and a coordinate may not have a w value of 1 after such a projection. If we try to do a translation or another type of transformation with that coordinate *after* we've done a projection and the w component is no longer 1, then we'll run into trouble and things will get distorted.

We've learned just enough about vector and matrix math to get us on our feet; let's go ahead and learn how to define an orthographic projection.

5.4 Defining an Orthographic Projection

To define an orthographic projection, we'll use Android's Matrix class, which resides in the android.opengl package. In that class there's a method called orthoM(), which will generate an orthographic projection for us. We'll use that projection to adjust the coordinate space, as we just discussed in *Adjusting to the Aspect Ratio*, on page 80, and as we'll soon see, an orthographic projection is very similar to a translation matrix.

Let's take a look at all of the parameters for orthoM():

orthoM(float[] m, int mOffset, float left, float right, float bottom, float top, float near, float far)

float[] m	The destination array—this array's length should be at least sixteen elements so it can store the orthographic projection matrix.
int mOffset	The offset into m into which the result is written
float left	The minimum range of the x-axis
float right	The maximum range of the x-axis
float bottom	The minimum range of the y-axis
float top	The maximum range of the y-axis
float near	The minimum range of the z-axis
float far	The maximum range of the z-axis

When we call this method, it should produce the following orthographic projection matrix:

$$\begin{bmatrix} \dfrac{2}{right-left} & 0 & 0 & -\dfrac{right+left}{right-left} \\ 0 & \dfrac{2}{top-bottom} & 0 & -\dfrac{top+bottom}{top-bottom} \\ 0 & 0 & \dfrac{-2}{far-near} & -\dfrac{far+near}{far-near} \\ 0 & 0 & 0 & 1 \end{bmatrix}$$

Don't let the fractions overwhelm you: this is very similar to the translation matrix that we saw in *Translations Using a Matrix*, on page 85. This orthographic projection matrix will map everything between left and right, bottom and top, and near and far into the range -1 to 1 in normalized device coordinates, and everything within this range will be visible on the screen.

The main difference is that the z-axis has a negative sign on it, which has the effect of *inverting* the z coordinate. This means that as things get further away, their z coordinate becomes more and more negative. The reason for this is entirely due to history and convention.

Left-Handed and Right-Handed Coordinate Systems

To better understand the issue with the z-axis, we need to understand the difference between a left-handed coordinate system and a right-handed coordinate system. To see whether a coordinate system is left-handed or right-handed, you take one of your hands and point your thumb along the positive x-axis. You then take your index finder and point it along the positive y-axis.

Now, point your middle finger along the z-axis. If you need to use your left hand to do this, then you're looking at a left-handed coordinate system. If you need to use your right hand, then this is a right-handed coordinate system.

Try this out with Figure 24, *Left-handed coordinate system*, on page 89 and Figure 25, *Right-handed coordinate system*, on page 89 by pointing your middle finger along the z-axis, and remember to point your thumb along the positive x-axis and your index finger along the positive y.

The choice of left-handed or right-handed really does not matter and is simply a matter of convention. While normalized device coordinates use a left-handed coordinate system, in earlier versions of OpenGL, everything else used the right-handed system by default, with negative z increasing into the distance. This is why Android's Matrix will generate matrices that invert the z by default.

If you would prefer to use a left-handed coordinate system everywhere and not just in normalized device coordinates, then you can just undo the inversion on the z-axis done by orthoM().

Now that we have a basic feel for matrix math, we're ready to add an orthographic projection to our code. If you'd like to review some specific examples, you can head to Section A1.1, *The Math Behind Orthographic Projections*, on page 297, and return here once you're ready to proceed with the next section.

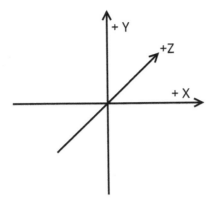

Figure 24—Left-handed coordinate system

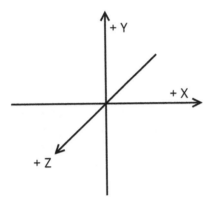

Figure 25—Right-handed coordinate system

5.5 Adding an Orthographic Projection

Let's update our code to add in an orthographic projection and fix that squashed table.

Updating the Shader

The first thing we need to do is update the shader so that it uses our matrix to transform our positions. If you don't yet have the AirHockeyOrtho project open (we created this project back at the beginning of this chapter), go ahead and open it up. Open simple_vertex_shader.glsl and update it as follows:

AirHockeyOrtho/res/raw/simple_vertex_shader.glsl

```
uniform mat4 u_Matrix;

attribute vec4 a_Position;
attribute vec4 a_Color;

varying vec4 v_Color;

void main()
{
    v_Color = a_Color;

    gl_Position = u_Matrix * a_Position;
    gl_PointSize = 10.0;
}
```

We've added a new uniform definition, u_Matrix, and we've defined it as a mat4, meaning that this uniform will represent a 4 x 4 matrix. We've also updated the line that assigns the position as follows:

AirHockeyOrtho/res/raw/simple_vertex_shader.glsl

```
gl_Position = u_Matrix * a_Position;
```

Instead of just passing through the position as we've defined it in our array, we now multiply the matrix with the position. This will do the same math as we talked about back in *Matrix-Vector Multiplication*, on page 84. It also means that our vertex array will no longer be interpreted as normalized device coordinates but will now be interpreted as existing in a virtual coordinate space, as defined by the matrix. The matrix will transform the coordinates from this virtual coordinate space back into normalized device coordinates.

Adding the Matrix Array and a New Uniform

Open up AirHockeyRenderer and add the following definition to the top of the class:

AirHockeyOrtho/src/com/airhockey/android/AirHockeyRenderer.java

```
private static final String U_MATRIX = "u_Matrix";
```

This holds the name of the new uniform that we defined in our vertex shader. We'll also need a floating point array to store the matrix:

AirHockeyOrtho/src/com/airhockey/android/AirHockeyRenderer.java

```
private final float[] projectionMatrix = new float[16];
```

We'll also need an integer to hold the location of the matrix uniform:

AirHockeyOrtho/src/com/airhockey/android/AirHockeyRenderer.java

```
private int uMatrixLocation;
```

Then we just need to add the following to onSurfaceCreated():

AirHockeyOrtho/src/com/airhockey/android/AirHockeyRenderer.java
```
uMatrixLocation = glGetUniformLocation(program, U_MATRIX);
```

Creating the Orthographic Projection Matrix

The next step will be to update onSurfaceChanged(). Add the following lines after the call to glViewport():

AirHockeyOrtho/src/com/airhockey/android/AirHockeyRenderer.java
```
final float aspectRatio = width > height ?
    (float) width / (float) height :
    (float) height / (float) width;

if (width > height) {
    // Landscape
    orthoM(projectionMatrix, 0, -aspectRatio, aspectRatio, -1f, 1f, -1f, 1f);
} else {
    // Portrait or square
    orthoM(projectionMatrix, 0, -1f, 1f, -aspectRatio, aspectRatio, -1f, 1f);
}
```

This code will create an orthographic projection matrix that will take the screen's current orientation into account. It will set up a virtual coordinate space the way we described in *Adjusting to the Aspect Ratio*, on page 80. There's more than one Matrix class in Android, so you'll want to make sure that you're importing android.opengl.Matrix.

First we calculate the aspect ratio by taking the greater of the width and height and dividing it by the smaller of the width and height. This value will be the same regardless of whether we're in portrait or landscape.

We then call orthoM(float[] m, int mOffset, float left, float right, float bottom, float top, float near, float far). If we're in landscape mode, we'll expand the coordinate space of the width so that instead of ranging from -1 to 1, the width will range from -aspectRatio to aspectRatio. The height will stay from -1 to 1. If we're in portrait mode, we expand the height instead and keep the width at -1 to 1.

Sending the Matrix to the Shader

The last change to do in AirHockeyRenderer is to send the orthographic projection matrix to the shader. We do that by adding the following line of code to onDrawFrame(), just after the call to glClear():

AirHockeyOrtho/src/com/airhockey/android/AirHockeyRenderer.java
```
glUniformMatrix4fv(uMatrixLocation, 1, false, projectionMatrix, 0);
```

Viewing Our Changes

We can now run the application and see what we have. It should look similar to the following figures in portrait mode and landscape mode:

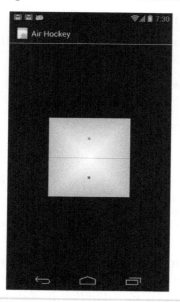

Figure 26—Air hockey in portrait mode using an orthographic projection

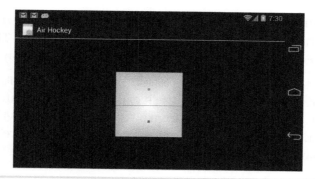

Figure 27—Air hockey in landscape mode using an orthographic projection

Updating the Table Data

Our table now looks the same in both portrait and landscape mode, which is what we wanted, but it still doesn't look quite right. What happened is that the table was being squished to appear narrower in portrait mode, and now that there's no more squishing we can see the table as we've defined it.

Let's update the table structure to make it taller (as seen in the next two figures); update *only* the *y* positions (the second column) of tableVerticesWithTriangles to match the data as follows:

AirHockeyOrtho/src/com/airhockey/android/AirHockeyRenderer.java
```
float[] tableVerticesWithTriangles = {
    // Order of coordinates: X, Y, R, G, B

    // Triangle Fan
      0f,    0f,   1f,    1f,    1f,
    -0.5f, -0.8f, 0.7f, 0.7f, 0.7f,
     0.5f, -0.8f, 0.7f, 0.7f, 0.7f,
     0.5f,  0.8f, 0.7f, 0.7f, 0.7f,
    -0.5f,  0.8f, 0.7f, 0.7f, 0.7f,
    -0.5f, -0.8f, 0.7f, 0.7f, 0.7f,

    // Line 1
    -0.5f, 0f, 1f, 0f, 0f,
     0.5f, 0f, 1f, 0f, 0f,

    // Mallets
    0f, -0.4f, 0f, 0f, 1f,
    0f,  0.4f, 1f, 0f, 0f
};
```

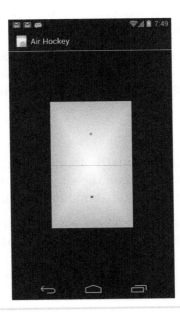

Figure 28—Air hockey in portrait mode, slightly taller

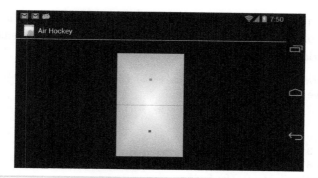

Figure 29—Air hockey in landscape mode, slightly taller

Now it looks a little more like the shape we'd expect of an air hockey table *and* it keeps its shape in both portrait and landscape modes.

5.6 A Review

We took the time to learn some of the basics behind linear algebra and used it to understand what happens when we multiply a matrix with a vector. We then learned how to define an orthographic projection matrix, which allows us to redefine our coordinate space, and we used this matrix to fix the distortion that we had whenever we rotated from portrait to landscape mode.

If any part of the matrix math appeared unclear, you might want to go back and review Section 5.3, *Linear Algebra 101*, on page 83; we'll be spending more and more time with vectors and matrices from here to the end of the book!

5.7 Exercises

Try adjusting the orthographic matrix to make the table appear larger and smaller, as well as pan it around on the screen. To make this happen, you'll want to play with the left, right, top, and bottom values passed to orthoM().

Once you've completed these exercises, get ready and hold on to your seat, because we're going to be entering the third dimension.

CHAPTER 6

Entering the Third Dimension

Imagine that you're at an arcade, standing in front of an air hockey table and looking over the table toward your opponent. What would the table look like from your perspective? Your end of the table would appear larger, and you would be looking down at the table from an angle, rather than from directly overhead. After all, nobody plays a game of air hockey by standing on top of the table and looking straight down.

OpenGL is great at rendering things in 2D, but it really begins to shine when we add a third dimension to the mix. In this chapter, we'll learn how to enter the third dimension so we can get that visual feel of staring down our opponent from across the table.

Here's our game plan for the chapter:

- First we'll learn about OpenGL's *perspective division* and how to use the w component to create the illusion of 3D on a 2D screen.

- Once we understand the w component, we'll learn how to set up a perspective projection so that we can see the table in 3D.

Let's start off by copying the project from last chapter over into a new project, called 'AirHockey3D'.

6.1 The Art of 3D

For centuries, artists have been fooling people into perceiving a flat two-dimensional painting as a complete three-dimensional scene. One of the tricks they use is called *linear projection*, and it works by joining together parallel lines at an imaginary vanishing point to create the illusion of perspective.

We can see a classic example of this effect when standing on a straight pair of railway tracks; as we look at the rails receding into the distance, they appear to get closer together, until they seem to vanish at a single point on the horizon:

The railroad ties also appear to get smaller as they get further away from us. If we measured the apparent size of each railroad tie, their measured size would decrease in proportion to their distance from our eyes.

In the following image, observe how the measured width of each railroad tie decreases with distance:

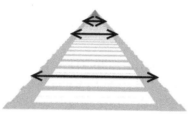

This trick is all that is needed to create a realistic 3D projection; let's go ahead and learn how OpenGL actually does it.

6.2 Transforming a Coordinate from the Shader to the Screen

We are now familiar with normalized device coordinates, and we know that in order for a vertex to display on the screen, its x, y, and z components all need to be in the range of [-1, 1]. Let's take a look at the following flow chart to review how a coordinate gets transformed from the original gl_Position written by the vertex shader to the final coordinate onscreen:

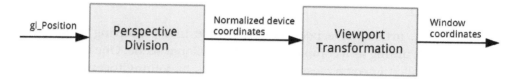

There are two transformation steps and three different coordinate spaces.

Clip Space

When the vertex shader writes a value out to gl_Position, OpenGL expects this position to be in *clip space*. The logic behind clip space is very simple: for any given position, the x, y, and z components all need to be between $-w$ and w for that position. For example, if a position's w is 1, then the x, y, and z components all need to be between -1 and 1. Anything outside this range will not be visible on the screen.

The reason why it depends on the position's w will be apparent once we learn about perspective division.

Perspective Division

Before a vertex position becomes a normalized device coordinate, OpenGL actually performs an extra step known as *perspective division*. After perspective division, positions will be in normalized device coordinates, in which every visible coordinate will lie in the range of [-1, 1] for the x, y, and z components, regardless of the size or shape of the rendering area.

To create the illusion of 3D on the screen, OpenGL will take each gl_Position and divide the x, y, and z components by the w component. When the w component is used to represent distance, this causes objects that are further away to be moved closer to the center of the rendering area, which then acts like a vanishing point. This is how OpenGL fools us into seeing a scene in 3D, using the same trick that artists have been using for centuries.

For example, let's say that we have an object with two vertices, each at the same location in 3D space, with the same x, y, and z components, but with different w components. Let's say these two coordinates are (1, 1, 1, 1) and (1, 1, 1, 2). Before OpenGL uses these as normalized device coordinates, it will do a perspective divide and divide the first three components by w; each coordinate will be divided as follows: (1/1, 1/1, 1/1) and (1/2, 1/2, 1/2). After this division, the normalized device coordinates will be (1, 1, 1) and (0.5, 0.5, 0.5). The coordinate with the larger w was moved closer to (0, 0, 0), the center of the rendering area in normalized device coordinates.

In the following image, we can see an example of this effect in action, as a coordinate with the same x, y, and z will be brought ever closer to the center as the w value increases:

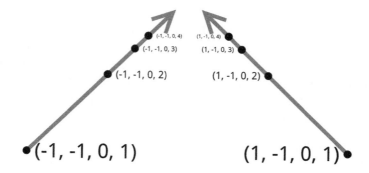

In OpenGL, the 3D effect is linear and done along straight lines. In real life, things are more complicated (imagine a fish-eye lens), but this sort of linear projection is a reasonable approximation.

Homogenous Coordinates

Because of the perspective division, coordinates in clip space are often referred to as *homogenous coordinates*,[1] introduced by August Ferdinand Möbius in 1827. The reason they are called *homogenous* is because several coordinates in clip space can map to the same point. For example, take the following points:

(1, 1, 1, 1), (2, 2, 2, 2), (3, 3, 3, 3), (4, 4, 4, 4), (5, 5, 5, 5)

After perspective division, all of these points will map to (1, 1, 1) in normalized device coordinates.

The Advantages of Dividing by *W*

You might be wondering why we don't simply divide by *z* instead. After all, if we interpret *z* as the distance and had two coordinates, (1, 1, 1) and (1, 1, 2), we could then divide by *z* to get two normalized coordinates of (1, 1) and (0.5, 0.5).

While this can work, there are additional advantages to adding *w* as a fourth component. We can decouple the perspective effect from the actual *z* coordinate, so we can switch between an orthographic and a perspective projection. There's also a benefit to preserving the *z* component as a depth buffer, which we'll cover in *Removing Hidden Surfaces with the Depth Buffer*, on page 245.

---

1.   http://en.wikipedia.org/wiki/Homogeneous_coordinates

Viewport Transformation

Before we can see the final result, OpenGL needs to map the *x* and *y* components of the normalized device coordinates to an area on the screen that the operating system has set aside for display, called the *viewport*; these mapped coordinates are known as *window coordinates*. We don't really need to be too concerned about these coordinates beyond telling OpenGL how to do the mapping. We're currently doing this in our code with a call to glViewport() in onSurfaceChanged().

When OpenGL does this mapping, it will map the range (-1, -1, -1) to (1, 1, 1) to the window that has been set aside for display. Normalized device coordinates outside of this range will be clipped. As we learned in Chapter 5, *Adjusting to the Screen's Aspect Ratio*, on page 77, this range is always the same, regardless of the width or height of the viewport.

6.3 Adding the *W* Component to Create Perspective

It will be easier to understand the effects of the *w* component if we actually see it in action, so let's add it to our table vertex data and see what happens. Since we'll now be specifying the *x*, *y*, *z*, and *w* components of a position, let's begin by updating POSITION_COMPONENT_COUNT as follows:

AirHockey3D/src/com/airhockey/android/AirHockeyRenderer.java
```
private static final int POSITION_COMPONENT_COUNT = 4;
```

We must always make sure that we're giving OpenGL the right component count for everything that we use; otherwise we'll either have a corrupt screen, nothing will display at all, or we might even crash our application.

The next step is to update all of our vertices:

AirHockey3D/src/com/airhockey/android/AirHockeyRenderer.java
```
float[] tableVerticesWithTriangles = {
    // Order of coordinates: X, Y, Z, W, R, G, B

    // Triangle Fan
       0f,    0f, 0f, 1.5f,   1f,   1f,   1f,
    -0.5f, -0.8f, 0f,   1f, 0.7f, 0.7f, 0.7f,
     0.5f, -0.8f, 0f,   1f, 0.7f, 0.7f, 0.7f,
     0.5f,  0.8f, 0f,   2f, 0.7f, 0.7f, 0.7f,
    -0.5f,  0.8f, 0f,   2f, 0.7f, 0.7f, 0.7f,
    -0.5f, -0.8f, 0f,   1f, 0.7f, 0.7f, 0.7f,

    // Line 1
    -0.5f, 0f, 0f, 1.5f, 1f, 0f, 0f,
     0.5f, 0f, 0f, 1.5f, 1f, 0f, 0f,
```

```
    // Mallets
    0f, -0.4f, 0f, 1.25f, 0f, 0f, 1f,
    0f,  0.4f, 0f, 1.75f, 1f, 0f, 0f
};
```

We added a z and a w component to our vertex data. We've updated all of the vertices so that the ones near the bottom of the screen have a w of 1 and the ones near the top of the screen have a w of 2; we also updated the line and the mallets to have a fractional w that's in between. This should have the effect of making the top part of the table appear smaller than the bottom, as if we were looking into the distance. We set all of our z components to zero, since we don't need to actually have anything in z to get the perspective effect.

OpenGL will automatically do the perspective divide for us using the w values that we've specified, and our current orthographic projection will just copy these w values over; so let's go ahead and run our project to see what it looks like. It should look similar to the next figure:

Things are starting to look more 3D! We were able to do this just by putting in our own w. However, what if we wanted to make things more dynamic, like changing the angle of the table or zooming in and out? Instead of hard-coding the w values, we'll use matrices to generate the values for us. Go ahead and revert the changes that we've made; in the next section, we'll learn how to use a perspective projection matrix to generate the w values automatically.

6.4   Moving to a Perspective Projection

Before we go into the matrix math behind a perspective projection, let's examine things at a visual level. In the previous chapter, we used an orthographic projection matrix to compensate for the aspect ratio of the screen by adjusting the width and height of the area that gets transformed into normalized device coordinates.

In the following image, we visualize an orthographic projection as a cube enclosing the entire scene, representing what OpenGL will end up rendering to the viewport and what we'll be able to see:

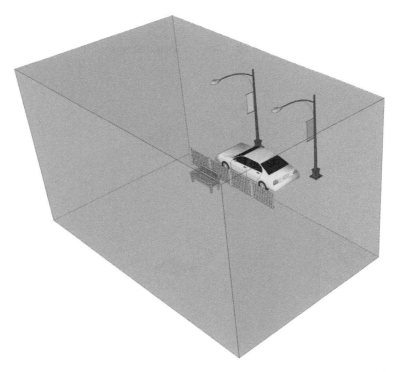

Figure 30, *The Projected Scene*, on page 102 shows the same scene from a different viewpoint:

The Frustum

Once we switch to a projection matrix, parallel lines in the scene will meet together at a vanishing point on the screen and objects will become smaller as they get further and further away. Instead of a cube, the region of space that we can see will look like Figure 31, *Projection through a Frustum*, on page 102.

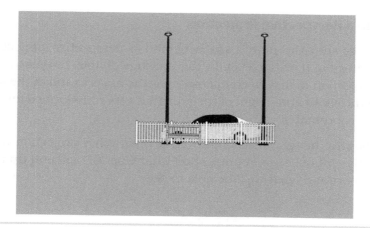

Figure 30—The Projected Scene

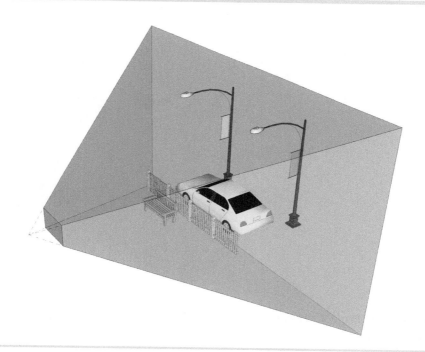

Figure 31—Projection through a Frustum

This shape is called a *frustum*,[2] and this viewing space is created with a perspective projection matrix and the perspective divide. A frustum is simply a

---

2. http://en.wikipedia.org/wiki/Frustum

cube that has been turned into a truncated pyramid by making the far side larger than the near side. The bigger the difference, the wider the field of view and the more that we can see.

With a frustum, there is also a focal point. This focal point can be found by following the lines that extend from the large end to the small end of the frustum and then following them past the small end until they meet together. When you view a scene with a perspective projection, that scene will appear as if your head was placed at this focal point. The distance between the focal point and the small end of the frustum is known as the *focal length*, and this influences the ratio between the small and large ends of the frustum and the corresponding field of vision.

In the following image, we can see the scene inside the frustum, as seen from the focal point:

Another interesting property of the focal point is that it is also the place where both ends of the frustum will *appear* to take up the same amount of space on the screen. The far end of the frustum is larger, but because it's also further away, it takes up the same amount of space. This is the same effect that we see during a solar eclipse: the moon is much smaller than the sun, but because it's also so much closer, it *appears* to be just large enough to cover up the disk of the sun! It all depends on our vantage point.

6.5 Defining a Perspective Projection

To recreate the magic of 3D, our perspective projection matrix needs to work together with the perspective divide. The projection matrix can't do the perspective divide by itself, and the perspective divide needs something to work with.

An object should move toward the center of the screen and decrease in size as it gets further away from us, so the most important task for our projection matrix is to create the proper values for w so that when OpenGL does the perspective divide, far objects will appear smaller than near objects. One of the ways that we can do that is by using the z component as the distance from the focal point and then mapping this distance to w. The greater the distance, the greater the w and the smaller the resulting object.

We won't go more into the math here, but if you want more details, you can jump ahead to Section A1.2, *The Math Behind Perspective Projections*, on page 300, and return here once you're ready to continue with the next section.

Adjusting for the Aspect Ratio and Field of Vision

Let's take a look at a more general-purpose projection matrix, which will allow us to adjust for the field of vision as well as for the screen's aspect ratio:

$$\begin{bmatrix} \dfrac{a}{aspect} & 0 & 0 & 0 \\ 0 & a & 0 & 0 \\ 0 & 0 & -\dfrac{f+n}{f-n} & -\dfrac{2fn}{f-n} \\ 0 & 0 & -1 & 0 \end{bmatrix}$$

Here's a quick explanation of the variables defined in this matrix:

a	If we imagine the scene as captured by a camera, then this variable represents the focal length of that camera. The focal length is calculated by *1/tangent of (field of vision/2)*. The field of vision must be less than 180 degrees.
	For example, with a field of vision of 90 degrees, the focal length will be set to *1/tangent of (90°/2)*, which is equal to 1/1, or 1.
aspect	This should be set to the aspect ratio of the screen, which is equal to width/height.
f	This should be set to the distance to the far plane and must be positive and greater than the distance to the near plane.
n	This should be set to the distance to the near plane and must be positive. For example, if this is set to 1, the near plane will be located at a z of -1.

Table 3—Projection matrix variables

As the field of vision gets smaller and the focal length gets longer, a smaller range of x and y values will map onto the range [-1, 1] in normalized device coordinates. This has the effect of making the frustum narrower.

In the following image, the frustum on the left has a field of vision of 90 degrees, while the frustum on the right has a field of vision of 45 degrees:

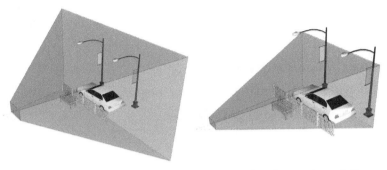

You can see that the focal length between the focal point and the near side of the frustum is slightly longer for the 45-degree frustum.

Here are the same frustums as seen from their points of focus:

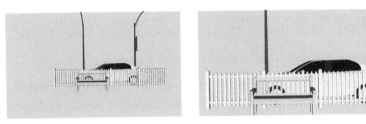

There are usually few distortion issues with a narrower field of vision. On the other hand, as the field of vision gets wider, the edges of the final image will appear more and more distorted. In real life, a wide field of vision would make everything look curved, like the effect seen from using a fish-eye lens on a camera. Since OpenGL uses linear projection along straight lines, the final image gets stretched out instead.

6.6 Creating a Projection Matrix in Our Code

We're now ready to add a perspective projection to our code. Android's Matrix class contains two methods for this, frustumM() and perspectiveM(). Unfortunately, frustumM() has a bug that affects some types of projections,[3] and perspectiveM() was only introduced in Android Ice Cream Sandwich and is not available on earlier versions of Android. We could simply target Ice Cream Sandwich and above, but then we'd be leaving out a large part of the market that still runs earlier versions of Android.

---

3. http://code.google.com/p/android/issues/detail?id=35646

Instead, we can create our own method to implement the matrix as defined in the previous section. Open up the project we created back at the beginning of this chapter and add a new class called MatrixHelper to the package com.airhockey.android.util. We'll implement a method very similar to the perspectiveM() in Android's Matrix class.

Creating Our Own perspectiveM

Add the following method signature to the beginning of MatrixHelper:

AirHockey3D/src/com/airhockey/android/util/MatrixHelper.java
```
public static void perspectiveM(float[] m, float yFovInDegrees, float aspect,
    float n, float f) {
```

Calculating the Focal Length

The first thing we'll do is calculate the focal length, which will be based on the field of vision across the y-axis. Add the following code just after the method signature:

AirHockey3D/src/com/airhockey/android/util/MatrixHelper.java
```
final float angleInRadians = (float) (yFovInDegrees * Math.PI / 180.0);

final float a = (float) (1.0 / Math.tan(angleInRadians / 2.0));
```

We use Java's Math class to calculate the tangent, and since it wants the angle in radians, we convert the field of vision from degrees to radians. We then calculate the focal length as described in the previous section.

Writing Out the Matrix

We can now write out the matrix values. Add the following code to complete the method:

AirHockey3D/src/com/airhockey/android/util/MatrixHelper.java
```
m[0] = a / aspect;
m[1] = 0f;
m[2] = 0f;
m[3] = 0f;

m[4] = 0f;
m[5] = a;
m[6] = 0f;
m[7] = 0f;

m[8] = 0f;
m[9] = 0f;
m[10] = -((f + n) / (f - n));
m[11] = -1f;
```

```
    m[12] = 0f;
    m[13] = 0f;
    m[14] = -((2f * f * n) / (f - n));
    m[15] = 0f;
}
```

This writes out the matrix data to the floating-point array defined in the argument m, which needs to have at least sixteen elements. OpenGL stores matrix data in *column-major* order, which means that we write out data one column at a time rather than one row at a time. The first four values refer to the first column, the second four values to the second column, and so on.

We've now finished our perspectiveM(), and we're ready to use it in our code. Our method is very similar to the one found in the Android source code,[4] with a few slight changes to make it more readable.

6.7 Switching to a Projection Matrix

We'll now switch to using the perspective projection matrix. Open up AirHockeyRenderer and remove all of the code from onSurfaceChanged(), except for the call to glViewport(). Add the following code:

AirHockey3D/src/com/airhockey/android/AirHockeyRenderer.java
```
MatrixHelper.perspectiveM(projectionMatrix, 45, (float) width
    / (float) height, 1f, 10f);
```

This will create a perspective projection with a field of vision of 45 degrees. The frustum will begin at a z of -1 and will end at a z of -10.

After adding the import for MatrixHelper, go ahead and run the program. You'll probably notice that our air hockey table has disappeared! Since we didn't specify a z position for our table, it's located at a z of 0 by default. Since our frustum begins at a z of -1, we won't be able to see the table unless we move it into the distance.

Instead of hard-coding the z values, let's use a translation matrix to move the table out before we project it using the projection matrix. By convention, we'll call this matrix the *model matrix*.

Moving Objects Around with a Model Matrix

Let's add the following matrix definition to the top of the class:

AirHockey3D/src/com/airhockey/android/AirHockeyRenderer.java
```
private final float[] modelMatrix = new float[16];
```

---

4. http://grepcode.com/file_/repository.grepcode.com/java/ext/com.google.android/android/4.0.4_r1.2/android/
   opengl/Matrix.java/?v=source

We'll use this matrix to move the air hockey table into the distance. At the end of onSurfaceChanged(), add the following code:

AirHockey3D/src/com/airhockey/android/AirHockeyRenderer.java
```
setIdentityM(modelMatrix, 0);
translateM(modelMatrix, 0, 0f, 0f, -2f);
```

This sets the model matrix to the identity matrix and then translates it by -2 along the z-axis. When we multiply our air hockey table coordinates with this matrix, they will end up getting moved by 2 units along the negative z-axis.

Multiplying Once Versus Multiplying Twice

We now have a choice: we still need to apply this matrix to each vertex, so our first option is to add the extra matrix to the vertex shader. We multiply each vertex by the model matrix to move it 2 units along the negative z-axis, and then we multiply each vertex by the projection matrix so that OpenGL can do the perspective divide and transform the vertices into normalized device coordinates.

Instead of going through all of this trouble, there's a better way: we can multiply the model and projection matrices together into a single matrix and then pass this matrix into the vertex shader. That way we can stay with one matrix in the shader.

Matrix Multiplication

Matrix-matrix multiplication works much like matrix-vector multiplication. For example, let's say that we had two generic matrices, as follows:

$$\begin{bmatrix} a_{11} & a_{12} & a_{13} & a_{14} \\ a_{21} & a_{22} & a_{23} & a_{24} \\ a_{31} & a_{32} & a_{33} & a_{34} \\ a_{41} & a_{42} & a_{43} & a_{44} \end{bmatrix} \begin{bmatrix} b_{11} & b_{12} & b_{13} & b_{14} \\ b_{21} & b_{22} & b_{23} & b_{24} \\ b_{31} & b_{32} & b_{33} & b_{34} \\ b_{41} & b_{42} & b_{43} & b_{44} \end{bmatrix}$$

To get the first element of the result, we multiply the first row of the first matrix by the first column of the second matrix and add together the results:

$$\begin{bmatrix} a_{11} & a_{12} & a_{13} & a_{14} \\ a_{21} & a_{22} & a_{23} & a_{24} \\ a_{31} & a_{32} & a_{33} & a_{34} \\ a_{41} & a_{42} & a_{43} & a_{44} \end{bmatrix} \begin{bmatrix} b_{11} & b_{12} & b_{13} & b_{14} \\ b_{21} & b_{22} & b_{23} & b_{24} \\ b_{31} & b_{32} & b_{33} & b_{34} \\ b_{41} & b_{42} & b_{43} & b_{44} \end{bmatrix} = \begin{bmatrix} a_{11}b_{11}+a_{12}b_{21}+a_{13}b_{31}+a_{14}b_{41} & ? & ? & ? \\ ? & ? & ? & ? \\ ? & ? & ? & ? \\ ? & ? & ? & ? \end{bmatrix}$$

Then for the second element of the result, we multiply the second row of the first matrix by the first column of the second matrix and add together the results:

$$\begin{bmatrix} a_{11} & a_{12} & a_{13} & a_{14} \\ a_{21} & a_{22} & a_{23} & a_{24} \\ a_{31} & a_{32} & a_{33} & a_{34} \\ a_{41} & a_{42} & a_{43} & a_{44} \end{bmatrix} \begin{bmatrix} b_{11} & b_{12} & b_{13} & b_{14} \\ b_{21} & b_{22} & b_{23} & b_{24} \\ b_{31} & b_{32} & b_{33} & b_{34} \\ b_{41} & b_{42} & b_{43} & b_{44} \end{bmatrix} = \begin{bmatrix} ? & ? & ? & ? \\ a_{21}b_{11}+a_{22}b_{21}+a_{23}b_{31}+a_{24}b_{41} & ? & ? & ? \\ ? & ? & ? & ? \\ ? & ? & ? & ? \end{bmatrix}$$

This continues for each subsequent element of the result matrix.

Order of Multiplication

Now that we know how to multiply two matrices together, we need to be careful to make sure that we multiply them in the right order. We can either multiply with the projection matrix on the left side and the model matrix on the right side, or with the model matrix on the left side and the projection matrix on the right side.

Unlike with regular multiplication, the order matters! If we get the order wrong, things might look weird or we might not see anything at all! The following is an example of two matrices multiplied in one particular order:

$$\begin{bmatrix} 1 & 2 \\ 3 & 4 \end{bmatrix} \begin{bmatrix} 4 & 3 \\ 2 & 1 \end{bmatrix} = \begin{bmatrix} 8 & 5 \\ 20 & 13 \end{bmatrix}$$

Here are the same two matrices multiplied in the reverse order:

$$\begin{bmatrix} 4 & 3 \\ 2 & 1 \end{bmatrix} \begin{bmatrix} 1 & 2 \\ 3 & 4 \end{bmatrix} = \begin{bmatrix} 13 & 20 \\ 5 & 8 \end{bmatrix}$$

With a different order, the results are also different.

Selecting the Appropriate Order

To figure out which order we should use, let's look at the math when we only use a projection matrix:

$vertex_{clip}$ = ProjectionMatrix * $vertex_{eye}$

$vertex_{eye}$ represents the position of the vertex in our scene before multiplying it with a projection matrix. Once we add a model matrix to move the table, the math looks like this:

$vertex_{eye}$ = ModelMatrix * $vertex_{model}$

$vertex_{clip}$ = ProjectionMatrix * $vertex_{eye}$

vertex$_{model}$ represents the position of the vertex before we use the model matrix to push it out into the scene. Combine the two expressions, and we end up with this:

vertex$_{clip}$ = ProjectionMatrix * ModelMatrix * vertex$_{model}$

To replace these two matrices with one, we have to multiply the projection matrix by the model matrix, with the projection matrix on the left side and the model matrix on the right side.

Updating the Code to Use One Matrix

Let's wrap up the new matrix code and add the following to onSurfaceChanged() after the call to translateM():

AirHockey3D/src/com/airhockey/android/AirHockeyRenderer.java
```
final float[] temp = new float[16];
multiplyMM(temp, 0, projectionMatrix, 0, modelMatrix, 0);
System.arraycopy(temp, 0, projectionMatrix, 0, temp.length);
```

Whenever we multiply two matrices, we need a temporary area to store the result. If we try to write the result directly, the results are undefined!

We first create a temporary floating-point array to store the temporary result; then we call multiplyMM() to multiply the projection matrix and model matrix together into this temporary array. Next we call System.arraycopy() to store the result back into projectionMatrix, which now contains the combined effects of the model matrix and the projection matrix.

If we run the application now, it should look like Figure 32, *Using a projection and a model matrix*, on page 111. Pushing the air hockey table into the distance brought it into our frustum, but the table is still standing upright. After a quick recap, we'll learn how to rotate the table so that we see it from an angle rather than upright.

A Quick Recap

Let's take a quick recap of what we've just covered in the past few sections:

- We learned how to use an extra matrix to move the air hockey table into the screen before passing it through the projection matrix.

- We learned how to multiply two matrices together.

- We then learned how to combine the projection and model matrices so that we don't have to modify the vertex shader to accept an additional matrix and multiply by both matrices every single time.

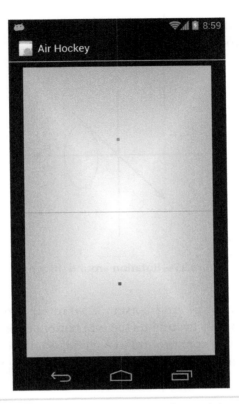

Figure 32—Using a projection and a model matrix

6.8 Adding Rotation

Now that we have a projection matrix configured and a model matrix in place to move our table around, all we need to do is rotate the table so that we're looking at it from across an angle. We'll be able to do this with one line of code using a rotation matrix. We haven't worked with rotations yet, so let's spend some time to learn more about how these rotations work.

The Direction of Rotation

The first thing we need to figure out is around which axis we need to rotate and by how much. Let's take another look at Figure 25, *Right-handed coordinate system*, on page 89. To figure out how an object would rotate around a given axis, we'll use the right-hand rule: take your right hand, make a fist, and point your thumb in the direction of the positive axis. The curl of your fingers shows you how an object would rotate around that axis, given a positive angle of rotation. Take a look at the next figure and see how when you point your thumb in the direction of the positive *x*-axis, the direction of rotation follows the curl of your fingers around the axis.

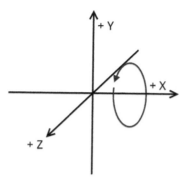

Figure 33—Rotation around the *x*-axis

Try this out with the *x*-, *y*-, and *z*-axes. If we rotate around the *y*-axis, our table will spin horizontally around its top and bottom ends. If we rotate around the *z*-axis, the table will spin around in a circle. What we want to do is rotate the table backward around the *x*-axis, as this will bring the table more level with our eyes.

Rotation Matrices

To do the actual rotation, we'll use a rotation matrix. Matrix rotation uses the trigonometric functions of sine and cosine to convert the rotation angle into scaling factors. The following is the matrix definition for a rotation around the *x*-axis:

$$\begin{bmatrix} 1 & 0 & 0 & 0 \\ 0 & \cos(a) & -\sin(a) & 0 \\ 0 & \sin(a) & \cos(a) & 0 \\ 0 & 0 & 0 & 1 \end{bmatrix}$$

Then you have a matrix for a rotation around the *y*-axis:

$$\begin{bmatrix} \cos(a) & 0 & \sin(a) & 0 \\ 0 & 1 & 0 & 0 \\ -\sin(a) & 0 & \cos(a) & 0 \\ 0 & 0 & 0 & 1 \end{bmatrix}$$

Finally, there's also one for a rotation around the *z*-axis:

$$\begin{bmatrix} \cos(a) & -\sin(a) & 0 & 0 \\ \sin(a) & \cos(a) & 0 & 0 \\ 0 & 0 & 1 & 0 \\ 0 & 0 & 0 & 1 \end{bmatrix}$$

It's also possible to combine all of these into a general rotation matrix based on an arbitrary angle and vector.[5]

Let's try out a rotation around the x-axis as a test. We'll start with a point that is one unit above the origin, with a y of 1, and rotate it 90 degrees around the x-axis. First, let's prepare the rotation matrix:

$$\begin{bmatrix} 1 & 0 & 0 & 0 \\ 0 & \cos(90) & -\sin(90) & 0 \\ 0 & \sin(90) & \cos(90) & 0 \\ 0 & 0 & 0 & 1 \end{bmatrix} = \begin{bmatrix} 1 & 0 & 0 & 0 \\ 0 & 0 & -1 & 0 \\ 0 & 1 & 0 & 0 \\ 0 & 0 & 0 & 1 \end{bmatrix}$$

Let's multiply this matrix with our point and see what happens:

$$\begin{bmatrix} 1 & 0 & 0 & 0 \\ 0 & 0 & -1 & 0 \\ 0 & 1 & 0 & 0 \\ 0 & 0 & 0 & 1 \end{bmatrix} \begin{bmatrix} 0 \\ 1 \\ 0 \\ 1 \end{bmatrix} = \begin{bmatrix} 0 \\ 0 \\ 1 \\ 1 \end{bmatrix}$$

The point has been moved from (0, 1, 0) to (0, 0, 1). If we look back at Figure 33, *Rotation around the x-axis*, on page 112, and use the right-hand rule with the x-axis, we can see how a positive rotation would move a point in a circle around the x-axis.

Adding the Rotation to Our Code

We're now ready to add the rotation to our code. Go back to onSurfaceChanged(), and adjust the translation and add a rotation as follows:

AirHockey3D/src/com/airhockey/android/AirHockeyRenderer.java
```
translateM(modelMatrix, 0, 0f, 0f, -2.5f);
rotateM(modelMatrix, 0, -60f, 1f, 0f, 0f);
```

We push the table a little farther, because once we rotate it the bottom end will be closer to us. We then rotate it by -60 degrees around the x-axis, which brings the table at a nice angle, as if we were standing in front of it.

The table should now look like the following:

---

5. http://en.wikipedia.org/wiki/Rotation_matrix#Rotation_matrix_from_axis_and_angle

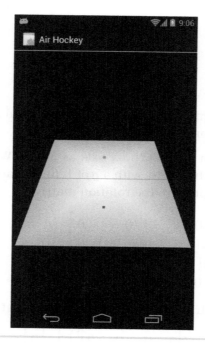

Figure 34—Air hockey table with a varying *w* component

6.9 A Review

This was a rather intense chapter. The matrix math got more involved as we learned about perspective projections and how they work with OpenGL's perspective divide. We then learned how to move and rotate our table with a second matrix.

The good news is that we don't need to have a perfect understanding of the underlying math and theory behind projections and rotations in order to use them. With just a basic understanding of what a frustum is and how matrices help us move stuff around, you will find it a lot easier to work with OpenGL down the road.

6.10 Exercises

Try adjusting the field of vision, and observe the effect that has on the air hockey table. You can also try moving the table around in different ways.

Once you've completed these exercises, we'll start making our table look nicer. In the next chapter we're going to start working with textures.

CHAPTER 7

Adding Detail with Textures

We've managed to get a lot done with just simple shapes and colors. There's something missing though: what if we could paint onto our shapes and add refined detail? Like artists, we can start out with basic shapes and color and add extra detail onto our surfaces by using *textures*. A texture is simply an image or a picture that has been uploaded into OpenGL.

We can add an incredible amount of detail with textures. Think of a beautiful 3D game you might have played recently. At the heart of things, the game is just using points, lines, and triangles, like any other 3D program. However, with the detail of textures and the touch of a skilled artist, these triangles can be textured to build a beautiful 3D scene.

Once we start using textures, we'll also start using more than one shader program. To make this easier to manage, we'll learn how to adapt our code so that we can use multiple shader programs and sources of vertex data and switch between them.

Here's our game plan for this chapter:

- We'll start out with an introduction to textures, and then we'll write code to load a texture into OpenGL.

- We'll learn how to display that texture, adapting our code to support multiple shader programs.

- We'll also cover the different texture filtering modes and what they do.

When we're done, our air hockey table should look like the next figure. Let's start off by copying the project from the last chapter over into a new project called 'AirHockeyTextured'.

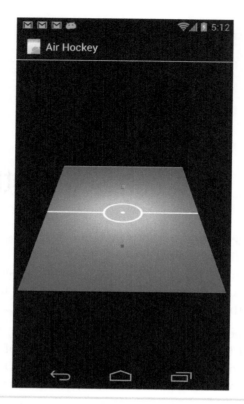

Figure 35—Air hockey table with a filtered texture

7.1 Understanding Textures

Textures in OpenGL can be used to represent images, pictures, and even fractal data that are generated by a mathematical algorithm. Each two-dimensional texture is composed of many small *texels*, which are small blocks of data analogous to the fragments and pixels that we've talked about previously. The most common way to use a texture is to load in the data directly from an image file.

We'll use the image in Figure 36, *The Surface Image*, on page 117 as our new air hockey table surface and load it in as a texture:

All of the images used in the code can be downloaded from this book's home page. I recommend storing the texture in your project's /res/drawable-nodpi/ folder.[1]

---

1. http://pragprog.com/book/kbogla

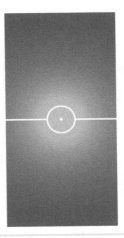

Figure 36—The Surface Image

Each two-dimensional texture has its own coordinate space, ranging from (0, 0) at one corner to (1, 1) at the other corner. By convention, one dimension is called *S* and the other is called *T*. When we want to apply a texture to a triangle or set of triangles, we'll specify a set of *ST* texture coordinates for each vertex so that OpenGL knows which parts of the texture it needs to draw across each triangle. These texture coordinates are also sometimes referred to as *UV* texture coordinates, as seen in Figure 37, *OpenGL 2D texture coordinates*, on page 118.

There is no inherent orientation for an OpenGL texture, since we can use different coordinates to orient it any which way we like. However, there *is* a default orientation for most computer image files: they are usually specified with the *y*-axis pointing downward (as seen in Figure 38, *Computer images: the y-axis points downward*, on page 118): the *y* value increases as we move toward the bottom of the image. This doesn't cause any trouble for us so long as we remember that if we want to view our image with the right orientation, then our texture coordinates need to take this into account.

In standard OpenGL ES 2.0, textures don't have to be square, but each dimension should be a power of two (POT). This means that each dimension should be a number like 128, 256, 512, and so on. The reason for this is that non-POT textures are very restricted in where they can be used, while POT textures are fine for all uses.

There is also a maximum texture size that varies from implementation to implementation but is usually something large, like 2048 x 2048.

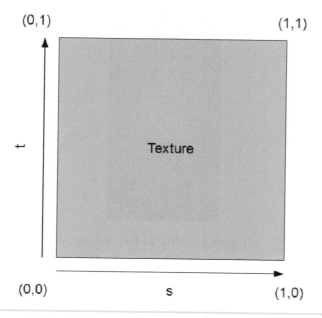

Figure 37—OpenGL 2D texture coordinates

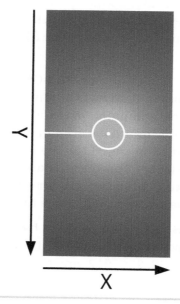

Figure 38—Computer images: the *y*-axis points downward

7.2 Loading Textures into OpenGL

Our first task will be to load data from an image file into an OpenGL texture. To start out, let's create a new class in the com.airhockey.android.util package called TextureHelper. We'll begin with the following method signature:

AirHockeyTextured/src/com/airhockey/android/util/TextureHelper.java
```
public static int loadTexture(Context context, int resourceId) {
```

This method will take in an Android context and a resource ID and will return the ID of the loaded OpenGL texture. To start off, we'll generate a new texture ID using the same type of pattern as when we've created other OpenGL objects:

AirHockeyTextured/src/com/airhockey/android/util/TextureHelper.java
```
final int[] textureObjectIds = new int[1];
glGenTextures(1, textureObjectIds, 0);

if (textureObjectIds[0] == 0) {
    if (LoggerConfig.ON) {
        Log.w(TAG, "Could not generate a new OpenGL texture object.");
    }
    return 0;
}
```

We generate one texture object by calling glGenTextures(1, textureObjectId, 0), passing in 1 as the first parameter. OpenGL will store the generated IDs in textureObjectIds. We also check that the call to glGenTextures() succeeded by continuing only if it's not equal to zero; otherwise we log the error and return 0. Since TAG is not yet defined, let's add a definition for it to the top of the class:

AirHockeyTextured/src/com/airhockey/android/util/TextureHelper.java
```
private static final String TAG = "TextureHelper";
```

Loading in Bitmap Data and Binding to the Texture

The next step is to use Android's APIs to read in the data from our image files. OpenGL can't read data from a PNG or JPEG file directly because these files are encoded into specific compressed formats. OpenGL needs the raw data in an uncompressed form, so we'll need to use Android's built-in bitmap decoder to decompress our image files into a form that OpenGL understands.

Let's continue implementing loadTexture() and decompress the image into an Android bitmap:

AirHockeyTextured/src/com/airhockey/android/util/TextureHelper.java
```
final BitmapFactory.Options options = new BitmapFactory.Options();
options.inScaled = false;

final Bitmap bitmap = BitmapFactory.decodeResource(
```

```
        context.getResources(), resourceId, options);

if (bitmap == null) {
    if (LoggerConfig.ON) {
        Log.w(TAG, "Resource ID " + resourceId + " could not be decoded.");
    }

    glDeleteTextures(1, textureObjectIds, 0);
    return 0;
}
```

We first create a new instance of BitmapFactory.Options called options, and we set inScaled to false. This tells Android that we want the original image data instead of a scaled version of the data.

We then call BitmapFactory.decodeResource() to do the actual decode, passing in the Android context, resource ID, and the decoding options that we've just defined. This call will decode the image into bitmap or will return null if it failed. We check against that failure and delete the OpenGL texture object if the bitmap is null. If the decode succeeded, we continue processing the texture.

Before we can do anything else with our newly generated texture object, we need to tell OpenGL that future texture calls should be applied to this texture object. We do that with a call to glBindTexture():

AirHockeyTextured/src/com/airhockey/android/util/TextureHelper.java
```
glBindTexture(GL_TEXTURE_2D, textureObjectIds[0]);
```

The first parameter, GL_TEXTURE_2D, tells OpenGL that this should be treated as a two-dimensional texture, and the second parameter tells OpenGL which texture object ID to bind to.

Understanding Texture Filtering

We'll also need to specify what should happen when the texture is expanded or reduced in size, using *texture filtering*. When we draw a texture onto the rendering surface, the texture's texels may not map exactly onto the fragments generated by OpenGL. There are two cases: "minification" and magnification. Minification happens when we try to cram several texels onto the same fragment, and magnification happens when we spread one texel across many fragments. We can configure OpenGL to use a texture filter for each case.

To start out, we'll cover two basic filtering modes: nearest-neighbor filtering and bilinear interpolation. There are additional filtering modes that we'll soon cover in more detail. We'll use the following image to illustrate each filtering mode:

Nearest-Neighbor Filtering

This selects the nearest texel for each fragment. When we magnify the texture, it will look rather blocky, as follows:

Each texel is clearly visible as a small square.

When we minify the texture, many of the details will be lost, as we don't have enough fragments for all of the texels:

Bilinear Filtering

Bilinear filtering uses bilinear interpolation to smooth the transitions between pixels. Instead of using the nearest texel for each fragment, OpenGL will use the four neighboring texels and interpolate them together using the same type of linear interpolation that we discussed back in *How Does a Varying Get Blended at Each Fragment?*, on page 66. We call it bilinear because it is done along two dimensions. The following is the same texture as before, magnified using bilinear interpolation:

The texture now looks much smoother than before. There's still some blockiness present because we've expanded the texture so much, but it's not as apparent as it was with nearest-neighbor filtering.

Mipmapping

While bilinear filtering works well for magnification, it doesn't work as well for minification beyond a certain size. The more we reduce the size of a texture on the rendering surface, the more texels will get crammed onto each fragment. Since OpenGL's bilinear filtering will only use four texels for each fragment, we still lose a lot of detail. This can cause noise and shimmering artifacts with moving objects as different texels get selected with each frame.

To combat these artifacts, we can use *mipmapping*, a technique that generates an optimized set of textures at different sizes. When generating the set of textures, OpenGL can use all of the texels to generate each level, ensuring that all of the texels will also be used when filtering the texture. At render time, OpenGL will select the most appropriate level for each fragment based on the number of texels per fragment.

Figure 39, *Mipmapped Textures*, on page 123 is a mipmapped set of textures combined onto a single image for clarity:

With mipmaps, more memory will be used, but the rendering can also be faster because the smaller levels take less space in the GPU's texture cache.

To better understand how mipmapping improves the quality of minification, let's compare and contrast our cute Android, minified to 12.5 percent of the original texel size using bilinear filtering, as shown in Figure 40, *Minified with Bilinear Filtering*, on page 123.

Figure 39—Mipmapped Textures

Figure 40—Minified with Bilinear Filtering

With this kind of quality, we may as well have stayed with nearest-neighbor filtering. Let's take a look at what we get when we add mipmaps Figure 41, *Minified with Mipmapping*, on page 124.

With mipmaps enabled, OpenGL will select the closest appropriate texture level and then do bilinear interpolation using that optimized texture. Each level was built with information from all of the texels, so the resulting image looks much better, with much more of the detail preserved.

Figure 41—Minified with Mipmapping

Trilinear Filtering

When we use mipmaps with bilinear filtering, we can sometimes see a noticeable jump or line in the rendered scene where OpenGL switches between different mipmap levels. We can switch to *trilinear filtering* to tell OpenGL to also interpolate between the two closest mipmap levels, using a total of eight texels per fragment. This helps to eliminate the transition between each mipmap level and results in a smoother image.

Setting Default Texture Filtering Parameters

Now that we know about texture filtering, let's continue loadTexture() and add the following code:

AirHockeyTextured/src/com/airhockey/android/util/TextureHelper.java
```
glTexParameteri(GL_TEXTURE_2D, GL_TEXTURE_MIN_FILTER, GL_LINEAR_MIPMAP_LINEAR);
glTexParameteri(GL_TEXTURE_2D, GL_TEXTURE_MAG_FILTER, GL_LINEAR);
```

We set each filter with a call to glTexParameteri(): GL_TEXTURE_MIN_FILTER refers to minification, while GL_TEXTURE_MAG_FILTER refers to magnification. For minification, we select GL_LINEAR_MIPMAP_LINEAR, which tells OpenGL to use trilinear filtering. We set the magnification filter to GL_LINEAR, which tells OpenGL to use bilinear filtering.

Table 4, *OpenGL texture filtering modes*, on page 125 and Table 5, *Allowable texture filtering modes for each case*, on page 125 explain the possible options as well as the valid options for minification and magnification.

GL_NEAREST	Nearest-neighbor filtering
GL_NEAREST_MIPMAP_NEAREST	Nearest-neighbor filtering with mipmaps
GL_NEAREST_MIPMAP_LINEAR	Nearest-neighbor filtering with interpolation between mipmap levels
GL_LINEAR	Bilinear filtering
GL_LINEAR_MIPMAP_NEAREST	Bilinear filtering with mipmaps
GL_LINEAR_MIPMAP_LINEAR	Trilinear filtering (bilinear filtering with interpolation between mipmap levels)

Table 4—OpenGL texture filtering modes

Minification	GL_NEAREST
	GL_NEAREST_MIPMAP_NEAREST
	GL_NEAREST_MIPMAP_LINEAR
	GL_LINEAR
	GL_LINEAR_MIPMAP_NEAREST
	GL_LINEAR_MIPMAP_LINEAR
Magnification	GL_NEAREST
	GL_LINEAR

Table 5—Allowable texture filtering modes for each case

Loading the Texture into OpenGL and Returning the ID

We can now load the bitmap data into OpenGL with an easy call to GLUtils. texImage2D():

AirHockeyTextured/src/com/airhockey/android/util/TextureHelper.java
```
texImage2D(GL_TEXTURE_2D, 0, bitmap, 0);
```

This call tells OpenGL to read in the bitmap data defined by bitmap and copy it over into the texture object that is currently bound.

Now that the data's been loaded into OpenGL, we no longer need to keep the Android bitmap around. Under normal circumstances, it might take a few garbage collection cycles for Dalvik to release this bitmap data, so we should call recycle() on the bitmap object to release the data immediately:

AirHockeyTextured/src/com/airhockey/android/util/TextureHelper.java
```
bitmap.recycle();
```

Generating mipmaps is also a cinch. We can tell OpenGL to generate all of the necessary levels with a quick call to glGenerateMipmap():

AirHockeyTextured/src/com/airhockey/android/util/TextureHelper.java
```
glGenerateMipmap(GL_TEXTURE_2D);
```

Now that we've finished loading the texture, a good practice is to then unbind from the texture so that we don't accidentally make further changes to this texture with other texture calls:

AirHockeyTextured/src/com/airhockey/android/util/TextureHelper.java
```
glBindTexture(GL_TEXTURE_2D, 0);
```

Passing 0 to glBindTexture() unbinds from the current texture. The last step is to return the texture object ID:

AirHockeyTextured/src/com/airhockey/android/util/TextureHelper.java
```
return textureObjectIds[0];
```

We now have a method that will be able to read in an image file from our resources folder and load the image data into OpenGL. We'll get back a texture ID that we can use as a reference to this texture or get 0 if the load failed.

7.3 Creating a New Set of Shaders

Before we can draw the texture to the screen, we'll have to create a new set of shaders that will accept a texture and apply it to the fragments being drawn. These new shaders will be similar to the ones we've been working with until now, with just a couple of slight changes to add support for texturing.

Creating the New Vertex Shader

Create a new file under your project's /res/raw/ directory, and call it texture_vertex_shader.glsl. Add the following contents:

AirHockeyTextured/res/raw/texture_vertex_shader.glsl
```
uniform mat4 u_Matrix;

attribute vec4 a_Position;
attribute vec2 a_TextureCoordinates;

varying vec2 v_TextureCoordinates;

void main()
{
    v_TextureCoordinates = a_TextureCoordinates;
    gl_Position = u_Matrix * a_Position;
}
```

Most of this shader code should look familiar: we've defined a uniform for our matrix, and we also have an attribute for our position. We use these to set the final gl_Position. Now for the new stuff: we've also added a new attribute for our texture coordinates, called a_TextureCoordinates. It's defined as a vec2 because there are two components: the S coordinate and the T coordinate. We send these coordinates on to the fragment shader as an interpolated varying called v_TextureCoordinates.

Creating the New Fragment Shader

In the same directory, create a new file called texture_fragment_shader.glsl, and add the following contents:

AirHockeyTextured/res/raw/texture_fragment_shader.glsl
```
precision mediump float;

uniform sampler2D u_TextureUnit;
varying vec2 v_TextureCoordinates;

void main()
{
    gl_FragColor = texture2D(u_TextureUnit, v_TextureCoordinates);
}
```

To draw the texture on an object, OpenGL will call the fragment shader for each fragment, and each call will receive the texture coordinates in v_Texture-Coordinates. The fragment shader will also receive the actual texture data via the uniform u_TextureUnit, which is defined as a sampler2D. This variable type refers to an array of two-dimensional texture data.

The interpolated texture coordinates and the texture data are passed in to the shader function texture2D(), which will read in the color value for the texture at that particular coordinate. We then set the fragment to that color by assigning the result to gl_FragColor.

The next couple of sections will be somewhat more involved: we're going to create a new set of classes and place our existing code for our table data and shader programs into these classes. We'll then switch between them at runtime.

7.4   Creating a New Class Structure for Our Vertex Data

We'll start off by separating our vertex data into separate classes, with one class to represent each type of physical object. We'll create one class for our table and another for our mallet. We won't need one for the line, since there's already a line on our texture.

We'll also create a separate class to encapsulate the actual vertex array and to reduce code duplication. Our class structure will look as follows:

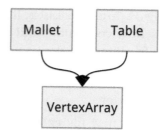

We'll create Mallet to manage the mallet data and Table to manage the table data; and each class will have an instance of VertexArray, which will encapsulate the FloatBuffer storing the vertex array.

We'll start off with VertexArray. Create a new package in your project called com.airhockey.android.data, and in that package, create a new class called VertexArray. Add the following code inside the class:

AirHockeyTextured/src/com/airhockey/android/data/VertexArray.java
```
private final FloatBuffer floatBuffer;

public VertexArray(float[] vertexData) {
    floatBuffer = ByteBuffer
        .allocateDirect(vertexData.length * BYTES_PER_FLOAT)
        .order(ByteOrder.nativeOrder())
        .asFloatBuffer()
        .put(vertexData);
}

public void setVertexAttribPointer(int dataOffset, int attributeLocation,
    int componentCount, int stride) {
    floatBuffer.position(dataOffset);
    glVertexAttribPointer(attributeLocation, componentCount, GL_FLOAT,
        false, stride, floatBuffer);
    glEnableVertexAttribArray(attributeLocation);

    floatBuffer.position(0);
}
```

This code contains a FloatBuffer that will be used to store our vertex array data in native code, as explained in Section 2.4, *Making the Data Accessible to OpenGL*, on page 26. The constructor takes in an array of Java floating-point data and writes it to the buffer.

We've also created a generic method to associate an attribute in our shader with the data. This follows the same pattern as we explained in *Associating an Array of Vertex Data with an Attribute*, on page 49.

Let's find a new place for BYTES_PER_FLOAT, since we'll end up using it in several classes. To do this, let's create a new class called Constants in com.airhockey.android and add the following code:

AirHockeyTextured/src/com/airhockey/android/Constants.java
```
package com.airhockey.android;

public class Constants {
    public static final int BYTES_PER_FLOAT = 4;
}
```

We can then update VertexArray to refer to the new constant.

Adding the Table Data

We'll now define a class to store our table data; this class will store the position data for our table, and we'll also add texture coordinates to apply the texture to the table.

Adding the Class Constants

Create a new package called com.airhockey.android.objects; in that new package, create a new class called Table and add the following code inside the class:

AirHockeyTextured/src/com/airhockey/android/objects/Table.java
```
private static final int POSITION_COMPONENT_COUNT = 2;
private static final int TEXTURE_COORDINATES_COMPONENT_COUNT = 2;
private static final int STRIDE = (POSITION_COMPONENT_COUNT
    + TEXTURE_COORDINATES_COMPONENT_COUNT) * BYTES_PER_FLOAT;
```

We defined our position component count, texture component count, and stride as shown.

Adding the Vertex Data

The next step is to define our vertex data with the following code:

AirHockeyTextured/src/com/airhockey/android/objects/Table.java
```
private static final float[] VERTEX_DATA = {
    // Order of coordinates: X, Y, S, T

    // Triangle Fan
       0f,    0f, 0.5f, 0.5f,
    -0.5f, -0.8f,   0f, 0.9f,
     0.5f, -0.8f,   1f, 0.9f,
     0.5f,  0.8f,   1f, 0.1f,
    -0.5f,  0.8f,   0f, 0.1f,
    -0.5f, -0.8f,   0f, 0.9f };
```

This array contains the vertex data for our air hockey table. We've defined the x and y positions and the S and T texture coordinates. You might notice that the *T* component is running in the opposite direction of the *y* component. This is so that the image is oriented with the right side up, as explained in Section 7.1, *Understanding Textures*, on page 116. It doesn't actually matter when we use a symmetrical texture, but it will matter in other cases, so it's a good rule to keep in mind.

Clipping the Texture

We also used *T* coordinates of 0.1f and 0.9f. Why? Well, our table is 1 unit wide and 1.6 units tall. Our texture image is 512 x 1024 in pixels, so if the width corresponds to 1 unit, the texture is actually 2 units tall. To avoid squashing the texture, we use the range 0.1 to 0.9 instead of 0.0 to 1.0 to clip the edges and just draw the center portion.

The following image illustrates the concept:

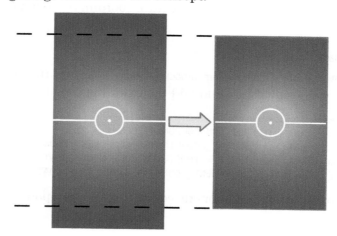

Instead of clipping, we could also stick with texture coordinates from 0.0 to 1.0 and *prestretch* our texture so that it looks correct after being squished onto the air hockey table. This way we won't use any memory on parts of the texture that won't be shown (Figure 42, *Prestretching*, on page 131).

Initializing and Drawing the Data

We'll now create a constructor for Table. This constructor will use VertexArray to copy the data over into a FloatBuffer in native memory.

AirHockeyTextured/src/com/airhockey/android/objects/Table.java

```
private final VertexArray vertexArray;

public Table() {
    vertexArray = new VertexArray(VERTEX_DATA);
}
```

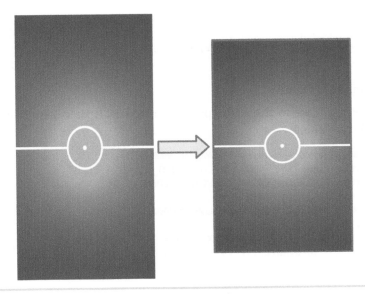

Figure 42—Prestretching

We'll also add a method to bind the vertex array to a shader program:

AirHockeyTextured/src/com/airhockey/android/objects/Table.java
```
public void bindData(TextureShaderProgram textureProgram) {
    vertexArray.setVertexAttribPointer(
        0,
        textureProgram.getPositionAttributeLocation(),
        POSITION_COMPONENT_COUNT,
        STRIDE);

    vertexArray.setVertexAttribPointer(
        POSITION_COMPONENT_COUNT,
        textureProgram.getTextureCoordinatesAttributeLocation(),
        TEXTURE_COORDINATES_COMPONENT_COUNT,
        STRIDE);
}
```

The method body calls setVertexAttribPointer() for each attribute, getting the location of each attribute from the shader program. This will bind the position data to the shader attribute referenced by getPositionAttributeLocation() and bind the texture coordinate data to the shader attribute referenced by getTextureCoordinatesAttributeLocation(). We'll define these methods when we create the shader classes.

We just need to add in one last method so we can draw the table:

AirHockeyTextured/src/com/airhockey/android/objects/Table.java
```java
public void draw() {
    glDrawArrays(GL_TRIANGLE_FAN, 0, 6);
}
```

Adding the Mallet Data

Create another class in the same package and call it Mallet. Add the following code inside the class:

AirHockeyTextured/src/com/airhockey/android/objects/Mallet.java
```java
private static final int POSITION_COMPONENT_COUNT = 2;
private static final int COLOR_COMPONENT_COUNT = 3;
private static final int STRIDE =
    (POSITION_COMPONENT_COUNT + COLOR_COMPONENT_COUNT)
    * BYTES_PER_FLOAT;
private static final float[] VERTEX_DATA = {
    // Order of coordinates: X, Y, R, G, B
    0f, -0.4f, 0f, 0f, 1f,
    0f,  0.4f, 1f, 0f, 0f };
private final VertexArray vertexArray;

public Mallet() {
    vertexArray = new VertexArray(VERTEX_DATA);
}

public void bindData(ColorShaderProgram colorProgram) {
    vertexArray.setVertexAttribPointer(
        0,
        colorProgram.getPositionAttributeLocation(),
        POSITION_COMPONENT_COUNT,
        STRIDE);
    vertexArray.setVertexAttribPointer(
        POSITION_COMPONENT_COUNT,
        colorProgram.getColorAttributeLocation(),
        COLOR_COMPONENT_COUNT,
        STRIDE);
}

public void draw() {
    glDrawArrays(GL_POINTS, 0, 2);
}
```

This follows the same pattern as the table, and we're still drawing the mallets as points, just like before.

Our vertex data is now defined: we have one class to represent the table data, another to represent the mallet data, and a third class to make it easier to manage the vertex data itself. Next up is defining classes for our shader programs.

7.5 Adding Classes for Our Shader Programs

In this section, we'll create one class for our texture shader program and another for our color shader program; we'll use the texture shader program to draw the table and use the color shader program to draw the mallets. We'll also create a base class for common functionality. We don't have to worry about the line anymore now that it's part of the texture.

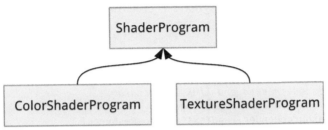

Let's start out by adding a helper function to ShaderHelper. Open up that class, and add the following method to the end:

AirHockeyTextured/src/com/airhockey/android/util/ShaderHelper.java

```java
public static int buildProgram(String vertexShaderSource,
    String fragmentShaderSource) {
    int program;

    // Compile the shaders.
    int vertexShader = compileVertexShader(vertexShaderSource);
    int fragmentShader = compileFragmentShader(fragmentShaderSource);

    // Link them into a shader program.
    program = linkProgram(vertexShader, fragmentShader);

    if (LoggerConfig.ON) {
        validateProgram(program);
    }

    return program;
}
```

This helper function will compile the shaders defined by vertexShaderSource and fragmentShaderSource and link them together into a program. If logging is turned on, it will also validate the program. We'll use this helper function to build up our base class.

Create a new package called com.airhockey.android.programs, and create a new class in that package called ShaderProgram. Add the following code inside the class:

AirHockeyTextured/src/com/airhockey/android/programs/ShaderProgram.java

```
// Uniform constants
protected static final String U_MATRIX = "u_Matrix";
protected static final String U_TEXTURE_UNIT = "u_TextureUnit";

// Attribute constants
protected static final String A_POSITION = "a_Position";
protected static final String A_COLOR = "a_Color";
protected static final String A_TEXTURE_COORDINATES = "a_TextureCoordinates";

// Shader program
protected final int program;
protected ShaderProgram(Context context, int vertexShaderResourceId,
    int fragmentShaderResourceId) {
    // Compile the shaders and link the program.
    program = ShaderHelper.buildProgram(
        TextResourceReader.readTextFileFromResource(
            context, vertexShaderResourceId),
        TextResourceReader.readTextFileFromResource(
            context, fragmentShaderResourceId));
}

public void useProgram() {
    // Set the current OpenGL shader program to this program.
    glUseProgram(program);
}
```

We start out the class by defining some common constants. In the constructor, we call the helper function that we've just defined, and we use it to build an OpenGL shader program with the specified shaders. We close off the class with useProgram(), which will call glUseProgram() to tell OpenGL to use program for subsequent rendering.

Adding the Texture Shader Program

We'll now define a class to set up and represent our texture shader program. Create a new class called TextureShaderProgram that extends ShaderProgram, and add the following code inside the class:

AirHockeyTextured/src/com/airhockey/android/programs/TextureShaderProgram.java

```
// Uniform locations
private final int uMatrixLocation;
private final int uTextureUnitLocation;

// Attribute locations
private final int aPositionLocation;
private final int aTextureCoordinatesLocation;
```

We've added four ints to hold the locations of our uniforms and attributes.

Initializing the Shader Program

The next step is to create a constructor to initialize the shader program. Let's add the following code:

AirHockeyTextured/src/com/airhockey/android/programs/TextureShaderProgram.java
```
public TextureShaderProgram(Context context) {
    super(context, R.raw.texture_vertex_shader,
        R.raw.texture_fragment_shader);

    // Retrieve uniform locations for the shader program.
    uMatrixLocation = glGetUniformLocation(program, U_MATRIX);
    uTextureUnitLocation = glGetUniformLocation(program, U_TEXTURE_UNIT);

    // Retrieve attribute locations for the shader program.
    aPositionLocation = glGetAttribLocation(program, A_POSITION);
    aTextureCoordinatesLocation =
        glGetAttribLocation(program, A_TEXTURE_COORDINATES);
}
```

This constructor will call the superclass with our selected resources, and the superclass will build the shader program. We'll then read in and save the uniform and attribute locations.

Setting Uniforms and Returning Attribute Locations

Next up is passing the matrix and texture into their uniforms. Let's add the following code:

AirHockeyTextured/src/com/airhockey/android/programs/TextureShaderProgram.java
```
public void setUniforms(float[] matrix, int textureId) {
    // Pass the matrix into the shader program.
    glUniformMatrix4fv(uMatrixLocation, 1, false, matrix, 0);

    // Set the active texture unit to texture unit 0.
    glActiveTexture(GL_TEXTURE0);

    // Bind the texture to this unit.
    glBindTexture(GL_TEXTURE_2D, textureId);

    // Tell the texture uniform sampler to use this texture in the shader by
    // telling it to read from texture unit 0.
    glUniform1i(uTextureUnitLocation, 0);
}
```

The first step is to pass the matrix in to its uniform, which is straightforward enough. The next part needs more explanation. When we draw using textures in OpenGL, we don't pass the texture directly in to the shader. Instead, we use a *texture unit* to hold the texture. We do this because a GPU can only draw so many textures at the same time. It uses these texture units to represent the active textures currently being drawn.

We can swap textures in and out of texture units if we need to switch textures, though this may slow down rendering if we do it too often. We can also use several texture units to draw more than one texture at the same time.

We start out this part by setting the active texture unit to texture unit 0 with a call to glActiveTexture(), and then we bind our texture to this unit with a call to glBindTexture(). We then pass in the selected texture unit to u_TextureUnit in the fragment shader by calling glUniform1i(uTextureUnitLocation, 0).

We're almost done with our texture shader class; we just need a way of getting the attribute locations so we can bind them to the correct vertex array data. Add the following code to finish off the class:

AirHockeyTextured/src/com/airhockey/android/programs/TextureShaderProgram.java
```java
public int getPositionAttributeLocation() {
    return aPositionLocation;
}

public int getTextureCoordinatesAttributeLocation() {
    return aTextureCoordinatesLocation;
}
```

Adding the Color Shader Program

Create another class in the same package and call it ColorShaderProgram. This class should also extend ShaderProgram, and it will follow the same pattern as TextureShaderProgram, with a constructor, a method to set uniforms, and methods to get attribute locations. Add the following code inside the class:

AirHockeyTextured/src/com/airhockey/android/programs/ColorShaderProgram.java
```java
// Uniform locations
private final int uMatrixLocation;

// Attribute locations
private final int aPositionLocation;
private final int aColorLocation;

public ColorShaderProgram(Context context) {
    super(context, R.raw.simple_vertex_shader,
        R.raw.simple_fragment_shader);
    // Retrieve uniform locations for the shader program.
    uMatrixLocation = glGetUniformLocation(program, U_MATRIX);
    // Retrieve attribute locations for the shader program.
    aPositionLocation = glGetAttribLocation(program, A_POSITION);
    aColorLocation = glGetAttribLocation(program, A_COLOR);
}
```

```java
public void setUniforms(float[] matrix) {
    // Pass the matrix into the shader program.
    glUniformMatrix4fv(uMatrixLocation, 1, false, matrix, 0);
}

public int getPositionAttributeLocation() {
    return aPositionLocation;
}

public int getColorAttributeLocation() {
    return aColorLocation;
}
```

We'll use this program for drawing our mallets.

By decoupling the shader programs from the data that gets drawn with these programs, we've made it easier to reuse our code. For example, we could draw any object with a color attribute using our color shader program, not just the mallets.

7.6 Drawing Our Texture

Now that we've divided our vertex data and shader programs into different classes, let's update our renderer class to draw using our texture. Open up AirHockeyRenderer, and delete everything except onSurfaceChanged(), as that's the only method we won't change. Add the following members and constructor:

AirHockeyTextured/src/com/airhockey/android/AirHockeyRenderer.java
```java
private final Context context;

private final float[] projectionMatrix = new float[16];
private final float[] modelMatrix = new float[16];

private Table table;
private Mallet mallet;

private TextureShaderProgram textureProgram;
private ColorShaderProgram colorProgram;

private int texture;

public AirHockeyRenderer(Context context) {
    this.context = context;
}
```

We've kept around variables for the context and matrices, and we've also added variables for our vertex arrays, shader programs, and texture. The constructor has been reduced to just saving a copy of the Android context.

Initializing Our Variables

Let's add the following onSurfaceCreated() to initialize our new variables:

```
AirHockeyTextured/src/com/airhockey/android/AirHockeyRenderer.java
@Override
public void onSurfaceCreated(GL10 glUnused, EGLConfig config) {
    glClearColor(0.0f, 0.0f, 0.0f, 0.0f);

    table = new Table();
    mallet = new Mallet();

    textureProgram = new TextureShaderProgram(context);
    colorProgram = new ColorShaderProgram(context);

    texture = TextureHelper.loadTexture(context, R.drawable.air_hockey_surface);
}
```

We set the clear color to black, initialize our vertex arrays and shader programs, and load in our texture using the helper function we defined back in Section 7.2, *Loading Textures into OpenGL*, on page 119.

Drawing with the Texture

We won't cover onSurfaceChanged() because it stays the same. Let's add the following onDrawFrame() to draw the table and mallets:

```
AirHockeyTextured/src/com/airhockey/android/AirHockeyRenderer.java
@Override
public void onDrawFrame(GL10 glUnused) {
    // Clear the rendering surface.
    glClear(GL_COLOR_BUFFER_BIT);

    // Draw the table.
    textureProgram.useProgram();
    textureProgram.setUniforms(projectionMatrix, texture);
    table.bindData(textureProgram);
    table.draw();

    // Draw the mallets.
    colorProgram.useProgram();
    colorProgram.setUniforms(projectionMatrix);
    mallet.bindData(colorProgram);
    mallet.draw();
}
```

We clear the rendering surface, and then the first thing we do is draw the table. First we call textureProgram.useProgram() to tell OpenGL to use this program, and then we pass in the uniforms with a call to textureProgram.setUniforms(). The next step is to bind the vertex array data and our shader program with a call to table.bindData(). We can then finally draw the table with a call to table.draw().

We repeat the same sequence with the color shader program to draw the mallets.

Running the Program and Seeing the Results

Go ahead and run the program; it should look just like Figure 35, *Air hockey table with a filtered texture*, on page 116. You might notice an error in your logcat debug log, such as E/IMGSRV(20095): :0: HardwareMipGen: Failed to generate texture mipmap levels (error=3), even though there will be no corresponding OpenGL error. This might mean that your implementation doesn't support non-square textures when calling glGenerateMipMap().

An easy fix for this is to squash the texture so that it is square. Because the texture is being applied onto a rectangular surface, it will get stretched out and will still look the same as before.

7.7   A Review

We now know how to load in a texture and display it on our air hockey table; we've also learned how to reorganize our program so that we can easily switch between multiple shader programs and vertex arrays in our code. We can adjust our textures to fit the shape they're being drawn on, either by adjusting the texture coordinates or by prestretching or squashing the texture itself.

Textures don't get drawn directly—they get bound to texture units, and then we pass in these texture units to the shaders. We can still draw different textures in our scene by swapping them in and out of texture units, but excessive swapping may degrade performance. We can also use more than one texture unit to draw several textures at the same time.

7.8   Exercises

Try loading in a different image, and use an additional texture unit to blend this image with the current one. You can try adding or multiplying the values together when you assign them to gl_FragColor in your fragment shader.

Once you've completed these exercises, we'll learn how to improve the look of our mallets in the next chapter.

CHAPTER 8

Building Simple Objects

We've come a long way with our air hockey project: our table is now at a good angle, and it looks better now that we have a texture. However, our mallets don't actually look anything like a real mallet, since we're currently drawing each one as a point. Could you imagine playing air hockey with a small dot as a mallet? Many applications combine simple shapes to build up more complicated objects, and we'll learn how to do that here so we can build a better mallet.

We're also missing an easy way to pan, rotate, and move around in the scene. Many 3D applications implement this by using a *view* matrix; changes made to this matrix affect the entire scene, as if we were looking at things from a moving camera. We'll add a view matrix to make it easier to rotate and move around.

Let's go over our game plan for the chapter:

- First we'll learn how to group triangles into triangle strips and fans and then combine these together into a single object.

- We'll also learn how to define the view matrix and integrate it into our matrix hierarchy.

Once we've finished these tasks, we'll be able to move the scene around with one line of code, and we'll also have mallets that look more like something we could actually use to hit a puck. Speaking of a puck, we don't have one yet, so we'll add that too.

To start out, let's copy our project from the previous chapter, and let's name the new project 'AirHockeyWithBetterMallets'.

8.1 Combining Triangle Strips and Triangle Fans

To build a mallet, or a puck for that matter, let's first try to imagine the shape at a higher level. A puck can be represented as a flat cylinder, as follows:

A mallet is just a bit more complex and can be represented as two cylinders, one on top of the other:

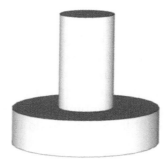

I know what you're thinking: a *real* air hockey mallet is more than just two cylinders stuck together. Bear with me; once we learn the basics, you may feel just confident enough to build up a more detailed mallet.

To figure out how to build these objects in OpenGL, let's imagine how we'd build this out of paper: first we'd cut out a circle for the cylinder top. We'd then take a flat piece of paper, cut it to the right size, and roll it into a tube. To make the cylinder, we could then put the circle on top of the tube. We would need one of these cylinders for the puck and two for the mallet.

It turns out that this is actually pretty easy to do with OpenGL. To build the circle, we can use a triangle fan. We first covered triangle fans back in Section 4.2, *Introducing Triangle Fans*, on page 61, when we used one to build our table out of six vertices and four triangles. We can also use a triangle fan to represent a circle; we just need to use a lot more triangles and arrange the outside vertices in the shape of a circle.

To build the side of the cylinder, we can use a related concept known as a *triangle strip*. Like a triangle fan, a triangle strip lets us define many triangles without duplicating the shared points over and over; but instead of fanning around in a circle, a triangle strip is built like a bridge girder, with the triangles laid out next to each other:

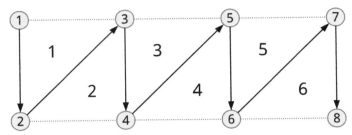

Like with the triangle fan, the first three vertices of a triangle strip define the first triangle. Each additional vertex after that defines an additional triangle. To build the side of the cylinder using a triangle strip, we just need to roll the strip around in a tube and make sure that the last two vertices line up with the first two.

8.2 Adding a Geometry Class

We now have a good idea of what we need to build a puck and a mallet: for the puck, we need one triangle fan for the top and one triangle strip for the side; for the mallet, we need two triangle fans and two triangle strips. To make it easier to build these objects, we'll define a Geometry class to hold some basic shape definitions and an ObjectBuilder to do the actual building.

> \|/ Joe asks:
> ʒͼ **Why Not Just Use a Library?**
>
> There are decent 3D libraries for Android out there, ranging from libgdx,[a] a thin open-source wrapper, to more advanced commercial frameworks such as Unity3D.[b] These libraries can help improve your productivity, but only once you've developed a basic understanding of OpenGL, 3D rendering, and how the pieces fit together at a low level; otherwise things will make little sense and you may as well be working with black magic. As an example, frameworks like Spring and Hibernate can make Java more productive, but it would be jumping the gun to start using them without knowing anything about how Java works.
>
> Studying these libraries can also be a great way to learn how to develop your own components. Java3D and jMonkeyEngine are among the more commonly used frameworks on the Java desktop; they are a good place to start, as their documentation is easily accessible online.[c]
>
> ――――――――
> a. http://code.google.com/p/libgdx/
> b. http://unity3d.com/
> c. http://www.oracle.com/technetwork/java/javase/tech/index-jsp-138252.html and http://jmonkeyengine.com/, respectively.

Let's start out with our Geometry class. Create a new class called Geometry in the package com.airhockey.android.util. Add the following code inside the class:

AirHockeyWithImprovedMallets/src/com/airhockey/android/util/Geometry.java

```
public static class Point {
    public final float x, y, z;
    public Point(float x, float y, float z) {
        this.x = x;
        this.y = y;
        this.z = z;
    }

    public Point translateY(float distance) {
        return new Point(x, y + distance, z);
    }
}
```

We've added a class to represent a point in 3D space, along with a helper function to translate the point along the y-axis. We'll also need a definition for a circle; add the following after Point:

AirHockeyWithImprovedMallets/src/com/airhockey/android/util/Geometry.java

```
public static class Circle {
    public final Point center;
    public final float radius;

    public Circle(Point center, float radius) {
        this.center = center;
        this.radius = radius;
    }

    public Circle scale(float scale) {
        return new Circle(center, radius * scale);
    }
}
```

We also have a helper function to scale the circle's radius. Last up is a definition for a cylinder:

AirHockeyWithImprovedMallets/src/com/airhockey/android/util/Geometry.java

```
public static class Cylinder {
    public final Point center;
    public final float radius;
    public final float height;

    public Cylinder(Point center, float radius, float height) {
        this.center = center;
        this.radius = radius;
        this.height = height;
    }
}
```

A cylinder is like an extended circle, so we have a center, a radius, and a height.

You'll probably have noticed that we've defined our geometry classes as *immutable*; whenever we make a change, we return a new object. This helps to make the code easier to work with and understand, but when you need top performance, you might want to stick with simple floating-point arrays and mutate them with static functions.

8.3 Adding an Object Builder

Now we can start writing our object builder class. Let's create a class in the package com.airhockey.android.objects called ObjectBuilder. Start out with the following code inside the class:

AirHockeyWithImprovedMallets/src/com/airhockey/android/objects/ObjectBuilder.java
```
private static final int FLOATS_PER_VERTEX = 3;
private final float[] vertexData;
private int offset = 0;

private ObjectBuilder(int sizeInVertices) {
    vertexData = new float[sizeInVertices * FLOATS_PER_VERTEX];
}
```

There's nothing too fancy here so far. We've defined a constant to represent how many floats we need for a vertex, an array to hold these vertices, and a variable to keep track of the position in the array for the next vertex. Our constructor initializes the array based on the required size in vertices.

We'll soon define a couple of static methods to generate a puck and a mallet. These static methods will create a new ObjectBuilder instance with the proper size, call instance methods on ObjectBuilder to add vertices to vertexData, and return the generated data back to the caller.

Let's set a few requirements for how our object builder should work:

- The caller can decide how many points the object should have. The more points, the smoother the puck or mallet will look.

- The object will be contained in one floating-point array. After the object is built, the caller will have one array to bind to OpenGL and one command to draw the object.

- The object will be centered at the caller's specified position and will lie flat on the *x-z* plane. In other words, the top of the object will point straight up.

Let's start out with a method to calculate the size of a cylinder top in vertices:

AirHockeyWithImprovedMallets/src/com/airhockey/android/objects/ObjectBuilder.java

```
private static int sizeOfCircleInVertices(int numPoints) {
    return 1 + (numPoints + 1);
}
```

A cylinder top is a circle built out of a triangle fan; it has one vertex in the center, one vertex for each point around the circle, and the first vertex around the circle is repeated twice so that we can close the circle off.

The following is a method to calculate the size of a cylinder side in vertices:

AirHockeyWithImprovedMallets/src/com/airhockey/android/objects/ObjectBuilder.java

```
private static int sizeOfOpenCylinderInVertices(int numPoints) {
    return (numPoints + 1) * 2;
}
```

A cylinder side is a rolled-up rectangle built out of a triangle strip, with *two* vertices for each point around the circle, and with the first two vertices repeated twice so that we can close off the tube.

Building a Puck with a Cylinder

We can now create a static method to generate a puck. Go ahead and create a new method called createPuck() and define it as follows:

AirHockeyWithImprovedMallets/src/com/airhockey/android/objects/ObjectBuilder.java

```
static GeneratedData createPuck(Cylinder puck, int numPoints) {
    int size = sizeOfCircleInVertices(numPoints)
               + sizeOfOpenCylinderInVertices(numPoints);

    ObjectBuilder builder = new ObjectBuilder(size);

    Circle puckTop = new Circle(
        puck.center.translateY(puck.height / 2f),
        puck.radius);

    builder.appendCircle(puckTop, numPoints);
    builder.appendOpenCylinder(puck, numPoints);

    return builder.build();
}
```

The first thing we do is figure out how many vertices we need to represent the puck, and then we instantiate a new ObjectBuilder with that size. A puck is built out of one cylinder top (equivalent to a circle) and one cylinder side, so the total size in vertices will be equal to sizeOfCircleInVertices(numPoints) + sizeOfOpenCylinderInVertices(numPoints).

We then calculate where the top of the puck should be and call appendCircle() to create it. We also generate the side of the puck by calling appendOpenCylinder(), and then we return the generated data by returning the results of build(). None of these methods exist yet, so we'll need to create them.

Why do we move the top of the puck by puck.height / 2f? Let's take a look at the following image:

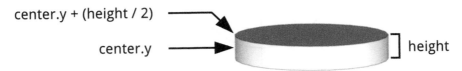

The puck is vertically centered at center.y, so it's fine to place the cylinder side there. The cylinder top, however, needs to be placed at the top of the puck. To do that, we move it up by half of the puck's overall height.

Building a Circle with a Triangle Fan

The next step is to write the code to build the top of the puck using a triangle fan. We'll write the data into vertexData, and we'll use offset to keep track of where we're writing in the array.

Create a new method called appendCircle(), and add the following code:

AirHockeyWithImprovedMallets/src/com/airhockey/android/objects/ObjectBuilder.java
```
private void appendCircle(Circle circle, int numPoints) {
    // Center point of fan
    vertexData[offset++] = circle.center.x;
    vertexData[offset++] = circle.center.y;
    vertexData[offset++] = circle.center.z;

    // Fan around center point. <= is used because we want to generate
    // the point at the starting angle twice to complete the fan.
    for (int i = 0; i <= numPoints; i++) {
        float angleInRadians =
            ((float) i / (float) numPoints)
            * ((float) Math.PI * 2f);

        vertexData[offset++] =
            circle.center.x
            + circle.radius * FloatMath.cos(angleInRadians);
        vertexData[offset++] = circle.center.y;
        vertexData[offset++] =
            circle.center.z
            + circle.radius * FloatMath.sin(angleInRadians);
    }
}
```

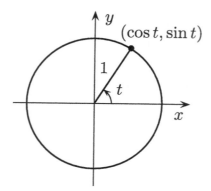

Figure 43—Unit circle

To build the triangle fan, we first define a center vertex at circle.center, and then we fan around the center point, taking care to repeat the first point around the circle twice. We then use trigonometry functions and the concept of a unit circle (see the preceding figure) to generate our points.

To generate points around a circle, we first need a loop that will range over the entire circle from 0 to 360 degrees, or 0 to 2 times pi in radians. To find the x position of a point around the circle, we call cos(angle), and to find the z position, we call sin(angle); we scale both by the circle's radius.

Since our circle is going to be lying flat on the x-z plane, the y component of the unit circle maps to our y position.

Adding a Draw Command for the Triangle Fan

We'll also need to tell OpenGL how to draw the top of the puck. Since a puck is built out of two primitives, a triangle fan for the top and a triangle strip for the side, we need a way to combine these draw commands together so that later on we can just call puck.draw(). One way we can do this is by adding each draw command into a *draw list*.

Let's create an interface to represent a single draw command. Add the following code to the top of ObjectBuilder:

AirHockeyWithImprovedMallets/src/com/airhockey/android/objects/ObjectBuilder.java
```
static interface DrawCommand {
    void draw();
}
```

We'll also need an instance variable to hold the collated draw commands. Add the following definition after vertexData:

AirHockeyWithImprovedMallets/src/com/airhockey/android/objects/ObjectBuilder.java
```
private final List<DrawCommand> drawList = new ArrayList<DrawCommand>();
```

We can now add a draw command for our triangle fan. Modify appendCircle() by adding the following variable definitions at the top:

AirHockeyWithImprovedMallets/src/com/airhockey/android/objects/ObjectBuilder.java
```
final int startVertex = offset / FLOATS_PER_VERTEX;
final int numVertices = sizeOfCircleInVertices(numPoints);
```

Since we're only using one array for the object, we need to tell OpenGL the right vertex offsets for each draw command. We calculate the offset and length and store them into startVertex and numVertices. Now we can add the following to the end of appendCircle():

AirHockeyWithImprovedMallets/src/com/airhockey/android/objects/ObjectBuilder.java
```
drawList.add(new DrawCommand() {
    @Override
    public void draw() {
        glDrawArrays(GL_TRIANGLE_FAN, startVertex, numVertices);
    }
});
```

With this code, we create a new inner class that calls glDrawArrays() and we add the inner class to our draw list. To draw the puck later, we just have to execute each draw() method in the list.

Building a Cylinder Side with a Triangle Strip

The next step is building the side of the puck with a triangle strip. Let's start off by adding the following code after appendCircle():

AirHockeyWithImprovedMallets/src/com/airhockey/android/objects/ObjectBuilder.java
```
private void appendOpenCylinder(Cylinder cylinder, int numPoints) {
    final int startVertex = offset / FLOATS_PER_VERTEX;
    final int numVertices = sizeOfOpenCylinderInVertices(numPoints);
    final float yStart = cylinder.center.y - (cylinder.height / 2f);
    final float yEnd = cylinder.center.y + (cylinder.height / 2f);
```

Just like before, we figure out the starting vertex and the number of vertices so that we can use them in our draw command. We also figure out where the puck should start and end—the positions should be as follows:

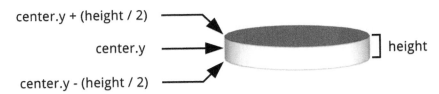

. Add the following code to generate the actual triangle strip:

AirHockeyWithImprovedMallets/src/com/airhockey/android/objects/ObjectBuilder.java
```
for (int i = 0; i <= numPoints; i++) {
    float angleInRadians =
            ((float) i / (float) numPoints)
        * ((float) Math.PI * 2f);

    float xPosition =
            cylinder.center.x
        + cylinder.radius * FloatMath.cos(angleInRadians);

    float zPosition =
            cylinder.center.z
        + cylinder.radius * FloatMath.sin(angleInRadians);

    vertexData[offset++] = xPosition;
    vertexData[offset++] = yStart;
    vertexData[offset++] = zPosition;

    vertexData[offset++] = xPosition;
    vertexData[offset++] = yEnd;
    vertexData[offset++] = zPosition;
}
```

We use the same math as before to generate vertices around the circle, except this time we generate two vertices for each point around the circle: one for the top of the cylinder and one for the bottom. We repeat the positions of the first two points so that we can close off the cylinder.

Add the following to finish the method:

AirHockeyWithImprovedMallets/src/com/airhockey/android/objects/ObjectBuilder.java
```
    drawList.add(new DrawCommand() {
        @Override
        public void draw() {
            glDrawArrays(GL_TRIANGLE_STRIP, startVertex, numVertices);
        }
    });
}
```

We use GL_TRIANGLE_STRIP to tell OpenGL to draw a triangle strip.

Returning the Generated Data

To make createPuck() work, we just need to define the build() method. We'll use this to return the generated data inside of a GeneratedData object. We haven't defined this class yet, so let's add the following class to the top of ObjectBuilder just after DrawCommand:

AirHockeyWithImprovedMallets/src/com/airhockey/android/objects/ObjectBuilder.java

```java
static class GeneratedData {
    final float[] vertexData;
    final List<DrawCommand> drawList;

    GeneratedData(float[] vertexData, List<DrawCommand> drawList) {
        this.vertexData = vertexData;
        this.drawList = drawList;
    }
}
```

This is just a holder class so that we can return both the vertex data and the draw list in a single object. Now we just need to define build():

AirHockeyWithImprovedMallets/src/com/airhockey/android/objects/ObjectBuilder.java

```java
private GeneratedData build() {
    return new GeneratedData(vertexData, drawList);
}
```

That's everything we need for createPuck() to work. Let's take a quick moment to review the flow:

- First we call the static method createPuck() from outside the class. This method creates a new ObjectBuilder with the right array size to hold all of the data for the puck. It also creates a display list so that we can draw the puck later on.

- Inside createPuck(), we call appendCircle() and appendOpenCylinder() to generate the top and sides of the puck. Each method adds its data to vertexData and a draw command to drawList.

- Finally, we call build() to return the generated data.

Building a Mallet with Two Cylinders

We can now use what we've learned to build a mallet. A mallet can be built out of two cylinders, so building a mallet is almost like building two pucks of different sizes. We'll define the mallet a certain way, as seen in Figure 44, *Mallet Definition*, on page 152.

The handle height will be about 75 percent of the overall height, and the base height will be 25 percent of the overall height. We can also say that the handle's width is about one-third the overall width. With these definitions in place, we'll be able to calculate where to place the two cylinders that make up the mallet.

When writing out these definitions, it sometimes helps to take a sheet of paper and draw the object out and then plot where everything is relative to the

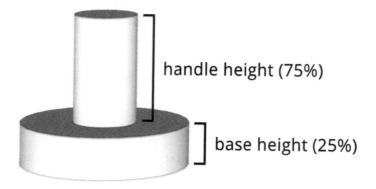

handle height (75%)

base height (25%)

Figure 44—Mallet Definition

center and sides of the objects. To create our mallet, we'll need to figure out the *y* position for each cylinder top as well as the center position for each cylinder.

Let's add a new method called createMallet() just after createPuck(). We'll start off with the following code:

AirHockeyWithImprovedMallets/src/com/airhockey/android/objects/ObjectBuilder.java

```
static GeneratedData createMallet(
    Point center, float radius, float height, int numPoints) {
    int size = sizeOfCircleInVertices(numPoints) * 2
            + sizeOfOpenCylinderInVertices(numPoints) * 2;

    ObjectBuilder builder = new ObjectBuilder(size);

    // First, generate the mallet base.
    float baseHeight = height * 0.25f;

    Circle baseCircle = new Circle(
        center.translateY(-baseHeight),
        radius);
    Cylinder baseCylinder = new Cylinder(
        baseCircle.center.translateY(-baseHeight / 2f),
        radius, baseHeight);

    builder.appendCircle(baseCircle, numPoints);
    builder.appendOpenCylinder(baseCylinder, numPoints);
```

We create a new ObjectBuilder of the proper size, and then we generate the base of the mallet. This code is quite similar to what we did in createPuck().

When you optimize imports, Eclipse might give you the choice to import com.airhockey.android.util.Geometry.Point, which is our Point class, or android.Graphics.Point, which is a different Point class in the Android SDK. You'll want to make sure to select *our* Point class.

Let's add the following code to generate the handle:

AirHockeyWithImprovedMallets/src/com/airhockey/android/objects/ObjectBuilder.java
```
float handleHeight = height * 0.75f;
float handleRadius = radius / 3f;

Circle handleCircle = new Circle(
    center.translateY(height * 0.5f),
    handleRadius);
Cylinder handleCylinder = new Cylinder(
    handleCircle.center.translateY(-handleHeight / 2f),
    handleRadius, handleHeight);

builder.appendCircle(handleCircle, numPoints);
builder.appendOpenCylinder(handleCylinder, numPoints);
```

We follow the same steps as before but with different coordinates and different sizes. Let's add a call to build() to complete the method:

AirHockeyWithImprovedMallets/src/com/airhockey/android/objects/ObjectBuilder.java
```
    return builder.build();
}
```

That's it for our ObjectBuilder class! We can now generate pucks and mallets; and when we want to draw them, all we need to do is bind the vertex data to OpenGL and call object.draw().

8.4 Updating Our Objects

Now that we have an object builder, we'll need to update our Mallet class since we're no longer drawing it as a point. We'll also need to add a new Puck class. Let's start with the puck. Create a new class in the same package called Puck, and add the following code to the class:

AirHockeyWithImprovedMallets/src/com/airhockey/android/objects/Puck.java
```
private static final int POSITION_COMPONENT_COUNT = 3;

public final float radius, height;

private final VertexArray vertexArray;
private final List<DrawCommand> drawList;

public Puck(float radius, float height, int numPointsAroundPuck) {
    GeneratedData generatedData = ObjectBuilder.createPuck(new Cylinder(
        new Point(0f, 0f, 0f), radius, height), numPointsAroundPuck);
```

```
        this.radius = radius;
        this.height = height;

        vertexArray = new VertexArray(generatedData.vertexData);
        drawList = generatedData.drawList;
    }
```

When a new Puck is created, it will generate the object data, store the vertices in a native buffer with vertexArray, and store the draw list in drawList.

Let's complete the class:

AirHockeyWithImprovedMallets/src/com/airhockey/android/objects/Puck.java
```
public void bindData(ColorShaderProgram colorProgram) {
    vertexArray.setVertexAttribPointer(0,
        colorProgram.getPositionAttributeLocation(),
        POSITION_COMPONENT_COUNT, 0);
}
public void draw() {
    for (DrawCommand drawCommand : drawList) {
        drawCommand.draw();
    }
}
```

The first method, bindData() follows the same pattern that we also follow with Table and Mallet: it binds the vertex data to the attributes defined by the shader program. The second method, draw(), just goes through the display list created by ObjectBuilder.createPuck().

We'll also need to update the Mallet class. Replace everything inside the class with the following code:

AirHockeyWithImprovedMallets/src/com/airhockey/android/objects/Mallet.java
```
private static final int POSITION_COMPONENT_COUNT = 3;

public final float radius;
public final float height;

private final VertexArray vertexArray;
private final List<DrawCommand> drawList;

public Mallet(float radius, float height, int numPointsAroundMallet) {
    GeneratedData generatedData = ObjectBuilder.createMallet(new Point(0f,
        0f, 0f), radius, height, numPointsAroundMallet);

    this.radius = radius;
    this.height = height;

    vertexArray = new VertexArray(generatedData.vertexData);
    drawList = generatedData.drawList;
}
```

```
public void bindData(ColorShaderProgram colorProgram) {
    vertexArray.setVertexAttribPointer(0,
        colorProgram.getPositionAttributeLocation(),
        POSITION_COMPONENT_COUNT, 0);
}
public void draw() {
    for (DrawCommand drawCommand : drawList) {
        drawCommand.draw();
    }
}
```

This follows the same pattern as for Puck.

8.5 Updating Shaders

We'll also need to update our color shader. We defined our puck and mallet with a per-vertex position but not with a per-vertex color. Instead we'll have to pass in the color as a uniform. The first thing we'll do to make these changes is add a new constant to ShaderProgram:

AirHockeyWithImprovedMallets/src/com/airhockey/android/programs/ShaderProgram.java
```
protected static final String U_COLOR = "u_Color";
```

The next step is to update ColorShaderProgram. Go ahead and remove all references to aColorLocation, including getColorAttributeLocation(), and then add the following uniform location definition:

AirHockeyWithImprovedMallets/src/com/airhockey/android/programs/ColorShaderProgram.java
```
private final int uColorLocation;
```

Update the constructor to set the uniform location:

```
uColorLocation = glGetUniformLocation(program, U_COLOR);
```

To complete the changes, update setUniforms() as follows:

```
public void setUniforms(float[] matrix, float r, float g, float b) {
    glUniformMatrix4fv(uMatrixLocation, 1, false, matrix, 0);
    glUniform4f(uColorLocation, r, g, b, 1f);
}
```

We'll also need to update the actual shaders. Update the contents of simple_vertex_shader.glsl as follows:

AirHockeyWithImprovedMallets/res/raw/simple_vertex_shader.glsl
```
uniform mat4 u_Matrix;
attribute vec4 a_Position;
void main()
{
    gl_Position = u_Matrix * a_Position;
}
```

Update simple_fragment_shader.glsl as follows:

```
precision mediump float;

uniform vec4 u_Color;

void main()
{
    gl_FragColor = u_Color;
}
```

Our shaders should now be up-to-date.

8.6 Integrating Our Changes

The hardest part of this chapter is done. We learned how to build a puck and a mallet out of simple geometric shapes, and we've also updated our shaders to reflect the changes. All that's left is to integrate the changes into AirHockeyRenderer; at the same time, we'll also learn how to add the concept of a camera by adding a view matrix.

So why would we want to add another matrix? When we first started our air hockey project, we originally didn't use any matrices at all. We first added an orthographic matrix to adjust for the aspect ratio, and then we switched to a perspective matrix to get a 3D projection. We then added a model matrix to start moving stuff around. A view matrix is really just an extension of a model matrix; it's used for the same purposes, but it applies equally to every object in the scene.

A Simple Matrix Hierarchy

Let's take a moment to review the three main types of matrices we'll use to get an object onto the screen:

Model matrix

A model matrix is used to place objects into world-space coordinates. For example, we might have our puck model and our mallet model initially centered at (0, 0, 0). Without a model matrix, our models will be stuck there: if we wanted to move them, we'd have to update each and every vertex ourselves. Instead of doing that, we can use a model matrix and transform our vertices by multiplying them with the matrix. If we want to move our puck to (5, 5), we just need to prepare a model matrix that will do this for us.

View matrix

A view matrix is used for the same reasons as a model matrix, but it equally affects every object in the scene. Because it affects everything, it is functionally equivalent to a camera: move the camera around, and you'll see things from a different viewpoint.

The advantage of using a separate matrix is that it lets us prebake a bunch of transformations into a single matrix. As an example, imagine we wanted to rotate the scene around and move it a certain amount into the distance. One way we could do this is by issuing the same rotate and translate calls for every single object. While that works, it's easier to just save these transformations into a separate matrix and apply that to every object.

Projection matrix

Finally, we have the projection matrix. This matrix helps to create the illusion of 3D, and it usually only changes whenever the screen changes orientation.

Let's also review how a vertex gets transformed from its original position to the screen:

$vertex_{model}$

This is a vertex in model coordinates. An example would be the positions contained inside the table vertices.

$vertex_{world}$

This is a vertex that has been positioned in the world with a model matrix.

$vertex_{eye}$

This is a vertex relative to our eyes or camera. We use a view matrix to move all vertices in the world around relative to our current viewing position.

$vertex_{clip}$

This is a vertex that has been processed with a projection matrix. The next step will be to do the perspective divide, as explained in *Perspective Division*, on page 97.

$vertex_{ndc}$

This is a vertex in normalized device coordinates. Once a vertex is in these coordinates, OpenGL will map it onto the viewport, and you'll be able to see it on your screen.

Here's what the chain looks like:

$$vertex_{clip} = ProjectionMatrix * vertex_{eye}$$

$$vertex_{clip} = ProjectionMatrix * ViewMatrix * vertex_{world}$$

$$vertex_{clip} = ProjectionMatrix * ViewMatrix * ModelMatrix * vertex_{model}$$

We'll need to apply each matrix in this order to get the right results.

Adding the New Objects to Our Air Hockey Table

Let's go ahead and add a view matrix to AirHockeyRender, and we'll also work in our new mallets and puck at the same time. We'll first add a few new matrix definitions to the top of the class:

AirHockeyWithImprovedMallets/src/com/airhockey/android/AirHockeyRenderer.java

```
private final float[] viewMatrix = new float[16];
private final float[] viewProjectionMatrix = new float[16];
private final float[] modelViewProjectionMatrix = new float[16];
```

We'll store our view matrix in viewMatrix, and the other two matrices will be used to hold the results of matrix multiplications. Let's also add a definition for our new puck just after mallet:

AirHockeyWithImprovedMallets/src/com/airhockey/android/AirHockeyRenderer.java

```
private Puck puck;
```

Don't forget to update your imports. The next step is to initialize our mallet and puck objects. We'll create them with a specific size in onSurfaceCreated(), as follows:

AirHockeyWithImprovedMallets/src/com/airhockey/android/AirHockeyRenderer.java

```
mallet = new Mallet(0.08f, 0.15f, 32);
puck = new Puck(0.06f, 0.02f, 32);
```

The radius and height for the puck and mallet are set to an arbitrary size so that they look proportionate to the table. Each object will be created with 32 points around the circle.

Initializing the New Matrices

The next step is to update onSurfaceChanged() and initialize the view matrix. Update onSurfaceChanged() to match the following contents:

AirHockeyWithImprovedMallets/src/com/airhockey/android/AirHockeyRenderer.java

```
@Override
public void onSurfaceChanged(GL10 glUnused, int width, int height) {
    // Set the OpenGL viewport to fill the entire surface.
    glViewport(0, 0, width, height);
    MatrixHelper.perspectiveM(projectionMatrix, 45, (float) width
        / (float) height, 1f, 10f);
    setLookAtM(viewMatrix, 0, 0f, 1.2f, 2.2f, 0f, 0f, 0f, 0f, 1f, 0f);
}
```

The first part of the method is pretty standard: we set the viewport, and we set up a projection matrix. The next part is new: we call setLookAtM() to create a special type of view matrix:

setLookAtM(float[] rm, int rmOffset, float eyeX, float eyeY, float eyeZ, float centerX, float centerY, float centerZ, float upX, float upY, float upZ)

float[] rm	This is the destination array. This array's length should be at least sixteen elements so that it can store the view matrix.
int rmOffset	setLookAtM() will begin writing the result at this offset into rm.
float eyeX, eyeY, eyeZ	This is where the eye will be. Everything in the scene will appear as if we're viewing it from this point.
float centerX, centerY, centerZ	This is where the eye is looking; this position will appear in the center of the scene.
float upX, upY, upZ	If we were talking about *your* eyes, then this is where your head would be pointing. An upY of 1 means your head would be pointing straight up.

Table 6—setLookAtM() parameters

We call setLookAtM() with an eye of (0, 1.2, 2.2), meaning your eye will be 1.2 units above the *x-z* plane and 2.2 units back. In other words, everything in the scene will appear 1.2 units below you and 2.2 units in front of you. A center of (0, 0, 0) means you'll be looking down toward the origin in front of you, and an up of (0, 1, 0) means that your head will be pointing straight up and the scene won't be rotated to either side.

Updating onDrawFrame

A couple of last changes remain before we can run our program and see the new changes. Add the following code to onDrawFrame() just after the call to glClear():

AirHockeyWithImprovedMallets/src/com/airhockey/android/AirHockeyRenderer.java
```
multiplyMM(viewProjectionMatrix, 0, projectionMatrix, 0, viewMatrix, 0);
```

This will cache the results of multiplying the projection and view matrices together into viewProjectionMatrix. Replace the rest of onDrawFrame() as follows:

AirHockeyWithImprovedMallets/src/com/airhockey/android/AirHockeyRenderer.java
```
positionTableInScene();
textureProgram.useProgram();
textureProgram.setUniforms(modelViewProjectionMatrix, texture);
table.bindData(textureProgram);
table.draw();

// Draw the mallets.
positionObjectInScene(0f, mallet.height / 2f, -0.4f);
colorProgram.useProgram();
colorProgram.setUniforms(modelViewProjectionMatrix, 1f, 0f, 0f);
mallet.bindData(colorProgram);
mallet.draw();

positionObjectInScene(0f, mallet.height / 2f, 0.4f);
colorProgram.setUniforms(modelViewProjectionMatrix, 0f, 0f, 1f);
// Note that we don't have to define the object data twice -- we just
// draw the same mallet again but in a different position and with a
// different color.
mallet.draw();

// Draw the puck.
positionObjectInScene(0f, puck.height / 2f, 0f);
colorProgram.setUniforms(modelViewProjectionMatrix, 0.8f, 0.8f, 1f);
puck.bindData(colorProgram);
puck.draw();
```

This code is mostly the same as it was in the last project, but there are a few key differences. The first difference is that we call positionTableInScene() and positionObjectInScene() before we draw those objects. We've also updated setUniforms() before drawing the mallets, and we've added code to draw the puck.

Did you also notice that we're drawing two mallets with the same mallet data? We could use the same set of vertices to draw hundreds of objects if we wanted to: all we have to do is update the model matrix before drawing each object.

Let's add the definition for positionTableInScene():

AirHockeyWithImprovedMallets/src/com/airhockey/android/AirHockeyRenderer.java
```
private void positionTableInScene() {
    // The table is defined in terms of X & Y coordinates, so we rotate it
    // 90 degrees to lie flat on the XZ plane.
    setIdentityM(modelMatrix, 0);
    rotateM(modelMatrix, 0, -90f, 1f, 0f, 0f);
    multiplyMM(modelViewProjectionMatrix, 0, viewProjectionMatrix,
        0, modelMatrix, 0);
}
```

The table is originally defined in terms of *x* and *y* coordinates, so to get it to lie flat on the ground, we rotate it 90 degrees back around the *x*-axis. Note that unlike previous lessons, we don't also translate the table into the distance because we want to keep the table at (0, 0, 0) in world coordinates, and the view matrix is already taking care of making the table visible for us.

The last step is to combine all the matrices together by multiplying viewProjectionMatrix and modelMatrix and storing the result in modelViewProjectionMatrix, which will then get passed into the shader program.

Let's also add the definition for positionObjectInScene():

AirHockeyWithImprovedMallets/src/com/airhockey/android/AirHockeyRenderer.java
```
private void positionObjectInScene(float x, float y, float z) {
    setIdentityM(modelMatrix, 0);
    translateM(modelMatrix, 0, x, y, z);
    multiplyMM(modelViewProjectionMatrix, 0, viewProjectionMatrix,
        0, modelMatrix, 0);
}
```

The mallets and puck are already defined to lie flat on the *x-z* plane, so there's no need for rotation. We translate them based on the parameters passed in so that they're placed at the proper position above the table.

Go ahead and run the program. If everything went according to plan, then it should look just like Figure 45, *Air hockey with improved mallets*, on page 162. The new mallets and puck should appear, with the view centered on the table. The mallets may appear a little *too* solid; we'll learn how to improve this in Chapter 13, *Lighting Up the World*, on page 253.

8.7 A Review

Congratulations on making it through another intense chapter! We learned all about generating triangle strips and triangle fans and how to put them together into objects. We also learned how to encapsulate the drawing calls when building these objects so that we can easily tie them together into a single command.

We also introduced the idea of a matrix hierarchy: one matrix for the projection, one for the camera, and one to move objects around in the world. Splitting things up in this way makes it easier to manipulate the scene and move stuff around.

8.8 Exercises

As your first exercise, rotate your viewpoint slowly around the table by adding one single method call to onDrawFrame().

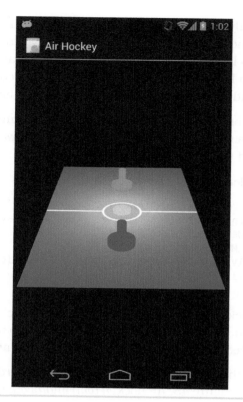

Figure 45—Air hockey with improved mallets

For a more challenging exercise, take a look at the following figure:

How would you update the mallet generator to more closely approximate this type of mallet? You can still build the mallet out of simple geometric shapes. Here's one way you might want to approach it:

- Two regular cylinder sides: one for the handle, one for the outside of the base

- Two rings: one for the top of the base and one for the inside of the base

- One sloped cylinder side for the inside of the base to connect the two rings

- A half-sphere to cap the top of the mallet

Of course, your imagination is the limit, and you can be as creative as you want to be. When you're ready, we'll learn how to move the mallets around with our fingers in the next chapter!

CHAPTER 9

Adding Touch Feedback: Interacting with Our Air Hockey Game

Good user interactivity through touch support is the cornerstone of many games and applications; it can give the user a sense of playing with something real, even if they're just looking at pixels on a screen. Some mobile games have become extremely popular just because they came up with a new touch paradigm; a certain game involving birds comes to mind.

We now have better-looking mallets in our air hockey game, but wouldn't it be nice if we could actually use them? In this chapter, we're going to start making our program more interactive by adding touch support. We'll learn how to add 3D intersection tests and collision detection so that we can grab our mallet and drag it around the screen.

Here's our game plan for the chapter:

- We'll begin by adding touch interactivity to our air hockey project. We'll go over the math and plumbing required to get this to work.

- We'll then learn how to make our mallet interact with the puck and stay within bounds.

When we've finished with the chapter, we'll be able to strike the puck with the mallet and watch it bounce around the table! To start out, let's copy our project from the previous chapter into a new project called 'AirHockeyTouch'.

9.1 Adding Touch Support to Our Activity

We'll begin by hooking into Android's touch event system. The first thing we'll need to do is hold onto a reference to our renderer, so let's open up AirHockey-Activity and modify the call to setRenderer() as follows:

AirHockeyTouch/src/com/airhockey/android/AirHockeyActivity.java
```
final AirHockeyRenderer airHockeyRenderer = new AirHockeyRenderer(this);

if (supportsEs2) {
    // ...
    glSurfaceView.setRenderer(airHockeyRenderer);
```

We'll refer to this reference in our touch handler to inform the renderer of new touch events.

Listening to Touch Events

Let's start writing our touch handler by adding the following code just before the call to setContentView():

AirHockeyTouch/src/com/airhockey/android/AirHockeyActivity.java
```
glSurfaceView.setOnTouchListener(new OnTouchListener() {
    @Override
    public boolean onTouch(View v, MotionEvent event) {
        if (event != null) {
            // Convert touch coordinates into normalized device
            // coordinates, keeping in mind that Android's Y
            // coordinates are inverted.
            final float normalizedX =
                (event.getX() / (float) v.getWidth()) * 2 - 1;
            final float normalizedY =
                -((event.getY() / (float) v.getHeight()) * 2 - 1);
```

In Android, we can listen in on a view's touch events by calling setOnTouchListener(). When a user touches that view, we'll receive a call to onTouch().

The first thing we do is check if there's an event to handle. In Android, the touch events will be in the view's coordinate space, so the upper left corner of the view will map to (0, 0), and the lower right corner will map to the view's dimensions. For example, if our view was 480 pixels wide by 800 pixels tall, then the lower right corner would map to (480, 800).

We'll need to work with normalized device coordinates in our renderer (see Section 5.1, *We Have an Aspect Ratio Problem*, on page 78, so we convert the touch event coordinates back into normalized device coordinates by inverting the y-axis and scaling each coordinate into the range [-1, 1].

Forwarding Touch Events to Our Renderer

Let's finish off the touch handler:

AirHockeyTouch/src/com/airhockey/android/AirHockeyActivity.java
```
            if (event.getAction() == MotionEvent.ACTION_DOWN) {
                glSurfaceView.queueEvent(new Runnable() {
                    @Override
```

```
            public void run() {
                airHockeyRenderer.handleTouchPress(
                    normalizedX, normalizedY);
            }
        });
    } else if (event.getAction() == MotionEvent.ACTION_MOVE) {
        glSurfaceView.queueEvent(new Runnable() {
            @Override
            public void run() {
                airHockeyRenderer.handleTouchDrag(
                    normalizedX, normalizedY);
            }
        });
    }

    return true;
} else {
    return false;
}
    }
});
```

We check to see if the event is either an initial press or a drag event, because we'll need to handle each case differently. An initial press corresponds to MotionEvent.ACTION_DOWN, and a drag corresponds to MotionEvent.ACTION_MOVE.

It's important to keep in mind that Android's UI runs in the main thread while GLSurfaceView runs OpenGL in a separate thread, so we need to communicate between the two using thread-safe techniques. We use queueEvent() to dispatch calls to the OpenGL thread, calling airHockeyRenderer.handleTouchPress() for a press and airHockeyRenderer.handleTouchDrag() for a drag. These methods don't exist at the moment, so we'll create them soon.

We finish off the handler by returning *true* to tell Android that we've consumed the touch event. If the event was null, then we return *false* instead.

Open up AirHockeyRenderer and add stubs for handleTouchPress() and handleTouchDrag():

AirHockeyTouch/src/com/airhockey/android/AirHockeyRenderer.java
```
public void handleTouchPress(float normalizedX, float normalizedY) {

}

public void handleTouchDrag(float normalizedX, float normalizedY) {

}
```

As a small exercise, add some logging statements here, run the application, and see what happens when you touch the screen.

9.2   Adding Intersection Tests

Now that we have the touched area of the screen in normalized device coordinates, we'll need to determine if that touched area contains the mallet. We'll need to perform an intersection test, a very important operation when working with 3D games and applications. Here's what we'll need to do:

1. First we'll need to convert the 2D screen coordinate back into 3D space and see what we're touching. We'll do this by casting the touched point into a ray that spans the 3D scene from our point of view.

2. We'll then need to check to see if this ray intersects with the mallet. To make things easier, we'll pretend that the mallet is actually a bounding sphere of around the same size and then we'll test against that sphere.

Let's start off by creating two new member variables:

AirHockeyTouch/src/com/airhockey/android/AirHockeyRenderer.java
```java
private boolean malletPressed = false;
private Point blueMalletPosition;
```

We'll use malletPressed to keep track of whether the mallet is currently pressed or not. We'll also store the mallet's position in blueMalletPosition. We'll need to initialize this to a default value, so let's add the following to onSurfaceCreated():

AirHockeyTouch/src/com/airhockey/android/AirHockeyRenderer.java
```java
blueMalletPosition = new Point(0f, mallet.height / 2f, 0.4f);
```

We can then update handleTouchPress() as follows:

AirHockeyTouch/src/com/airhockey/android/AirHockeyRenderer.java
```java
public void handleTouchPress(float normalizedX, float normalizedY) {
    Ray ray = convertNormalized2DPointToRay(normalizedX, normalizedY);

    // Now test if this ray intersects with the mallet by creating a
    // bounding sphere that wraps the mallet.
    Sphere malletBoundingSphere = new Sphere(new Point(
            blueMalletPosition.x,
            blueMalletPosition.y,
            blueMalletPosition.z),
        mallet.height / 2f);

    // If the ray intersects (if the user touched a part of the screen that
    // intersects the mallet's bounding sphere), then set malletPressed =
    // true.
    malletPressed = Geometry.intersects(malletBoundingSphere, ray);
}
```

To see if the touched point intersects the mallet, we first cast the touched point to a ray, wrap the mallet with a bounding sphere, and then test to see if the ray intersects that sphere.

This might make more sense if we look at things visually. Let's consider an imaginary scene with our air hockey table, a puck, and two mallets, and let's imagine that we're touching the screen at the darkened circle in the following image:

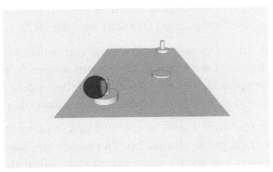

We're clearly touching one of the mallets. However, our touched area is in 2D space and the mallet is in 3D space. How do we test if the touched point intersects with the mallet?

To test this, we first convert the 2D point into two 3D points: one at the near end of the 3D frustum and one at the far end of the 3D frustum (if the word "frustum" is making your head a little foggy, now might be a good time to head back to *The Frustum*, on page 101, and take a few moments to review). We then draw a line between these two points to create a *ray*. If we look at our scene from the side, here's how the ray would intersect the 3D scene:

To make the math easier, we'll pretend that the mallet is a sphere when we do the test.

Let's start off by defining convertNormalized2DPointToRay() and solving the first part of the puzzle: converting the touched point into a 3D ray.

Extending a Two-Dimensional Point into a Three-Dimensional Line

Normally when we project a 3D scene onto a 2D screen, we use a perspective projection and the perspective divide to transform our vertices into normalized device coordinates (see *Perspective Division*, on page 97).

Now we want to go the other way: we have the normalized device coordinates of the touched point, and we want to figure out where in the 3D world that touched point corresponds to. To convert a touched point into a 3D ray, we essentially need to undo the perspective projection and the perspective divide.

We currently have touched x and y coordinates, but we have no idea how near or far the touched point should be. To resolve the ambiguity, we'll map the touched point to a line in 3D space: the near end of the line will map to the near end of the frustum defined by our projection matrix, and the far end of the line will map to the far end of the frustum.

To do this conversion, we'll need an inverted matrix that will undo the effects of the view and projection matrices. Let's add the following definition to the list of matrix definitions:

AirHockeyTouch/src/com/airhockey/android/AirHockeyRenderer.java
```
private final float[] invertedViewProjectionMatrix = new float[16];
```

In onDrawFrame(), add the following line of code after the call to multiplyMM():

AirHockeyTouch/src/com/airhockey/android/AirHockeyRenderer.java
```
invertM(invertedViewProjectionMatrix, 0, viewProjectionMatrix, 0);
```

This call will create an inverted matrix that we'll be able to use to convert the two-dimensional touch point into a pair of three-dimensional coordinates. If we move around in our scene, it will affect which part of the scene is underneath our fingers, so we also want to take the view matrix into account. We do this by taking the inverse of the combined view and projection matrices.

Reversing the Perspective Projection and Perspective Divide

Now we can start defining convertNormalized2DPointToRay(). Let's start out with the following code:

AirHockeyTouch/src/com/airhockey/android/AirHockeyRenderer.java

```java
private Ray convertNormalized2DPointToRay(
    float normalizedX, float normalizedY) {
    // We'll convert these normalized device coordinates into world-space
    // coordinates. We'll pick a point on the near and far planes, and draw a
    // line between them. To do this transform, we need to first multiply by
    // the inverse matrix, and then we need to undo the perspective divide.
    final float[] nearPointNdc = {normalizedX, normalizedY, -1, 1};
    final float[] farPointNdc =  {normalizedX, normalizedY,  1, 1};

    final float[] nearPointWorld = new float[4];
    final float[] farPointWorld = new float[4];

    multiplyMV(
        nearPointWorld, 0, invertedViewProjectionMatrix, 0, nearPointNdc, 0);
    multiplyMV(
        farPointWorld, 0, invertedViewProjectionMatrix, 0, farPointNdc, 0);
```

To map the touched point to a ray, we set up two points in normalized device coordinates: one point is the touched point with a z of -1, and the other point is the touched point with a z of +1. We store these points in nearPointNdc and farPointNdc, respectively. Since we have no idea what the w component should be, we put a w of 1 for both. We then multiply each point with invertedViewProjectionMatrix to get a coordinate in world space.

We also need to undo the perspective divide. There's an interesting property of the inverted view projection matrix: after we multiply our vertices with the inverted view projection matrix, nearPointWorld and farPointWorld will actually contain an inverted w value. This is because normally the whole point of a projection matrix is to create different w values so that the perspective divide can do its magic; so if we use an *inverted* projection matrix, we'll also get an inverted w. All we need to do is divide x, y, and z with these inverted w's, and we'll undo the perspective divide.

Let's continue the definition for convertNormalized2DPointToRay():

AirHockeyTouch/src/com/airhockey/android/AirHockeyRenderer.java

```java
divideByW(nearPointWorld);
divideByW(farPointWorld);
```

We'll also need to define divideByW():

AirHockeyTouch/src/com/airhockey/android/AirHockeyRenderer.java

```java
private void divideByW(float[] vector) {
    vector[0] /= vector[3];
    vector[1] /= vector[3];
    vector[2] /= vector[3];
}
```

Defining a Ray

We've now successfully converted a touched point into two points in world space. We can now use these two points to define a ray that spans the 3D scene. Let's finish off convertNormalized2DPointToRay():

AirHockeyTouch/src/com/airhockey/android/AirHockeyRenderer.java

```java
    Point nearPointRay =
        new Point(nearPointWorld[0], nearPointWorld[1], nearPointWorld[2]);

    Point farPointRay =
        new Point(farPointWorld[0], farPointWorld[1], farPointWorld[2]);

    return new Ray(nearPointRay,
                Geometry.vectorBetween(nearPointRay, farPointRay));
}
```

We'll also need to add a definition for Ray. Let's add the following to our Geometry class:

AirHockeyTouch/src/com/airhockey/android/util/Geometry.java

```java
public static class Ray {
    public final Point point;
    public final Vector vector;

    public Ray(Point point, Vector vector) {
        this.point = point;
        this.vector = vector;
    }
}
```

A ray consists of a starting point and a vector representing the direction of the ray. To create this vector, we call vectorBetween() to create a vector ranging from the near point to the far point.

Let's add a basic definition for Vector to our Geometry class:

AirHockeyTouch/src/com/airhockey/android/util/Geometry.java

```java
public static class Vector  {
    public final float x, y, z;

    public Vector(float x, float y, float z) {
        this.x = x;
        this.y = y;
        this.z = z;
    }
}
```

We'll also need a definition for vectorBetween():

```
AirHockeyTouch/src/com/airhockey/android/util/Geometry.java
public static Vector vectorBetween(Point from, Point to) {
    return new Vector(
        to.x - from.x,
        to.y - from.y,
        to.z - from.z);
}
```

We've now finished the first part of the puzzle: converting a touched point into a 3D ray. Now we need to add the intersection test.

Performing the Intersection Test

Earlier we mentioned that doing the intersection test would be much easier if we pretended that our mallet was a sphere. In fact, if we look back at handle-TouchPress(), we're defining a bounding sphere with similar dimensions as the mallet:

```
AirHockeyTouch/src/com/airhockey/android/AirHockeyRenderer.java
Sphere malletBoundingSphere = new Sphere(new Point(
        blueMalletPosition.x,
        blueMalletPosition.y,
        blueMalletPosition.z),
    mallet.height / 2f);
```

We still need to define Sphere, so let's go ahead and add the following code to our Geometry class:

```
AirHockeyTouch/src/com/airhockey/android/util/Geometry.java
public static class Sphere {
    public final Point center;
    public final float radius;

    public Sphere(Point center, float radius) {
        this.center = center;
        this.radius = radius;
    }
}
```

Taking another look at handleTouchPress(), we still need to cover the intersection test:

```
AirHockeyTouch/src/com/airhockey/android/AirHockeyRenderer.java
malletPressed = Geometry.intersects(malletBoundingSphere, ray);
```

Using a Triangle to Calculate the Distance

Before we define the code for this, let's visualize the intersection test, as it will make things easier to understand:

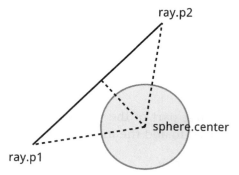

To do this test, we need to follow these steps:

1. We need to figure out the distance between the sphere and the ray. We do this by first defining two points on the ray: the initial point and the end point, found by adding the ray's vector to the initial point. We then create an imaginary triangle between these two points and the center of the sphere, and then we get the distance by calculating the height of that triangle.

2. We then compare that distance to the sphere's radius. If that distance is smaller than the radius, then the ray intersects the sphere.

A more detailed explanation behind this algorithm can be found on Wolfram MathWorld.[1]

Let's start writing out the code. Add the following method to the Geometry class:

AirHockeyTouch/src/com/airhockey/android/util/Geometry.java

```
public static boolean intersects(Sphere sphere, Ray ray) {
    return distanceBetween(sphere.center, ray) < sphere.radius;
}
```

This method will determine the distance between the sphere center and the ray and check if that distance is less than the sphere radius. If it is, then the sphere and the ray intersect.

Calculating the Distance with Vector Math

Go ahead and write out the following code for distanceBetween():

AirHockeyTouch/src/com/airhockey/android/util/Geometry.java

```
public static float distanceBetween(Point point, Ray ray) {
    Vector p1ToPoint = vectorBetween(ray.point, point);
    Vector p2ToPoint = vectorBetween(ray.point.translate(ray.vector), point);
```

---

1. http://mathworld.wolfram.com/Point-LineDistance3-Dimensional.html

```
// The length of the cross product gives the area of an imaginary
// parallelogram having the two vectors as sides. A parallelogram can be
// thought of as consisting of two triangles, so this is the same as
// twice the area of the triangle defined by the two vectors.
// http://en.wikipedia.org/wiki/Cross_product#Geometric_meaning
float areaOfTriangleTimesTwo = p1ToPoint.crossProduct(p2ToPoint).length();
float lengthOfBase = ray.vector.length();

// The area of a triangle is also equal to (base * height) / 2. In
// other words, the height is equal to (area * 2) / base. The height
// of this triangle is the distance from the point to the ray.
float distanceFromPointToRay = areaOfTriangleTimesTwo / lengthOfBase;
return distanceFromPointToRay;
}
```

This method may look a little intense, but it's only doing the triangle method that we just mentioned.

First we define two vectors: one from the first point of the ray to the sphere center and one from the second point of the ray to the sphere center. These two vectors together define a triangle.

To get the area of this triangle, we first need to calculate the cross product of these two vectors.[2] Calculating the cross product will give us a third vector that is perpendicular to the first two vectors, but more importantly for us, the length of this vector will be equal to twice the area of the triangle defined by the first two vectors.

Once we have the area of the triangle, we can use the triangle formula to calculate the height of the triangle, which will give us the distance from the ray to the center of the sphere. The height will be equal to (area * 2) / lengthOfBase. We have the area * 2 in areaOfTriangleTimesTwo, and we can calculate the length of the base by taking the length of ray.vector. To calculate the height of the triangle, we just need to divide one by the other. Once we have this distance, we can compare it to the sphere's radius to see if the ray intersects the sphere.

To get this to work, we'll need to add a new method to Point:

AirHockeyTouch/src/com/airhockey/android/util/Geometry.java
```
public Point translate(Vector vector) {
    return new Point(
        x + vector.x,
        y + vector.y,
        z + vector.z);
}
```

---

2. http://en.wikipedia.org/wiki/Cross_product

We'll also need to add a couple of extra methods to our Vector class:

AirHockeyTouch/src/com/airhockey/android/util/Geometry.java
```
public float length() {
    return FloatMath.sqrt(
        x * x
      + y * y
      + z * z);
}
```

```
// http://en.wikipedia.org/wiki/Cross_product
public Vector crossProduct(Vector other) {
    return new Vector(
        (y * other.z) - (z * other.y),
        (z * other.x) - (x * other.z),
        (x * other.y) - (y * other.x));
}
```

The first method, length(), returns the length of a vector by applying Pythagoras's theorem.[3] The second, crossProduct(), calculates the cross product between two vectors.[4]

An Example of a Ray-Sphere Intersection Test

Let's walk through the code with an actual example, using the following image for our coordinate points:

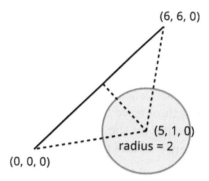

We have a ray located at (0, 0, 0) with a vector of (6, 6, 0). Since we need two points, we add the vector to the first point, which gives us a second point at (6, 6, 0). We also have a sphere with a radius of 2 and a center point at (5, 1, 0).

The first thing we do is assign the vectors p1ToPoint and p2ToPoint. For p1ToPoint, we'll set it to the vector between the ray's starting point and the center of the

---

3.   http://en.wikipedia.org/wiki/Pythagorean_theorem
4.   http://en.wikipedia.org/wiki/Cross_product

sphere, so we'll set it to (5, 1, 0) - (0, 0, 0) = (5, 1, 0). For p2ToPoint, we set it to the vector between the ray's second point and the center of the sphere, so we'll set it to (5, 1, 0) - (6, 6, 0) = (-1, -5, 0).

The next step is to get the height of the triangle. First we get the double area by taking the length of the cross product of p1ToPoint and p2ToPoint. We won't go through all of the intermediary steps, but if you follow the math, you should end up with a cross product of (0, 0, -24) and a length of 24. In other words, the area of the triangle is equal to 24 divided by 2.

To get the height of the triangle, we need to multiply the area by 2 and divide that by the base. The area multiplied by 2 is equal to 24, so now we just need to find the base by taking the length of the ray vector, (6, 6, 0). The length of this vector is approximately 8.49, so if we solve for the height, we end up with 24 / 8.49 = 2.82.

Now we can do our final test. 2.82 is greater than the radius of 2, so this ray definitely does not intersect with this sphere.

Our definition for handleTouchPress() is now complete. Give the application a run, and add some debug statements to see what happens when you tap on the mallet with your finger.

9.3 Moving Around an Object by Dragging

Now that we're able to test if the mallet has been touched, we'll work on solving the next part of the puzzle: Where does the mallet go when we drag it around? We can think of things in this way: the mallet lies flat on the table, so when we move our finger around, the mallet should move with our finger and continue to lie flat on the table. We can figure out the right position by doing a ray-plane intersection test.

Let's complete the definition for handleTouchDrag():

AirHockeyTouch/src/com/airhockey/android/AirHockeyRenderer.java
```java
public void handleTouchDrag(float normalizedX, float normalizedY) {
    if (malletPressed) {
        Ray ray = convertNormalized2DPointToRay(normalizedX, normalizedY);
        // Define a plane representing our air hockey table.
        Plane plane = new Plane(new Point(0, 0, 0), new Vector(0, 1, 0));
        // Find out where the touched point intersects the plane
        // representing our table. We'll move the mallet along this plane.
        Point touchedPoint = Geometry.intersectionPoint(ray, plane);
        blueMalletPosition =
            new Point(touchedPoint.x, mallet.height / 2f, touchedPoint.z);
    }
}
```

We only want to drag the mallet around if we had initially pressed on it with a finger, so first we check to see that malletPressed is true. If it is, then we do the same ray conversion that we were doing in handleTouchPress(). Once we have the ray representing the touched point, we find out where that ray intersects with the plane represented by our air hockey table, and then we move the mallet to that point.

Let's add the code for Plane to Geometry:

AirHockeyTouch/src/com/airhockey/android/util/Geometry.java
```
public static class Plane {
    public final Point point;
    public final Vector normal;

    public Plane(Point point, Vector normal) {
        this.point = point;
        this.normal = normal;
    }
}
```

This definition of a plane is very simple: it consists of a *normal* vector and a point on that plane; the normal vector of a plane is simply a vector that is perpendicular to that plane. There are other possible definitions of a plane, but this is the one that we'll work with.

In the following image, we can see an example of a plane located at (0, 0, 0) with a normal of (0, 1, 0):

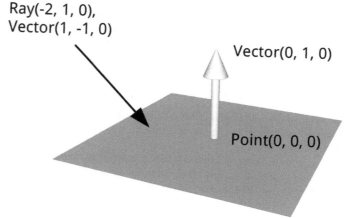

There's also a ray at (-2, 1, 0) with a vector of (1, -1, 0). We'll use this plane and ray to explain the intersection test. Let's add the following code to calculate the intersection point:

AirHockeyTouch/src/com/airhockey/android/util/Geometry.java
```
public static Point intersectionPoint(Ray ray, Plane plane) {
    Vector rayToPlaneVector = vectorBetween(ray.point, plane.point);

    float scaleFactor = rayToPlaneVector.dotProduct(plane.normal)
                      / ray.vector.dotProduct(plane.normal);

    Point intersectionPoint = ray.point.translate(ray.vector.scale(scaleFactor));
    return intersectionPoint;
}
```

To calculate the intersection point, we need to figure out how much we need to scale the ray's vector until it touches the plane exactly; this is the *scaling factor*. We can then translate the ray's point by this scaled vector to find the intersection point.

To calculate the scaling factor, we first create a vector between the ray's starting point and a point on the plane. We then calculate the dot product between that vector and the plane's normal.[5]

The dot product of two vectors is directly related to (though usually not equivalent to) the cosine between those two vectors. As an example, if we had two parallel vectors of (1, 0, 0) and (1, 0, 0), then the angle between them would be 0 degrees and the cosine of this angle would be 1. If we had two perpendicular vectors of (1, 0, 0) and (0, 0, 1), then the angle between them would be 90 degrees and the cosine of this angle would be 0.

To figure out the scaling amount, we can take the dot product between the ray-to-plane vector and the plane normal and divide that by the dot product between the ray vector and the plane normal. This will give us the scaling factor that we need.

A special case happens when the ray is parallel to the plane: in this case, there is no possible intersection point between the ray and the plane. The ray will be perpendicular to the plane normal, the dot product will be 0, and we'll get a division by 0 when we try to calculate the scaling factor. We'll end up with an intersection point that is full of floating-point *NaN*s, which is shorthand for "not a number."

Don't worry if you don't understand this in complete detail. The important part is that it works; for the mathematically curious, there's a good explanation on Wikipedia that you can read to learn more.[6]

---

5. http://en.wikipedia.org/wiki/Dot_product
6. http://en.wikipedia.org/wiki/Line-plane_intersection

We'll need to fill in the missing blanks by adding the following code to Vector:

AirHockeyTouch/src/com/airhockey/android/util/Geometry.java
```
public float dotProduct(Vector other) {
    return x * other.x
         + y * other.y
         + z * other.z;
}

public Vector scale(float f) {
    return new Vector(
        x * f,
        y * f,
        z * f);
}
```

The first method, dotProduct(), calculates the dot product between two vectors.[7] The second, scale(), scales each component of the vector evenly by the scale amount.

An Example of a Ray-Plane Intersection Test

As before, we'll also walk through an example just to see how the numbers pan out. Let's use the following example of a plane with a ray:

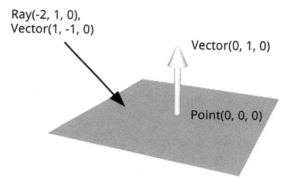

We have a plane at (0, 0, 0) with a normal of (0, 1, 0), and we have a ray at (-2, 1, 0) with a vector of (1, -1, 0). If we extend the vector far enough, where would this ray hit the plane? Let's go through the math and find out.

First we need to assign rayToPlaneVector to the vector between the plane and the ray. This should get set to (0, 0, 0) - (-2, 1, 0) = (2, -1, 0).

Then the next step is to calculate scaleFactor. Once we calculate the dot products, the equation reduces to -1/-1, which gives us a scaling factor of 1.

---

7.   http://en.wikipedia.org/wiki/Dot_product

To get the intersection point, we just need to translate the ray point by the scaled ray vector. The ray vector is scaled by 1, so we can just add the vector to the point to get (-2, 1, 0) + (1, -1, 0) = (-1, 0, 0). This is where the ray intersects with the plane.

We've now added everything we needed to get handleTouchDrag() to work. There's only one part left: we need to go back to AirHockeyRenderer and actually use the new point when drawing the blue mallet. Let's update onDrawFrame() and update the second call to positionObjectInScene() as follows:

AirHockeyTouch/src/com/airhockey/android/AirHockeyRenderer.java
```
positionObjectInScene(blueMalletPosition.x, blueMalletPosition.y,
    blueMalletPosition.z);
```

Go ahead and give this a run; you should now be able to drag the mallet around on the screen and watch it follow your fingertip!

9.4 Adding Collision Detection

Now that you've had a chance to have a bit of fun and drag the mallet around, you've probably noticed our first problem: the mallet can go way out of bounds, as seen in Figure 46, *An out-of-bounds mallet*, on page 182. In this section, we'll add some basic collision detection to keep our mallet where it belongs. We'll also add some really basic physics to let us smack the puck around the table.

Keeping the Player's Mallet Within Bounds

Let's start off by adding the following bounds definitions to AirHockeyRenderer:

AirHockeyTouch/src/com/airhockey/android/AirHockeyRenderer.java
```
private final float leftBound = -0.5f;
private final float rightBound = 0.5f;
private final float farBound = -0.8f;
private final float nearBound = 0.8f;
```

These correspond to the edges of the air hockey table. Now we can update handleTouchDrag() and replace the current assignment to blueMalletPosition with the following code:

AirHockeyTouch/src/com/airhockey/android/AirHockeyRenderer.java
```
blueMalletPosition = new Point(
    clamp(touchedPoint.x,
        leftBound + mallet.radius,
        rightBound - mallet.radius),
    mallet.height / 2f,
    clamp(touchedPoint.z,
        0f + mallet.radius,
        nearBound - mallet.radius));
```

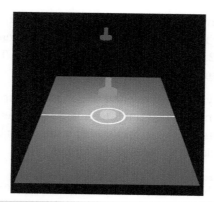

Figure 46—An out-of-bounds mallet

If we look back and review handleTouchDrag(), we'll remember that touchedPoint represents the intersection between where we touched the screen and the plane that the air hockey table lies on. The mallet wants to move to this point.

To keep the mallet from exceeding the bounds of the table, we clamp touchedPoint to the table bounds. The mallet can't surpass either edge of the table. We also take the dividing line of the table into account by using 0f instead of farBound, so that the player cannot cross over to the other side, and we also take the mallet's radius into account, so that the edge of the mallet cannot go beyond the edge of the player's bounds.

We also need to add a definition for clamp():

AirHockeyTouch/src/com/airhockey/android/AirHockeyRenderer.java
```
private float clamp(float value, float min, float max) {
    return Math.min(max, Math.max(value, min));
}
```

Go ahead and give the application another run. You should now find that your blue mallet refuses to go out of bounds.

Adding Velocity and Direction

Now we can add some code to smack the puck with the mallet. To get an idea of how the puck should react, we need to answer a couple of questions:

- How fast is the mallet going?
- In which direction is the mallet moving?

To be able to answer these questions, we need to keep track of how the mallet is moving over time. The first thing we'll do is add a new member variable to AirHockeyRenderer called previousBlueMalletPosition:

AirHockeyTouch/src/com/airhockey/android/AirHockeyRenderer.java
```
private Point previousBlueMalletPosition;
```

We'll set a value by adding the following code to handleTouchDrag(), just before the assignment to blueMalletPosition:

AirHockeyTouch/src/com/airhockey/android/AirHockeyRenderer.java
```
previousBlueMalletPosition = blueMalletPosition;
```

Now the next step is to store a position for the puck as well as a velocity and direction. Add the following member variables to AirHockeyRenderer:

AirHockeyTouch/src/com/airhockey/android/AirHockeyRenderer.java
```
private Point puckPosition;
private Vector puckVector;
```

We'll use the vector to store both the speed and the direction of the puck. We need to initialize these variables, so let's add the following to onSurfaceCreated():

AirHockeyTouch/src/com/airhockey/android/AirHockeyRenderer.java
```
puckPosition = new Point(0f, puck.height / 2f, 0f);
puckVector = new Vector(0f, 0f, 0f);
```

Now we can add the following collision code to the end of handleTouchDrag(), making sure to keep it inside if (malletPressed) {:

AirHockeyTouch/src/com/airhockey/android/AirHockeyRenderer.java
```
float distance =
    Geometry.vectorBetween(blueMalletPosition, puckPosition).length();

if (distance < (puck.radius + mallet.radius)) {
    // The mallet has struck the puck. Now send the puck flying
    // based on the mallet velocity.
    puckVector = Geometry.vectorBetween(
        previousBlueMalletPosition, blueMalletPosition);
}
```

This code will first check the distance between the blue mallet and the puck, and then it will see if that distance is less than both of their radii put together. If it is, then the mallet has struck the puck and we take the previous mallet position and the current mallet position to create a direction vector for the puck. The faster the mallet is going, the bigger that vector is going to be and the faster the puck is going to go.

We'll need to update onDrawFrame() so that the puck moves on each frame. Let's add the following code to the beginning of onDrawFrame():

AirHockeyTouch/src/com/airhockey/android/AirHockeyRenderer.java
```
puckPosition = puckPosition.translate(puckVector);
```

As the last step, we'll also need to update the call to positionObjectInScene() just before we draw the puck, as follows:

AirHockeyTouch/src/com/airhockey/android/AirHockeyRenderer.java
```
positionObjectInScene(puckPosition.x, puckPosition.y, puckPosition.z);
```

Run the program another time, and check what happens when you hit the puck with your mallet.

Adding Reflection Against Boundaries

Now we have another problem: our puck can move, but as we can see in Figure 47, *An out-of-bounds puck*, on page 185, it just keeps going, and going, and going...

To fix this, we'll have to add bounds checking to the puck as well and bounce it off the sides of the table whenever it hits one of the sides.

We can add the following code to onDrawFrame() after the call to puckPosition.translate():

AirHockeyTouch/src/com/airhockey/android/AirHockeyRenderer.java
```
if (puckPosition.x < leftBound + puck.radius
 || puckPosition.x > rightBound - puck.radius) {
    puckVector = new Vector(-puckVector.x, puckVector.y, puckVector.z);
}
if (puckPosition.z < farBound + puck.radius
 || puckPosition.z > nearBound - puck.radius) {
    puckVector = new Vector(puckVector.x, puckVector.y, -puckVector.z);
}
// Clamp the puck position.
puckPosition = new Point(
    clamp(puckPosition.x, leftBound + puck.radius, rightBound - puck.radius),
    puckPosition.y,
    clamp(puckPosition.z, farBound + puck.radius, nearBound - puck.radius)
);
```

We first check if the puck has gone either too far to the left or too far to the right. If it has, then we reverse its direction by inverting the x component of the vector.

We then check if the puck has gone past the near or far edges of the table. In that case, we reverse its direction by inverting the z component of the vector. Don't get confused by the z checks—the further away something is, the smaller the z, since negative z points into the distance.

Finally, we bring the puck back within the confines of the table by clamping it to the table bounds. If we try things again, our puck should now bounce around inside the table instead of flying off the edge.

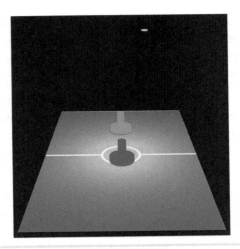

Figure 47—An out-of-bounds puck

Adding Friction

There's still one big problem with the way that the puck moves: it never slows down! That doesn't look very realistic, so we'll add some dampening code to slow the puck over time. At the end of the puck-related code in onDrawFrame(), add the following method to slow down the puck each frame:

AirHockeyTouch/src/com/airhockey/android/AirHockeyRenderer.java
```
puckVector = puckVector.scale(0.99f);
```

If we run it again, we'll see the puck slow down and eventually come to a stop. We can make things more realistic by adding an additional dampening to the bounces. Add the following code twice, once inside the body of each bounce check:

AirHockeyTouch/src/com/airhockey/android/AirHockeyRenderer.java
```
puckVector = puckVector.scale(0.9f);
```

We'll now see the puck slow down some more when it bounces off the sides.

9.5 A Review and Wrap-Up

We covered some interesting topics in this chapter: first we learned how to grab and move a mallet around with our fingers, and then we learned how to get the puck bouncing around the table. You might have noticed an overlapping problem along the way; we'll learn how to take care of that in *Removing Hidden Surfaces with the Depth Buffer*, on page 245.

Some of the math might have been above our heads, but the important part is to understand the concepts at a high level so that we know how to use them. There are many great libraries out there to make things easier, such as Bullet Physics and JBox2D.[8]

There are many ways to extend what we've learned: for example, you could create a bowling game where a ball gets flung by the player and you watch that ball head down the lane to knock out the pins at the far side. Touch interaction is what really sets mobile apart, and there are many ways to be imaginative.

We've now come to the end of our air hockey project. Take a moment to sit back and reflect on everything that we've learned, as we really have come a long way. We are not that far off from having a complete game either; all we'd need is some sounds, a basic opponent AI, a menu, a few effects here and there, and we'd be good to go. There are libraries out there that can take care of some of these tasks, such as libgdx.[9] You can also explore these aspects of game development in more detail with a book like *Beginning Android Games [Zec12]*.

We've also learned quite a few important concepts along the way. We started out by figuring out how shaders work, and we built things up by learning about colors, matrices, and textures, and we even learned how to build simple objects and move them with our fingers. Feel proud of what you have learned and accomplished, as we've come this way all on our own, working directly with OpenGL at a low level.

9.6 Exercises

Before we head on to the next part of the book, let's take some time to complete the following exercises:

- Since we're not changing the view matrix on every frame, what could you do to optimize the updates to viewProjectionMatrix and invertedViewProjectionMatrix?

- The puck currently reacts the same whether the mallet strikes it directly or on the side. Update the collision code to take the striking angle into account; Figure 43, *Unit circle*, on page 148, might give you an idea of how to approach this.

- Update the collision code so that the puck also interacts with the mallets when it's moving on its own; for bonus points, make its motion frame-rate independent. Hint: Store your movement vector as units per second,

---

8. http://bulletphysics.org/ and http://www.jbox2d.org/, respectively.
9. https://code.google.com/p/libgdx/

and figure out how much time has elapsed between each frame to calculate the movement delta for that frame.

For future reference, it's also a good idea to spend some time researching cross products and dot products online, looking at visual examples to better understand how they work.

Once you've completed these exercises, let's head to the next chapter.

Part II

Building a 3D World

CHAPTER 10

Spicing Things Up with Particles

We're going to change directions and start exploring more of the art behind OpenGL. Over the next few chapters, we'll start building up a landscape with mountains, clouds, and a few effects thrown in just for fun.

As we reach the end of this project, we'll wrap things up by turning this landscape into a 3D live wallpaper that can run on your Android's home screen. Like 3D games, 3D live wallpapers have really exploded in popularity as Android phones get faster and ship with larger and more vibrant screens. These live wallpapers are also easier to create in some ways, as the focus is more on the art and the aesthetics, and there's usually no game logic to worry about.

Beauty is in the eye of the beholder, and the skills that help in programming aren't necessarily the same ones that help in being an artist. However, we'll learn many of the techniques that we can use to make things look nice and realistic. We'll learn how to use lighting, blending, and more, and how we can put them together to create a scene. By the time we complete this part of the book, our project will look like Figure 48, *A simple scene, with point lights against a night backdrop*, on page 192.

In this chapter, we'll start off our new project by exploring the world of particles—simple objects drawn as a set of points. With particles, we can use a combination of basic physics and rendering to come up with some really neat effects. We can create fountains that shoot droplets in the air and watch them fall back to earth. We can simulate the effects of rain, or we can create explosions and fireworks. The math behind particles doesn't need to be complicated, making them easy to add to any 3D scene.

Before we get started, let's review our game plan for this chapter:

Figure 48—A simple scene, with point lights against a night backdrop

- First we'll cover what we need to set up a particle system.

- We'll then add a few fountains to shoot some particles up into the air.

- We'll also learn how to improve the look of the particles by using techniques such as blending and point sprites.

We can reuse a lot of our code from AirHockeyTouch, but we'll need to do some cleanup first. To start off our project, copy AirHockeyTouch over into a new project called 'Particles', and then follow these steps to get things spruced up:

1. Rename the base package to com.particles.android. You'll need to update your Java packages and the references in AndroidManifest.xml.

2. Rename the activity to ParticlesActivity and the renderer to ParticlesRenderer.

3. Remove all classes from com.particles.android.objects.

4. Remove ColorShaderProgram and TextureShaderProgram from com.particles.android.programs.

5. Remove the contents of ParticlesRenderer, leaving only the constructor and empty method definitions for the Renderer interface methods. We'll build these up as we work through this chapter.

6. Remove the touch listener from ParticlesActivity.

7. Change the app name to 'Particles' by modifying the value of app_name in strings.xml.

8. Finally, remove everything from the /res/raw/ and /res/drawable-nodpi/ folders.

We now have a clean base from which to get started.

10.1 Creating a Set of Shaders for a Simple Particle System

Let's start things off by adding a very simple particle system to represent a fountain. We can imagine this as a fountain of water lit up by a light underneath, or we can imagine it as a fireworks fountain, like we might see at a fireworks show. To get this fountain started, we'll need to take care of a few technical details.

First, we need some way of representing all of the particles in memory. We could use an array of Java objects for this, but it can be expensive to create and delete a bunch of objects during runtime, and there's no easy way to send the data over to OpenGL. We can store all of the particle data inline instead, inside a single array, such as seen in Figure 49, *Layout of the particles in memory*, on page 194. To add a particle, we'll just need to increase the particle count, write the data to our particle array, and copy over the changed contents to our native buffer. When we run out of space, we can recycle the array by starting over at the beginning.

We'll also need a way to draw each particle. We can represent each particle as a single vertex and draw these vertices as a set of points, each with a unique position and color.

Finally, we'll also need some way of updating the particles. We can do some of this work on the GPU by putting the logic in a shader program. We'll store a direction vector and a creation time for each particle; with the creation time, we can figure out how much time has elapsed since the particle was created, and then we can use the elapsed time with the direction vector and the position to figure out the particle's current position. We'll use a floating-point number to store the time, with 0.0 representing when we began running our particle system.

With these basic requirements in place, we can come up with an initial set of specifications for our shader program. First we'll need a uniform for the

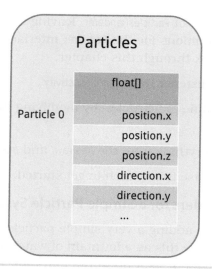

Figure 49—Layout of the particles in memory

projection matrix and a uniform for the current time, so that the shader can figure out how much time has elapsed since each particle was created. We'll also need four attributes corresponding to the particle's properties: position, color, direction vector, and creation time.

Adding the Code for the Shaders

Let's start things off by adding the code for the shaders. Go ahead and create a new vertex shader called particle_vertex_shader.glsl inside of the /res/raw/ folder. First we'll start off with the definitions:

Particles/res/raw/particle_vertex_shader.glsl
```
uniform mat4 u_Matrix;
uniform float u_Time;

attribute vec3 a_Position;
attribute vec3 a_Color;
attribute vec3 a_DirectionVector;
attribute float a_ParticleStartTime;

varying vec3 v_Color;
varying float v_ElapsedTime;
```

These definitions implement our requirements for the particle shader. We'll need to use the color and the elapsed time in the fragment shader as well, so we've also created two varyings for these two variables. Let's complete the vertex shader:

Particles/res/raw/particle_vertex_shader.glsl

```
void main()
{
    v_Color = a_Color;
    v_ElapsedTime = u_Time - a_ParticleStartTime;
    vec3 currentPosition = a_Position + (a_DirectionVector * v_ElapsedTime);
    gl_Position = u_Matrix * vec4(currentPosition, 1.0);
    gl_PointSize = 10.0;
}
```

We first send the color on to the fragment shader, as seen on the third line, and then we calculate how much time has elapsed since this particle was created and send that on to the fragment shader as well. To calculate the current position of the particle, we multiply the direction vector with the elapsed time and add that to the position. The more time elapses, the further the particle will go.

To complete the shader code, we project the particle with the matrix, and since we're rendering the particle as a point, we set the point size to 10 pixels.

It's important to ensure that we don't accidentally mess up the w component when doing our math, so we use 3-component vectors to represent the position and the direction, converting to a full 4-component vector only when we need to multiply it with u_Matrix. This ensures that our math above only affects the x, y, and z components.

Now we can go ahead and add the fragment shader. Create a new file called particle_fragment_shader.glsl in the same place as the vertex shader and add the following code:

Particles/res/raw/particle_fragment_shader.glsl

```
precision mediump float;
varying vec3 v_Color;
varying float v_ElapsedTime;
void main()
{
    gl_FragColor = vec4(v_Color / v_ElapsedTime, 1.0);
}
```

This shader will brighten up young particles and dim old particles by dividing the color by the elapsed time. What happens if there's a divide by zero? According to the specification, this can lead to an unspecified result but must not lead to termination of the shader program.[1] For a more predictable result, you can always add a small number to the denominator.

---

1. http://www.khronos.org/registry/gles/specs/2.0/GLSL_ES_Specification_1.0.17.pdf

Wrapping the Shaders with a Java Class

With the shader code completed, we can now wrap the shader using a Java class using the same pattern that we used in the first part of the book. First let's add some new constants to ShaderProgram:

Particles/src/com/particles/android/programs/ShaderProgram.java

```
protected static final String U_TIME = "u_Time";

protected static final String A_DIRECTION_VECTOR = "a_DirectionVector";
protected static final String A_PARTICLE_START_TIME = "a_ParticleStartTime";
```

With these new constants in place, we can go ahead and add a new class to the package com.particles.android.programs called ParticleShaderProgram, which extends ShaderProgram and starts out with the following code inside the class:

Particles/src/com/particles/android/programs/ParticleShaderProgram.java

```
// Uniform locations
private final int uMatrixLocation;
private final int uTimeLocation;

// Attribute locations
private final int aPositionLocation;
private final int aColorLocation;
private final int aDirectionVectorLocation;
private final int aParticleStartTimeLocation;
```

Let's complete the class definition:

Particles/src/com/particles/android/programs/ParticleShaderProgram.java

```
public ParticleShaderProgram(Context context) {
    super(context, R.raw.particle_vertex_shader,
        R.raw.particle_fragment_shader);

    // Retrieve uniform locations for the shader program.
    uMatrixLocation = glGetUniformLocation(program, U_MATRIX);
    uTimeLocation = glGetUniformLocation(program, U_TIME);

    // Retrieve attribute locations for the shader program.
    aPositionLocation = glGetAttribLocation(program, A_POSITION);
    aColorLocation = glGetAttribLocation(program, A_COLOR);
    aDirectionVectorLocation = glGetAttribLocation(program, A_DIRECTION_VECTOR);
    aParticleStartTimeLocation =
        glGetAttribLocation(program, A_PARTICLE_START_TIME);
}

public void setUniforms(float[] matrix, float elapsedTime) {
    glUniformMatrix4fv(uMatrixLocation, 1, false, matrix, 0);
    glUniform1f(uTimeLocation, elapsedTime);
}
```

```java
public int getPositionAttributeLocation() {
    return aPositionLocation;
}
public int getColorAttributeLocation() {
    return aColorLocation;
}
public int getDirectionVectorAttributeLocation() {
    return aDirectionVectorLocation;
}
public int getParticleStartTimeAttributeLocation() {
    return aParticleStartTimeLocation;
}
```

This wraps up the class using the same patterns from Part I.

10.2 Adding the Particle System

Now we can start creating the particle system. Let's create a new class called ParticleSystem inside the package com.particles.android.objects, starting off with the following code in the class:

Particles/src/com/particles/android/objects/ParticleSystem.java
```java
private static final int POSITION_COMPONENT_COUNT = 3;
private static final int COLOR_COMPONENT_COUNT = 3;
private static final int VECTOR_COMPONENT_COUNT = 3;
private static final int PARTICLE_START_TIME_COMPONENT_COUNT = 1;

private static final int TOTAL_COMPONENT_COUNT =
      POSITION_COMPONENT_COUNT
    + COLOR_COMPONENT_COUNT
    + VECTOR_COMPONENT_COUNT
    + PARTICLE_START_TIME_COMPONENT_COUNT;

private static final int STRIDE = TOTAL_COMPONENT_COUNT * BYTES_PER_FLOAT;
```

So far we just have some basic definitions for the component counts and the stride between particles. Let's continue to build out the class:

Particles/src/com/particles/android/objects/ParticleSystem.java
```java
private final float[] particles;
private final VertexArray vertexArray;
private final int maxParticleCount;

private int currentParticleCount;
private int nextParticle;

public ParticleSystem(int maxParticleCount) {
    particles = new float[maxParticleCount * TOTAL_COMPONENT_COUNT];
    vertexArray = new VertexArray(particles);
    this.maxParticleCount = maxParticleCount;
}
```

We now have a floating-point array to store the particles, a VertexArray to represent the data that we'll send to OpenGL, and maxParticleCount to hold the maximum number of particles, since the size of the array is fixed. We'll use currentParticleCount and nextParticle to keep track of the particles in the array.

Let's start building up a new method called addParticle():

```
Particles/src/com/particles/android/objects/ParticleSystem.java
public void addParticle(Point position, int color, Vector direction,
    float particleStartTime) {
    final int particleOffset = nextParticle * TOTAL_COMPONENT_COUNT;

    int currentOffset = particleOffset;
    nextParticle++;

    if (currentParticleCount < maxParticleCount) {
        currentParticleCount++;
    }

    if (nextParticle == maxParticleCount) {
        // Start over at the beginning, but keep currentParticleCount so
        // that all the other particles still get drawn.
        nextParticle = 0;
    }
```

To create the new particle, we first pass in the position, color, direction, and the particle creation time. The color is passed in as an Android color, and we'll use Android's Color class to parse the color into its separate components.

Before we can add a new particle to our array, we need to calculate where it needs to go. Our array is sort of like an amorphous blob, with all of the particles stored together. To calculate the right offset, we use nextParticle to store the number of the next particle, with the first particle starting at zero. We can then get the offset by multiplying nextParticle by the number of components per particle. We store this offset in particleOffset and currentOffset; we'll use particleOffset to remember where our new particle started, and currentOffset to remember the position for each attribute of the new particle.

Each time a new particle is added, we increment nextParticle by 1, and when we reach the end, we start over at 0 so we can recycle the oldest particles. We also need to keep track of how many particles need to be drawn, and we do this by incrementing currentParticleCount each time a new particle is added, keeping it clamped to the maximum.

Now that we've updated our bookkeeping, let's write out the new particle data to our array:

Particles/src/com/particles/android/objects/ParticleSystem.java
```
particles[currentOffset++] = position.x;
particles[currentOffset++] = position.y;
particles[currentOffset++] = position.z;

particles[currentOffset++] = Color.red(color) / 255f;
particles[currentOffset++] = Color.green(color) / 255f;
particles[currentOffset++] = Color.blue(color) / 255f;

particles[currentOffset++] = direction.x;
particles[currentOffset++] = direction.y;
particles[currentOffset++] = direction.z;

particles[currentOffset++] = particleStartTime;
```

First we write out the position, then the color (using Android's Color class to
parse each component), then the direction vector, and finally the particle
creation time. Android's Color class returns components in a range from 0 to
255, while OpenGL expects the color to be from 0 to 1, so we convert from
Android to OpenGL by dividing each component by 255 (see *Converting Colors
Using Android's Color Class*, on page 64, for more detail).

We still need to copy the new particle over to our native buffer so that OpenGL
can access the new data, so let's finish up addParticle() with the following method
call:

Particles/src/com/particles/android/objects/ParticleSystem.java
```
vertexArray.updateBuffer(particles, particleOffset, TOTAL_COMPONENT_COUNT);
```

We want to copy over only the new data so that we don't waste time copying
over data that hasn't changed, so we pass in the start offset for the new particle and the count. We'll also need to add the definition for updateBuffer() as a
new method inside of VertexArray. Let's do that by adding the following code to
the end of that class:

Particles/src/com/particles/android/data/VertexArray.java
```
public void updateBuffer(float[] vertexData, int start, int count) {
    floatBuffer.position(start);
    floatBuffer.put(vertexData, start, count);
    floatBuffer.position(0);
}
```

Now we can return to ParticleSystem and add a binding function:

Particles/src/com/particles/android/objects/ParticleSystem.java
```
public void bindData(ParticleShaderProgram particleProgram) {
    int dataOffset = 0;
    vertexArray.setVertexAttribPointer(dataOffset,
        particleProgram.getPositionAttributeLocation(),
```

```
        POSITION_COMPONENT_COUNT, STRIDE);
    dataOffset += POSITION_COMPONENT_COUNT;

    vertexArray.setVertexAttribPointer(dataOffset,
        particleProgram.getColorAttributeLocation(),
        COLOR_COMPONENT_COUNT, STRIDE);
    dataOffset += COLOR_COMPONENT_COUNT;

    vertexArray.setVertexAttribPointer(dataOffset,
        particleProgram.getDirectionVectorAttributeLocation(),
        VECTOR_COMPONENT_COUNT, STRIDE);
    dataOffset += VECTOR_COMPONENT_COUNT;

    vertexArray.setVertexAttribPointer(dataOffset,
        particleProgram.getParticleStartTimeAttributeLocation(),
        PARTICLE_START_TIME_COMPONENT_COUNT, STRIDE);
}
```

This is just some more boiler-plate code that follows the same pattern as in previous chapters, binding our vertex data to the right attributes in the shader program and taking care to respect the same ordering as the one we used in addParticle(). If we mix up the color with the direction vector or make a similar sort of mistake, we'll get rather funny results when we try to draw the particles.

Let's finish up the class by adding a draw function:

Particles/src/com/particles/android/objects/ParticleSystem.java
```
public void draw() {
    glDrawArrays(GL_POINTS, 0, currentParticleCount);
}
```

We now have a particle system in place. This system will let us add particles up to a certain limit, recycle old particles, and efficiently locate the particles next to each other in memory.

Adding a Particle Fountain

With the particle system in place, we now need something that will actually generate some particles for us and add them to the particle system. Let's start creating our particle fountain by adding a new class called ParticleShooter to the same package as ParticleSystem with the following code:

Particles/src/com/particles/android/objects/ParticleShooter.java
```
private final Point position;
private final Vector direction;
private final int color;
```

```
public ParticleShooter(Point position, Vector direction, int color) {
    this.position = position;
    this.direction = direction;
    this.color = color;
}
```

We've given our particle shooter its own position, direction, and color; we'll just pass these over directly to the particle system when we create the new particles. Let's continue the particle shooter:

Particles/src/com/particles/android/objects/ParticleShooter.java
```
public void addParticles(ParticleSystem particleSystem, float currentTime,
    int count) {
    for (int i = 0; i < count; i++) {
        particleSystem.addParticle(position, color, direction, currentTime);
    }
}
```

In addParticles(), we pass in the particle system and how many particles we want to add, as well as the current time for the particle system. We now have all of our components in place, and we just need to add a few calls to our renderer class to glue everything together.

10.3 Drawing the Particle System

We just need to add some code to ParticlesRenderer and then we can finally see our particles in action. Let's start out with the following definitions:

Particles/src/com/particles/android/ParticlesRenderer.java
```
private final Context context;

private final float[] projectionMatrix = new float[16];
private final float[] viewMatrix = new float[16];
private final float[] viewProjectionMatrix = new float[16];

private ParticleShaderProgram particleProgram;
private ParticleSystem particleSystem;
private ParticleShooter redParticleShooter;
private ParticleShooter greenParticleShooter;
private ParticleShooter blueParticleShooter;
private long globalStartTime;

public ParticlesRenderer(Context context) {
    this.context = context;
}
```

We have our standard variables for the Android context and our matrices, and we have our particle shader, system, and three particle shooters. We also have a variable for the global start time and a standard constructor.

Let's define the body for onSurfaceCreated():

```
Particles/src/com/particles/android/ParticlesRenderer.java
@Override
public void onSurfaceCreated(GL10 glUnused, EGLConfig config) {
    glClearColor(0.0f, 0.0f, 0.0f, 0.0f);

    particleProgram = new ParticleShaderProgram(context);
    particleSystem = new ParticleSystem(10000);
    globalStartTime = System.nanoTime();

    final Vector particleDirection = new Vector(0f, 0.5f, 0f);

    redParticleShooter = new ParticleShooter(
        new Point(-1f, 0f, 0f),
        particleDirection,
        Color.rgb(255, 50, 5));

    greenParticleShooter = new ParticleShooter(
        new Point(0f, 0f, 0f),
        particleDirection,
        Color.rgb(25, 255, 25));

    blueParticleShooter = new ParticleShooter(
        new Point(1f, 0f, 0f),
        particleDirection,
        Color.rgb(5, 50, 255));
}
```

We set the clear color to black, initialize our particle shader program, and initialize a new particle system with a maximum limit of ten thousand particles, and then we set the global start time to the current system time using System.nanoTime() as the base. We want the particle system to run on a floating-point time basis so that when the particle system is initialized, the current time will be 0.0 and a particle created at that time will have a creation time of 0.0. Five seconds later, a new particle will have a creation time of 5.0. To do this, we can take the difference between the current system time and globalStartTime, and since System.nanoTime() returns the time in nanoseconds, we'll just need to divide the difference by 1 trillion to convert this into seconds.

The next part of the method sets up our three particle fountains. Each fountain is represented by a particle shooter, and each shooter will shoot its particles in the direction of particleDirection, or straight up along the y-axis. We've aligned the three fountains from left to right, and we've set the colors so that the first one is red, the second is green, and the third is blue.

Let's add the definition for onSurfaceChanged():

Particles/src/com/particles/android/ParticlesRenderer.java

```
@Override
public void onSurfaceChanged(GL10 glUnused, int width, int height) {
    glViewport(0, 0, width, height);

    MatrixHelper.perspectiveM(projectionMatrix, 45, (float) width
        / (float) height, 1f, 10f);

    setIdentityM(viewMatrix, 0);
    translateM(viewMatrix, 0, 0f, -1.5f, -5f);
    multiplyMM(viewProjectionMatrix, 0, projectionMatrix, 0,
        viewMatrix, 0);
}
```

This is a standard definition, with a regular perspective projection and a view matrix that pushes things down and into the distance.

Let's complete the renderer by adding the following definition for onDrawFrame():

Particles/src/com/particles/android/ParticlesRenderer.java

```
@Override
public void onDrawFrame(GL10 glUnused) {
    glClear(GL_COLOR_BUFFER_BIT);

    float currentTime = (System.nanoTime() - globalStartTime) / 1000000000f;

    redParticleShooter.addParticles(particleSystem, currentTime, 5);
    greenParticleShooter.addParticles(particleSystem, currentTime, 5);
    blueParticleShooter.addParticles(particleSystem, currentTime, 5);

    particleProgram.useProgram();
    particleProgram.setUniforms(viewProjectionMatrix, currentTime);
    particleSystem.bindData(particleProgram);
    particleSystem.draw();
}
```

Each time a new frame is drawn, we calculate the current time and pass it into the shader. That will tell the shader how far each particle has moved since it was created. We also generate five new particles for each fountain, and then we draw the particles with the particle shader program.

Go ahead and run the program. After a few seconds, it should look like Figure 50, *Particles, first pass*, on page 204.

We now have something that works, and we can see the brightening and dimming effect as a particle ages, but it still looks strange, doesn't it? Shouldn't the particles spread out as they move upward, and shouldn't they also fall back down as gravity takes hold? We'll solve these problems and more in the next few steps.

Figure 50—Particles, first pass

10.4 Spreading Out the Particles

The first thing we'll do is spread out our particles, and we'll also vary the speed of each particle to give each particle fountain some more variety. Let's go back to ParticleShooter and add the following member variables to the class:

Particles/src/com/particles/android/objects/ParticleShooter.java
```
private final float angleVariance;
private final float speedVariance;

private final Random random = new Random();

private float[] rotationMatrix = new float[16];
private float[] directionVector = new float[4];
private float[] resultVector = new float[4];
```

Each shooter will have an angle variance that will control the spread of particles and a speed variance to alter the speed of each particle. We also have a matrix and two vectors, so we can use Android's Matrix class to do some math.

Let's update the constructor signature as follows:

Particles/src/com/particles/android/objects/ParticleShooter.java
```
public ParticleShooter(
    Point position, Vector direction, int color,
    float angleVarianceInDegrees, float speedVariance) {
```

We can then add the following code to assign the new member variables:

Particles/src/com/particles/android/objects/ParticleShooter.java
```
this.angleVariance = angleVarianceInDegrees;
this.speedVariance = speedVariance;

directionVector[0] = direction.x;
directionVector[1] = direction.y;
directionVector[2] = direction.z;
```

Now we just need to update addParticles() to apply the angle and speed variance. Update the body of the for loop as follows:

Particles/src/com/particles/android/objects/ParticleShooter.java
```
setRotateEulerM(rotationMatrix, 0,
    (random.nextFloat() - 0.5f) * angleVariance,
    (random.nextFloat() - 0.5f) * angleVariance,
    (random.nextFloat() - 0.5f) * angleVariance);

multiplyMV(
    resultVector, 0,
    rotationMatrix, 0,
    directionVector, 0);

float speedAdjustment = 1f + random.nextFloat() * speedVariance;

Vector thisDirection = new Vector(
    resultVector[0] * speedAdjustment,
    resultVector[1] * speedAdjustment,
    resultVector[2] * speedAdjustment);

particleSystem.addParticle(position, color, thisDirection, currentTime);
```

To alter the shooting angle, we use Android's Matrix.setRotateEulerM() to create a rotation matrix that will alter the angle by a random amount of angleVariance, which is in degrees. We then multiply this matrix with the direction vector to get a slightly rotated vector. To adjust the speed, we multiply each component of the direction vector with an equal random adjustment of speedVariance. Once that's done, we add the new particle by calling particleSystem.addParticle().

With these changes, we no longer need to keep around the direction member variable, so go ahead and remove that. We now need to update ParticlesRenderer to adjust for the new constructor parameters. Modify onSurfaceCreated() so that the particle shooters are created as follows:

```
Particles/src/com/particles/android/ParticlesRenderer.java
final float angleVarianceInDegrees = 5f;
final float speedVariance = 1f;

redParticleShooter = new ParticleShooter(
    new Point(-1f, 0f, 0f),
    particleDirection,
    Color.rgb(255, 50, 5),
    angleVarianceInDegrees,
    speedVariance);

greenParticleShooter = new ParticleShooter(
    new Point(0f, 0f, 0f),
    particleDirection,
    Color.rgb(25, 255, 25),
    angleVarianceInDegrees,
    speedVariance);

blueParticleShooter = new ParticleShooter(
    new Point(1f, 0f, 0f),
    particleDirection,
    Color.rgb(5, 50, 255),
    angleVarianceInDegrees,
    speedVariance);
```

We've set things up so that each particle fountain has an angle variance of 5 degrees and a speed variance of 1 unit. Go ahead and run the app to see what we get this time. It should look like Figure 51, *Particles with angle and speed variance*, on page 207.

Things are already looking a lot better! Now we need to add some gravity to pull those particles back down to earth.

10.5 Adding Gravity

What goes up must come down. Isaac Newton became famous because he observed the effects of gravity on apples falling from a tree; our particles will look better if we add some gravity to them as well.

On earth, everyone feels an acceleration of 9.8 meters per second squared, and if we ignore the effects of wind resistance, then the longer something falls, the faster it goes. We can easily reproduce this effect in our code by adding a gravity adjustment to our vertex shader. Let's open up particle_vertex_shader.glsl and add the following line of code after the assignment to v_ElapsedTime:

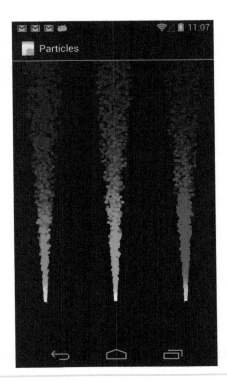

Figure 51—Particles with angle and speed variance

Particles/res/raw/particle_vertex_shader.glsl
```
float gravityFactor = v_ElapsedTime * v_ElapsedTime / 8.0;
```

This will calculate an accelerating gravity factor by applying the gravitational acceleration formula and squaring the elapsed time; we also divide things by 8 to dampen the effect. The number 8 is arbitrary: we could use any other number that also makes things look good on the screen. Now we need to apply the gravity to our current position, so let's add the following code to the vertex shader after the assignment to currentPosition:

Particles/res/raw/particle_vertex_shader.glsl
```
currentPosition.y -= gravityFactor;
```

Let's run the app again and see what happens. It should look like Figure 52, *Adding gravity to the particles*, on page 208.

Now we can see that each particle slows down as it moves upward, and eventually it starts falling back down toward earth. We can still improve the look: some of the darker particles overlap the brighter ones, and that looks kind of strange.

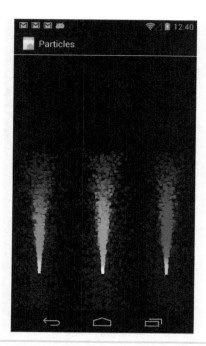

Figure 52—Adding gravity to the particles

10.6 Mixing the Particles with Additive Blending

When we do different effects in OpenGL, we often have to think back to the effect that we're trying to reproduce. If we imagine our three particle streams as a fireworks fountain, like the one we'd see at a fireworks show, then we'd expect the particles to give off light; and the more of them there are, the brighter things should be. One of the ways that we can reproduce this effect is by using additive blending.

Let's enable blending by adding the following code to ParticlesRenderer in the onSurfaceCreated() method:

Particles/src/com/particles/android/ParticlesRenderer.java
```
glEnable(GL_BLEND);
glBlendFunc(GL_ONE, GL_ONE);
```

That's it! First we enable blending, and then we set the blending mode to additive blending. To better understand how this works, let's look at OpenGL's default blending equation:

output = (source factor * source fragment) + (destination factor * destination fragment)

In OpenGL, blending works by blending the result of the fragment shader with the color that's already there in the frame buffer. The value for *source fragment* comes from our fragment shader, *destination fragment* is what's already there in the frame buffer, and the values for *source factor* and *destination factor* are configured by calling glBlendFunc(). In the code that we just added, we called glBlendFunc() with each factor set to GL_ONE, which changes the blending equation as follows:

output = (GL_ONE * source fragment) + (GL_ONE * destination fragment)

GL_ONE is just a placeholder for 1, and since multiplying anything by 1 results in the same number, the equation can be simplified as follows:

output = source fragment + destination fragment

With this blending mode, the fragments from our fragment shader will be added to the fragments already on the screen, and that's how we get additive blending. There are many more blending modes possible, which you can review online at the Khronos website.[2]

Let's run our particle app again and see how things look; they should now look like Figure 53, *Blending the particles together with additive blending*, on page 210.

Our particles now look brightened up, and they blend together. Something to keep in mind is that OpenGL clamps the value of each color component, so if we add solid green to solid green, we'll still have solid green. However, if we add just a tiny bit of red and add the colors together enough times, we'll actually shift the hue and end up with yellow. Add in a bit of blue to the yellow enough times and we end up with white.

We can come up with some neat effects by taking OpenGL's clamping behavior into consideration. For example, in the next figure, our red fireworks fountain actually becomes somewhat yellow where it's brightest, and this is because we added in a bit of green and a bit less blue to the base color.

10.7 Customizing the Appearance of Our Points

You may have noticed that our points are being rendered as small squares, with the number of pixels on each side equal to the value of gl_PointSize. Using another special OpenGL variable, gl_PointCoord, we can actually customize the appearance of our points. For each point, when the fragment shader is run, we'll get a two-dimensional gl_PointCoord coordinate with each component

---

2.   http://www.khronos.org/opengles/sdk/docs/man/xhtml/glBlendFunc.xml

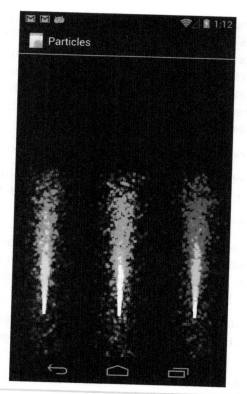

Figure 53—Blending the particles together with additive blending

ranging from 0 to 1 on each axis, depending on which fragment in the point is currently being rendered.

To see how this works, we'll first use gl_PointCoord to draw our fragments as circles instead of squares. How can we do this? Well, each point will be rendered with fragments that range from 0 to 1 on each axis relative to gl_PointCoord, so that places the center of the point at (0.5, 0.5), with 0.5 units of room on each side. In other words, we can say that the radius of the point is also 0.5. To draw a circle, all we need to do is draw only the fragments that lie within that radius.

First let's crank up the point size so that this will be easier to see. Let's update the value of gl_PointSize in particle_vertex_shader.glsl as follows:

Particles/res/raw/particle_vertex_shader.glsl
```
gl_PointSize = 25.0;
```

Now let's update the fragment shader as follows:

Particles/res/raw/particle_fragment_shader.glsl

```
precision mediump float;
varying vec3 v_Color;
varying float v_ElapsedTime;
void main()
{
    float xDistance = 0.5 - gl_PointCoord.x;
    float yDistance = 0.5 - gl_PointCoord.y;
    float distanceFromCenter =
        sqrt(xDistance * xDistance + yDistance * yDistance);

    if (distanceFromCenter > 0.5) {
        discard;
    } else {
        gl_FragColor = vec4(v_Color / v_ElapsedTime, 1.0);
    }
}
```

This is a somewhat expensive way of drawing a point as a circle, but it works. The way this works is that for each fragment, we calculate the distance to the center of the point with Pythagoras's theorem.[3] If that distance is greater than the radius of 0.5, then the current fragment is not part of the circle and we use the special keyword discard to tell OpenGL to forget about this fragment. Otherwise, we draw the fragment as before.

Let's give things another run; our app should now look like Figure 54, *Particles drawn as circles*, on page 212.

10.8 Drawing Each Point as a Sprite

The technique we just learned works, but sometimes a texture works better. Using the same gl_PointCoord and a texture, we can actually draw each point as a point sprite. We'll change our particle shader to use the texture shown in Figure 55, *Texture for Particles*, on page 212 for each particle.

This texture (particle_texture.png) and all of the textures that we'll use in future chapters can be downloaded from this book's home page. I recommend storing this texture in your project's /res/drawable-nodpi/ folder.[4]

We'll use the knowledge that we've learned in Chapter 7, *Adding Detail with Textures*, on page 115, to implement texturing in this project. First let's update the fragment shader by adding the following uniform:

Particles/res/raw/particle_fragment_shader.glsl

```
uniform sampler2D u_TextureUnit;
```

---

3. http://en.wikipedia.org/wiki/Pythagorean_theorem
4. http://pragprog.com/book/kbogla

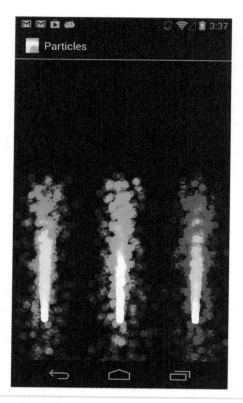

Figure 54—Particles drawn as circles

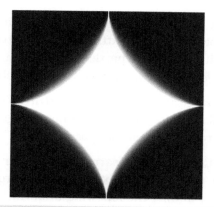

Figure 55—Texture for Particles

Remove all the circle logic that we added in the previous section, and update the assignment to gl_FragColor as follows:

Particles/res/raw/particle_fragment_shader.glsl
```
gl_FragColor = vec4(v_Color / v_ElapsedTime, 1.0)
            * texture2D(u_TextureUnit, gl_PointCoord);
```

This will draw a texture on the point using gl_PointCoord for the texture coordinates. The texture color will be multiplied with the point color, so the points will be colored the same way as before.

Now we need to add the new uniform to ParticleShaderProgram. First add the following member variable:

Particles/src/com/particles/android/programs/ParticleShaderProgram.java
```
private final int uTextureUnitLocation;
```

Now add the following to the end of the constructor:

Particles/src/com/particles/android/programs/ParticleShaderProgram.java
```
uTextureUnitLocation = glGetUniformLocation(program, U_TEXTURE_UNIT);
```

We need to update the signature for setUniforms() as follows:

Particles/src/com/particles/android/programs/ParticleShaderProgram.java
```
public void setUniforms(float[] matrix, float elapsedTime, int textureId) {
```

We also need to add the following to the end of setUniforms():

Particles/src/com/particles/android/programs/ParticleShaderProgram.java
```
glActiveTexture(GL_TEXTURE0);
glBindTexture(GL_TEXTURE_2D, textureId);
glUniform1i(uTextureUnitLocation, 0);
```

This texture binding is explained in more detail in *Setting Uniforms and Returning Attribute Locations*, on page 135.

We just need to load in the new texture, and we'll be ready to run the app. Open up ParticlesRenderer, and add the following new member variable:

Particles/src/com/particles/android/ParticlesRenderer.java
```
private int texture;
```

Add the following to the end of onSurfaceCreated():

Particles/src/com/particles/android/ParticlesRenderer.java
```
texture = TextureHelper.loadTexture(context, R.drawable.particle_texture);
```

Now we can update the call to particleProgram.setUniforms() in onDrawFrame() as follows:

Particles/src/com/particles/android/ParticlesRenderer.java
```
particleProgram.setUniforms(viewProjectionMatrix, currentTime, texture);
```

Run the app again; things should look similar to the following figure:

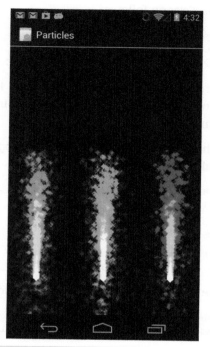

Figure 56—Drawing the particles as point sprites

10.9 A Review

We've covered some of the basics of a particle system, but really we've only scratched the surface. So much can be done with particles, including realistic-looking flames, rain and snow effects, and more. We've learned how to draw particles with OpenGL's GL_POINTS mode, but we also went into further detail by learning how to use gl_PointCoord with the discard keyword to come up with custom point shapes; we can also customize the appearance of our points even further by using textures. With these capabilities, we can come up with some really neat effects.

10.10 Exercises

Now that we've covered the basics of a particle system, let's take it further and create some firework bursts in the air. Depending on how you implement things, your app might look as shown in the next figure.

Here are some challenges that you'll want to consider as you work on this exercise:

- How does one create the trails? Will you update the particle positions in Java code and use that to create new particles? Or can you modify the particle creation times and create effects with that?

- There's a tradeoff between particle count and size and what the device is capable of. At some point, too many particles will slow down the frame rate.

- Should the fireworks create smoke?

As a research exercise, do some more reading on particle systems and on how particles can be generated on the CPU and GPU. Using your favorite search engine, read up on how these particles can be used for many different effects, including fire, rain, snow, and smoke.

Figure 57—A particle fireworks example

When you're ready, let's move on to the next chapter!

CHAPTER 11

Adding a Skybox

We started out with a dark void, and then we added some visual form by adding three particle fountains to the scene. However, our world is still mostly black and void. Our fountains are floating in the dark, with no surface to keep the particles from falling into the abyss.

To start things off, we'll learn how to add a backdrop to our scene, which will help to provide a sense of visual context. Many games and wallpapers use a combination of 2D art and 3D techniques to come up with their backdrops, and in this chapter, we'll learn how to set our fountains against a sky backdrop by using a *skybox*, which is a technique we can use to add a 360-degree panorama. These skyboxes were first seen in many popular games in the late 90s, and they continue to be used today. They're also used plenty outside of the game world; the 360-degree panorama that we can see when using Google Street View is just one example.

Let's take a look at our game plan for this chapter:

- We'll learn how to define a skybox using *cube mapping*, a method of stitching together six different textures into a cube.

- We'll also take our first look at *index arrays*, a way of reducing vertex duplication by storing only unique vertices in a vertex array and linking them together by *referring* to those vertices with index offsets instead of duplicating the vertex data. Index arrays can reduce memory use and increase performance when there is a lot of vertex reuse.

To get started, we'll continue the project we began in the last chapter. Let's copy that over into a new project called 'Skybox'.

11.1 Creating a Skybox

A skybox is a way of representing a 3D panorama that can be seen in every direction, no matter which way you turn your head. One of the most classic ways of rendering a skybox is to use a cube surrounding the viewer, with a detailed texture on each face of the cube; this is also known as a *cube map*. When we draw the skybox, we just need to make sure that it appears behind everything else in the scene.

When we use a skybox, we use a cube to represent the sky, so normally we'd expect the sky to look like a giant cube, with highly visible joints between each face. However, there's a trick that makes the edges of the cube disappear: each face of the cube is a picture taken with a 90-degree field of view and a planar projection, the same type that we'd expect from OpenGL itself.[1] When we position the viewer in the middle of the cube and use a perspective projection with a regular field of vision, everything lines up just right, the edges of the cube disappear, and we have a seamless panorama.

Even though the images themselves should be created with a field of vision of 90 degrees, the OpenGL scene itself can use a wide range of angles, such as 45 degrees or 60 degrees. The trick will work well as long as excessive angles are not used, as the rectilinear nature of OpenGL's perspective projection will cause increasing distortion around the edges.[2]

In the next figure, we can see an example of the six faces of a cube map texture lined up next to each other, showing how each face blends with the one next to it.

1.   http://en.wikipedia.org/wiki/Planar_projection
2.   http://en.wikipedia.org/wiki/Rectilinear_lens

To create the skybox in our scene, we'll store each face of the cube in a separate texture, and then we'll tell OpenGL to stitch these textures into a cube
map and apply it to a cube. When OpenGL renders the cube with linear
interpolation enabled, many GPUs will actually blend the texels between
neighboring faces, making the cube edges seamless. In fact, seamless cube
mapping support is guaranteed on OpenGL ES 3.0.

The Advantages and Disadvantages of Skybox Techniques

While a cube map by itself works great for a simple skybox, there are a few disadvan-
tages that come with the simplicity. The effect only works well if the skybox is rendered
from the center of the cube, so anything that's part of the skybox will always appear
to be at the same distance from viewers, no matter how far they travel. Since the
skybox is usually composed of prerendered textures, the scene is also necessarily
static, with clouds that don't move. And depending on the viewer's field of vision, the
cube map textures might need to be very high resolution to look good on the screen,
eating up a lot of texture memory and bandwidth.

Many modern games and applications usually work around these limitations by
complementing the traditional skybox technique with a separate 3D scene with its
own dynamic elements and clouds. This separate 3D scene will still be rendered
behind everything else; but the camera can also move around this separate scene
and elements inside that scene can be animated, giving the viewer the illusion of
being in a gigantic 3D world.

11.2 Loading a Cube Map into OpenGL

In the accompanying online resources for this chapter, you'll find the example
cube map separated into six separate textures in the /res/drawable-nodpi/ folder,
one for each face of the cube. Let's add a new method to our TextureHelper class
to load these textures into an OpenGL cube map. We'll call this method load-
CubeMap(), and we'll start off with the following code:

Skybox/src/com/particles/android/util/TextureHelper.java
```
public static int loadCubeMap(Context context, int[] cubeResources) {
    final int[] textureObjectIds = new int[1];
    glGenTextures(1, textureObjectIds, 0);

    if (textureObjectIds[0] == 0) {
        if (LoggerConfig.ON) {
            Log.w(TAG, "Could not generate a new OpenGL texture object.");
        }
        return 0;
    }
    final BitmapFactory.Options options = new BitmapFactory.Options();
    options.inScaled = false;
    final Bitmap[] cubeBitmaps = new Bitmap[6];
```

When we call this method, we'll pass in six image resources, one for each face of the cube. The order matters, so we'll use these images in a standard order that we can document in the comments for the method. To start things off, we create one OpenGL texture object, just like we do when loading a regular texture. We also have six bitmaps to temporarily hold the image resource data in memory as we lead each image from its resource and transfer the data over to OpenGL.

Let's load the images into the bitmap array:

Skybox/src/com/particles/android/util/TextureHelper.java
```
for (int i = 0; i < 6; i++) {
    cubeBitmaps[i] =
        BitmapFactory.decodeResource(context.getResources(),
            cubeResources[i], options);

    if (cubeBitmaps[i] == null) {
        if (LoggerConfig.ON) {
            Log.w(TAG, "Resource ID " + cubeResources[i]
                + " could not be decoded.");
        }
        glDeleteTextures(1, textureObjectIds, 0);
        return 0;
    }
}
```

We decode all six images into memory, making sure that each load was a success before continuing. Next we'll configure the texture filters:

Skybox/src/com/particles/android/util/TextureHelper.java
```
glBindTexture(GL_TEXTURE_CUBE_MAP, textureObjectIds[0]);

glTexParameteri(GL_TEXTURE_CUBE_MAP, GL_TEXTURE_MIN_FILTER, GL_LINEAR);
glTexParameteri(GL_TEXTURE_CUBE_MAP, GL_TEXTURE_MAG_FILTER, GL_LINEAR);
```

Since each cube map texture will always be viewed from the same viewpoint, it's less necessary to use the mipmapping technique described in *Mipmapping*, on page 122, so we can just use regular bilinear filtering and save on texture memory. If we know that the cube map resolution is significantly higher than the device resolution, then we can also shrink each texture before uploading it to OpenGL.

Let's add the following code to associate each image with the appropriate face of the cube map:

Skybox/src/com/particles/android/util/TextureHelper.java
```
texImage2D(GL_TEXTURE_CUBE_MAP_NEGATIVE_X, 0, cubeBitmaps[0], 0);
texImage2D(GL_TEXTURE_CUBE_MAP_POSITIVE_X, 0, cubeBitmaps[1], 0);
```

```
texImage2D(GL_TEXTURE_CUBE_MAP_NEGATIVE_Y, 0, cubeBitmaps[2], 0);
texImage2D(GL_TEXTURE_CUBE_MAP_POSITIVE_Y, 0, cubeBitmaps[3], 0);

texImage2D(GL_TEXTURE_CUBE_MAP_NEGATIVE_Z, 0, cubeBitmaps[4], 0);
texImage2D(GL_TEXTURE_CUBE_MAP_POSITIVE_Z, 0, cubeBitmaps[5], 0);
```

When we call this method, we'll pass in the cube faces in this order: left, right, bottom, top, front, and back. So long as the caller of this method also passes in the faces in the same order, we're good.

First we map the left and right textures to the negative and positive x faces, the bottom and top textures to the negative and positive y faces, and the front texture to the negative z and the back texture to the positive z, as if we were using a left-handed coordinate system. The convention for a cube map is to use a left-handed coordinate system when inside the cube and a right-handed coordinate system when outside the cube.[3] This will matter when we render our skybox: if we mix up the conventions, our skybox will appear flipped across the z-axis.

Let's wrap up the method with the following code:

Skybox/src/com/particles/android/util/TextureHelper.java
```
    glBindTexture(GL_TEXTURE_2D, 0);

    for (Bitmap bitmap : cubeBitmaps) {
        bitmap.recycle();
    }

    return textureObjectIds[0];
}
```

We unbind from the texture, recycle all of the bitmaps, and return the OpenGL texture object ID back to the caller.

When dealing with large cube map textures, this style of loading the textures can be memory-intensive, so if you know you'll be running on memory-constrained devices, one alternative is to load one bitmap at a time and load it into the appropriate face, reusing the bitmap for each subsequent face.

11.3 Creating a Cube

For our next task, we're going to create a new cube object for our skybox, and we'll also create our first index array. A cube is a good candidate for indexing because it only has 8 unique vertices. With 3 position components per vertex, we'll need 24 floats to store these vertices.

---

3. http://www.opengl.org/registry/specs/ARB/texture_cube_map.txt

Let's say that we decide to draw the cube with 2 triangles per face, so we have 12 triangles in all. With 3 vertices per triangle, if we were drawing the cube with a vertex array alone, we'd need 36 vertices or 108 floats, with a lot of the data duplicated. With an index array, we don't need to repeat all of the vertex data. Instead, we only need to repeat the indices. This allows us to reduce the overall size of the data.

Let's create a new class under com.particles.android.objects called Skybox, starting off with the following code inside the class:

Skybox/src/com/particles/android/objects/Skybox.java
```
private static final int POSITION_COMPONENT_COUNT = 3;
private final VertexArray vertexArray;
private final ByteBuffer indexArray;

public Skybox() {
    // Create a unit cube.
    vertexArray = new VertexArray(new float[] {
        -1,  1,  1,     // (0) Top-left near
         1,  1,  1,     // (1) Top-right near
        -1, -1,  1,     // (2) Bottom-left near
         1, -1,  1,     // (3) Bottom-right near
        -1,  1, -1,     // (4) Top-left far
         1,  1, -1,     // (5) Top-right far
        -1, -1, -1,     // (6) Bottom-left far
         1, -1, -1      // (7) Bottom-right far
    });
```

The VertexArray holds our vertex array, and we'll soon use the ByteBuffer to hold our index array. Let's finish the constructor with the following code:

Skybox/src/com/particles/android/objects/Skybox.java
```
    indexArray = ByteBuffer.allocateDirect(6 * 6)
        .put(new byte[] {
            // Front
            1, 3, 0,
            0, 3, 2,

            // Back
            4, 6, 5,
            5, 6, 7,

            // Left
            0, 2, 4,
            4, 2, 6,

            // Right
            5, 7, 1,
            1, 7, 3,
```

```
        // Top
        5, 1, 4,
        4, 1, 0,

        // Bottom
        6, 2, 7,
        7, 2, 3
    });
    indexArray.position(0);
}
```

This index array refers to each vertex by an index offset. For example, 0 refers to the first vertex in the vertex array, and 1 refers to the second vertex. With this index array, we've bound all of the vertices into groups of triangles, with two triangles per face of the cube.

Let's take a closer look at the difference by examining just the front face of the cube:

Skybox/src/com/particles/android/objects/Skybox.java
```
1, 3, 0,
0, 3, 2,
```

Now let's look at how we would have defined it if we were only using a vertex array:

```
 1,  1,  1,          // Top-right near
 1, -1,  1,          // Bottom-right near
-1,  1,  1,          // Top-left near
-1,  1,  1,          // Top-left near
 1, -1,  1,          // Bottom-right near
-1, -1,  1,          // Bottom-left near
```

With an index array, we can refer to each vertex by position instead of repeating the same vertex data over and over.

Let's add the following code to finish up the class:

Skybox/src/com/particles/android/objects/Skybox.java
```
public void bindData(SkyboxShaderProgram skyboxProgram) {
    vertexArray.setVertexAttribPointer(0,
        skyboxProgram.getPositionAttributeLocation(),
        POSITION_COMPONENT_COUNT, 0);
}

public void draw() {
    glDrawElements(GL_TRIANGLES, 36, GL_UNSIGNED_BYTE, indexArray);
}
```

The bindData() method is standard, and all we're missing is the skybox shader class for it to compile. To draw the cube, we call glDrawElements(GL_TRIANGLES, 36,

GL_UNSIGNED_BYTE, indices), which tells OpenGL to draw the vertices that we bound in bindData() with the index array defined by indices and to interpret the indices as unsigned bytes. With OpenGL ES 2, indices need to either be unsigned bytes (8-bit integers with a range of 0–255), or unsigned shorts (16-bit integers with a range of 0–65535).

Earlier on we had defined our index array as a ByteBuffer, so we tell OpenGL to interpret this data as a stream of unsigned bytes. Java's byte is actually *signed*, meaning it ranges from -128 to 127, but this won't be a problem so long as we stick to the positive part of that range.

11.4 Adding a Skybox Shader Program

Let's continue by creating a vertex shader for our skybox. Create a new file in your raw resource folder called skybox_vertex_shader.glsl, and add the following contents:

```
Skybox/res/raw/skybox_vertex_shader.glsl
uniform mat4 u_Matrix;
attribute vec3 a_Position;
varying vec3 v_Position;

void main()
{
    v_Position = a_Position;
    v_Position.z = -v_Position.z;

    gl_Position = u_Matrix * vec4(a_Position, 1.0);
    gl_Position = gl_Position.xyww;
}
```

First we pass on the vertex position to the fragment shader, as seen on the first line inside main(), and then we invert the position's z component on the next line; this gives the fragment shader a position that will be interpolated across each face of the cube so that we can later use this position to look up the right part of the skybox texture. The z component is flipped so that we can convert from the world's right-handed coordinate space to the left-handed coordinate space expected for the skybox. If we skip this step, the skybox will still work, but the textures will appear flipped.

After we project the position into clip coordinates by multiplying a_Position with the matrix, we set the z component to be equal to the w component with the following code:

```
Skybox/res/raw/skybox_vertex_shader.glsl
gl_Position = gl_Position.xyww;
```

Converting Between Signed and Unsigned Data Types

Sometimes sticking to the signed part of a data type's range isn't possible. When we're working with unsigned bytes, we can store any number from 0 to 255. However, Java will normally only let us store numbers in the range of -128 to 127, and 255 is definitely outside of that range. While we can't write code that says byte b = 255;, there *is* a way to fool Java into interpreting the number as a signed byte.

Let's take a look at the binary value for 255: in binary, we would represent this number as 11111111. We just need to find a way of telling Java to put these bits into the byte. It turns out that we can do this if we use Java's bit masking to mask off the last eight bits of the number 255 as follows:

```
byte b = (byte) (255 & 0xff);
```

This works because Java will interpret the number literal of 255 as being a 32-bit integer, which is big enough to hold the number 255. However, once we've assigned 255 to the byte, Java will actually see this byte as -1 instead of as 255, because to Java this byte is signed, and it will interpret the value using two's complement.[a] However, OpenGL or anywhere else expecting unsigned numbers will see the byte as 255.

To read the value back in Java, we can't just read it directly because Java sees it as -1. Instead, we need to use a larger Java data type to hold the result. For example, we could do the conversion with the following code:

```
short s = (short) (b & 0xff);
```

We can't just use short s = b; because Java will do *sign extension* and our short will still be -1. By telling Java to mask off the last eight bits, we implicitly convert to an integer, and then Java will correctly interpret the last eight bits of that integer as 255. Our short will then be set to 255, as we expected.

---

a.   http://en.wikipedia.org/wiki/Two's_complement

This is a trick that makes sure that every part of the skybox will lie on the far plane in normalized device coordinates and thus behind everything else in the scene. This trick works because perspective division divides everything by w, and w divided by itself will equal 1. After the perspective divide, z will end up on the far plane of 1.

This "trick" might seem unnecessary right now, since if we wanted the skybox to appear behind everything else we could just draw it first and then draw everything else on top of it. There are performance reasons behind this trick though, which we'll cover in more detail in *Removing Hidden Surfaces with the Depth Buffer*, on page 245.

Let's continue with the fragment shader. Add a new file called skybox_fragment_shader.glsl, and add the following code:

Skybox/res/raw/skybox_fragment_shader.glsl

```
precision mediump float;

uniform samplerCube u_TextureUnit;
varying vec3 v_Position;

void main()
{
        gl_FragColor = textureCube(u_TextureUnit, v_Position);
}
```

To draw the skybox using the cube texture, we call textureCube() with the interpolated cube face position as the texture coordinates for that fragment.

Let's add the matching Java class to wrap this shader program by adding a new class called SkyboxShaderProgram that extends ShaderProgram to the package com.particles.android.programs, with the following code inside the class:

Skybox/src/com/particles/android/programs/SkyboxShaderProgram.java

```
private final int uMatrixLocation;
private final int uTextureUnitLocation;
private final int aPositionLocation;

public SkyboxShaderProgram(Context context) {
    super(context, R.raw.skybox_vertex_shader,
        R.raw.skybox_fragment_shader);

    uMatrixLocation = glGetUniformLocation(program, U_MATRIX);
    uTextureUnitLocation = glGetUniformLocation(program, U_TEXTURE_UNIT);
    aPositionLocation = glGetAttribLocation(program, A_POSITION);
}

public void setUniforms(float[] matrix, int textureId) {
    glUniformMatrix4fv(uMatrixLocation, 1, false, matrix, 0);

    glActiveTexture(GL_TEXTURE0);
    glBindTexture(GL_TEXTURE_CUBE_MAP, textureId);
    glUniform1i(uTextureUnitLocation, 0);
}

public int getPositionAttributeLocation() {
    return aPositionLocation;
}
```

By now we're getting used to wrapping our shader programs and this is all pretty straightforward. Since we're using a cube map texture, we bind the texture with GL_TEXTURE_CUBE_MAP.

11.5 Adding the Skybox to Our Scene

Now that we have the cube model and shader code written up, let's add the skybox to our scene. Open up ParticlesRenderer, and add the following members to the top of the class:

Skybox/src/com/particles/android/ParticlesRenderer.java

```
private SkyboxShaderProgram skyboxProgram;
private Skybox skybox;
private int skyboxTexture;
```

At the same time, rename the existing texture member variable from the last chapter to particleTexture. Bring in any missing imports, and then we'll initialize these new variables in onSurfaceCreated() with the following code:

Skybox/src/com/particles/android/ParticlesRenderer.java

```
skyboxProgram = new SkyboxShaderProgram(context);
skybox = new Skybox();
skyboxTexture = TextureHelper.loadCubeMap(context,
    new int[] { R.drawable.left, R.drawable.right,
                R.drawable.bottom, R.drawable.top,
                R.drawable.front, R.drawable.back});
```

Now that we're using a skybox, we don't want translations applied to the scene to also apply to the skybox. For that reason, we'll need to use a different matrix for the skybox and for the particles, so remove all of the lines after the call to perspectiveM() in onSurfaceChanged(); we'll set these matrices up in onDrawFrame() instead. Let's update onDrawFrame() as follows:

Skybox/src/com/particles/android/ParticlesRenderer.java

```
@Override
public void onDrawFrame(GL10 glUnused) {
    glClear(GL_COLOR_BUFFER_BIT);
    drawSkybox();
    drawParticles();
}
```

First we'll draw the skybox, and then we'll draw the particles on top of the skybox. Let's add the method to draw the skybox:

Skybox/src/com/particles/android/ParticlesRenderer.java

```
private void drawSkybox() {
    setIdentityM(viewMatrix, 0);
    multiplyMM(viewProjectionMatrix, 0, projectionMatrix, 0, viewMatrix, 0);
    skyboxProgram.useProgram();
    skyboxProgram.setUniforms(viewProjectionMatrix, skyboxTexture);
    skybox.bindData(skyboxProgram);
    skybox.draw();
}
```

We'll draw the skybox centered around (0, 0, 0) so that we'll appear to be in the middle of the skybox and everything will appear visually correct.

Let's add the code to draw the particles:

Skybox/src/com/particles/android/ParticlesRenderer.java
```
private void drawParticles() {
    float currentTime = (System.nanoTime() - globalStartTime) / 1000000000f;

    redParticleShooter.addParticles(particleSystem, currentTime, 1);
    greenParticleShooter.addParticles(particleSystem, currentTime, 1);
    blueParticleShooter.addParticles(particleSystem, currentTime, 1);

    setIdentityM(viewMatrix, 0);
    translateM(viewMatrix, 0, 0f, -1.5f, -5f);
    multiplyMM(viewProjectionMatrix, 0, projectionMatrix, 0, viewMatrix, 0);

    glEnable(GL_BLEND);
    glBlendFunc(GL_ONE, GL_ONE);

    particleProgram.useProgram();
    particleProgram.setUniforms(viewProjectionMatrix, currentTime, particleTexture);
    particleSystem.bindData(particleProgram);
    particleSystem.draw();

    glDisable(GL_BLEND);
}
```

This is similar to the last chapter, with the particle fountains being pushed down and into the distance, except that we now do the matrix update inside of drawParticles(), and we turn blending on and off within the method itself. We do this because we don't want blending turned on when we draw the skybox itself.

Now that we're enabling and disabling blending only when drawing the particles, go ahead and remove the calls to glEnable(GL_BLEND) and glBlendFunc() from onSurfaceCreated().

Let's test out our new skybox and see what we get. If all goes well, then it should look like Figure 58, *A stormy skybox*, on page 229.

We now have a stormy sky backdrop to complement our scene! It still looks somewhat strange to see those fountains floating in the middle of the air, but we'll address that soon by adding in some terrain in the next chapter.

11.6 Panning the Camera Around the Scene

Currently we can only see a very small part of the skybox on our screen. Wouldn't it be nice if we could pan around and see the rest of the skybox?

Figure 58—A stormy skybox

We can easily do that by listening for touch events and using those touch events to rotate the skybox and scene together.

Open up ParticlesActivity, and add the following code before the call to setContentView():

Skybox/src/com/particles/android/ParticlesActivity.java
```
glSurfaceView.setOnTouchListener(new OnTouchListener() {
    float previousX, previousY;

    @Override
    public boolean onTouch(View v, MotionEvent event) {
        if (event != null) {
            if (event.getAction() == MotionEvent.ACTION_DOWN) {
                previousX = event.getX();
                previousY = event.getY();
            } else if (event.getAction() == MotionEvent.ACTION_MOVE) {
                final float deltaX = event.getX() - previousX;
                final float deltaY = event.getY() - previousY;
```

```
                previousX = event.getX();
                previousY = event.getY();

                glSurfaceView.queueEvent(new Runnable() {
                    @Override
                    public void run() {
                        particlesRenderer.handleTouchDrag(
                            deltaX, deltaY);
                    }
                });
            }

            return true;
        } else {
            return false;
        }
    }
});
```

This code defines a touch listener that will measure how far you've dragged your finger between each successive call to onTouch(). When you first touch the screen, the current touch position will be recorded in previousX and previousY.

As you drag your finger across the screen, you'll get a bunch of drag events, and each time you do, you'll first take the difference between the new position and the old position and store that into deltaX and deltaY, and then you'll update previousX and previousY. The deltas will be passed into the particle renderer by calling handleTouchDrag(). We need to create this method, so let's return to ParticlesRenderer and add the following to the class:

Skybox/src/com/particles/android/ParticlesRenderer.java
```
private float xRotation, yRotation;

public void handleTouchDrag(float deltaX, float deltaY) {
    xRotation += deltaX / 16f;
    yRotation += deltaY / 16f;

    if (yRotation < -90) {
        yRotation = -90;
    } else if (yRotation > 90) {
        yRotation = 90;
    }
}
```

This method will take in the distance the user dragged in each direction and add it to xRotation and yRotation, which represent the rotation in degrees. We don't want the touch to be too sensitive, so we scale down the effect by 16, and we don't want to rotate too far up and down, so we clamp the y rotation between +90 degrees and -90 degrees.

Let's apply the rotations to our skybox and scene. First let's update drawSkybox() by replacing the current matrix code with the following code:

Skybox/src/com/particles/android/ParticlesRenderer.java

```
setIdentityM(viewMatrix, 0);
rotateM(viewMatrix, 0, -yRotation, 1f, 0f, 0f);
rotateM(viewMatrix, 0, -xRotation, 0f, 1f, 0f);
multiplyMM(viewProjectionMatrix, 0, projectionMatrix, 0, viewMatrix, 0);
```

Now we just need to rotate the particles as well:

Skybox/src/com/particles/android/ParticlesRenderer.java

```
setIdentityM(viewMatrix, 0);
rotateM(viewMatrix, 0, -yRotation, 1f, 0f, 0f);
rotateM(viewMatrix, 0, -xRotation, 0f, 1f, 0f);
translateM(viewMatrix, 0, 0f, -1.5f, -5f);
multiplyMM(viewProjectionMatrix, 0, projectionMatrix, 0, viewMatrix, 0);
```

Rotating the matrix by the y rotation first and the x rotation second gives you an "FPS-style" rotation (where FPS stands for first person shooter), so rotating up or down always brings you toward your head or your feet, and rotating left or right always rotates you around in a circle about your feet.

Now if you give the app another run and drag your finger across the screen, you can pan the camera around and see other parts of the skybox, as seen in the next figure:

11.7 A Review

In this chapter we learned how to add a skybox by using a cube and cube mapping to apply a skybox texture onto the cube. We also learned about index arrays and how they can help reduce memory usage when an object has a lot of shared vertices.

While we used cube maps in this chapter for the skybox, they can be used for other things too. A cube map can also be used as an *environment map* on an object to make it appear reflective or shiny. Index arrays will also come quite in handy when dealing with more complex objects and scenes, though it is always best to benchmark and compare the choices and then use the one that performs the best.

11.8 Exercises

As your first exercise, add a small cube to the scene and apply the cube map to this cube. For a more advanced exercise, add movement to the camera (you could use the volume keys to move forward and backward, for example) to move the scene without also moving the skybox.

When you're ready, let's move on to the next chapter.

CHAPTER 12

Adding Terrain

Now that we have a nice backdrop with some stormy clouds on the horizon, it's time for us to start adding in some substance to our world. In this chapter, we'll learn how to use a height map to add some terrain to the scene. As we do this, we'll touch many new areas of OpenGL and learn how to use the depth buffer for preventing overdraw, and we'll also learn how to store vertex and index data directly on the GPU for better performance.

Height maps are an easy way to add terrain to a scene, and they can easily be generated or edited using a regular paint program. The depth buffer itself is a fundamental part of OpenGL, and it helps us easily render more complex scenes without worrying too much about how that scene is put together.

Here's our game plan:

- First we'll look at how to create a height map and load it into our application using vertex buffer objects and index buffer objects.

- We'll then take our first look at culling and the depth buffer, two techniques for occluding hidden objects.

Let's continue the project from last chapter by copying the code over into a new project called 'Heightmap'.

12.1 Creating a Height Map

A height map is simply a two-dimensional map of heights, much like a topography map that you can find in an atlas. A simple way to create a height map is to use a grayscale image, with the light areas representing high ground and the dark areas representing low ground. Since it's just an image, we can draw our own height map using any regular paint program and end up with something like the next figure. You can even download height maps of real terrain off the Internet from places like the National Elevation Dataset.[1]

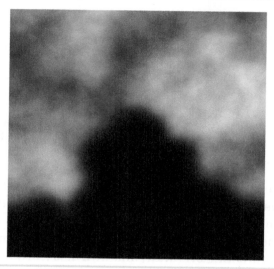

Figure 59—A height map example

We'll use the height map from the preceding figure for this project, which can be downloaded from this book's website.[2] Place this image in your project's /res/drawable-nodpi/ folder; in the next step, we'll load this height map data in.

12.2 Creating Vertex and Index Buffer Objects

To load in the height map, we're going to use two new OpenGL objects: a vertex buffer object and an index buffer object. These two objects are analogous to the vertex arrays and index arrays that we've been using in previous chapters, except that the graphics driver can choose to place them directly in the GPU's memory. This can lead to better performance for objects that we don't change often once they've been created, such as a height map. These buffer objects aren't always faster, though, so it does pay to compare both options.

Creating a Vertex Buffer Object

To load in these buffer objects, we'll need to create some supporting code. Let's create a new class called VertexBuffer in the com.particles.android.data, with the following member variable and constructor:

---

1.   http://ned.usgs.gov/
2.   http://pragprog.com/book/kbogla/

```java
private final int bufferId;

public VertexBuffer(float[] vertexData) {
    // Allocate a buffer.
    final int buffers[] = new int[1];
    glGenBuffers(buffers.length, buffers, 0);
    if (buffers[0] == 0) {
        throw new RuntimeException("Could not create a new vertex buffer object.");
    }
    bufferId = buffers[0];

    // Bind to the buffer.
    glBindBuffer(GL_ARRAY_BUFFER, buffers[0]);

    // Transfer data to native memory.
    FloatBuffer vertexArray = ByteBuffer
        .allocateDirect(vertexData.length * BYTES_PER_FLOAT)
        .order(ByteOrder.nativeOrder())
        .asFloatBuffer()
        .put(vertexData);
    vertexArray.position(0);

    // Transfer data from native memory to the GPU buffer.
    glBufferData(GL_ARRAY_BUFFER, vertexArray.capacity() * BYTES_PER_FLOAT,
        vertexArray, GL_STATIC_DRAW);

    // IMPORTANT: Unbind from the buffer when we're done with it.
    glBindBuffer(GL_ARRAY_BUFFER, 0);
}
```

To send vertex data into a vertex buffer object, we first create a new buffer object using glGenBuffers(). This method takes in an array, so we create a new one-element array to store the new buffer ID. We then bind to the buffer with a call to glBindBuffer(), passing in GL_ARRAY_BUFFER to tell OpenGL that this is a vertex buffer.

To copy the data into the buffer object, we have to first transfer it into native memory just like we used to do with VertexArray. Once it's there, we can transfer the data into the buffer object with a call to glBufferData(). Let's take a look at this method's parameters in more detail (see Table 7, *glBufferData parameters*, on page 236).

When we're done loading data into the buffer, we need to make sure that we unbind from the buffer by calling glBindBuffer() with 0 as the buffer ID; otherwise calls to functions like glVertexAttribPointer() elsewhere in our code will not work properly.

glBufferData(int target, int size, Buffer data, int usage)

int target	This should be GL_ARRAY_BUFFER for a vertex buffer object, or GL_ELEMENT_ARRAY_BUFFER for an index buffer object.
int size	This is the size of the data in bytes.
Buffer data	This should be a Buffer object that was created with allocateDirect().
int usage	This tells OpenGL the expected usage pattern for this buffer object. Here are the options:

GL_STREAM_DRAW

This object will only be modified once and only used a few times.

GL_STATIC_DRAW

This object will be modified once, but it will be used many times.

GL_DYNAMIC_DRAW

This object will be both modified and used many times.

These are hints rather than constraints so that OpenGL can do optimizations on its end. We'll want to use GL_STATIC_DRAW most of the time.

Table 7—glBufferData parameters

We'll also need a wrapper to glVertexAttribPointer() like we had with our old VertexArray class, so let's add a new method called setVertexAttribPointer():

Heightmap/src/com/particles/android/data/VertexBuffer.java
```
public void setVertexAttribPointer(int dataOffset, int attributeLocation,
    int componentCount, int stride) {
    glBindBuffer(GL_ARRAY_BUFFER, bufferId);
    glVertexAttribPointer(attributeLocation, componentCount, GL_FLOAT,
        false, stride, dataOffset);
    glEnableVertexAttribArray(attributeLocation);
    glBindBuffer(GL_ARRAY_BUFFER, 0);
}
```

The main differences here are that we now need to bind to the buffer before calling glVertexAttribPointer(), and we use a slightly different glVertexAttribPointer() that takes in an int instead of a Buffer as the last parameter. This integer tells OpenGL the offset in bytes for the current attribute; this could be 0 for the first attribute or a specific byte offset for subsequent attributes.

As before, we make sure to unbind from the buffer before returning from the method.

Creating an Index Buffer Object

We'll also need a wrapper class for the index buffer, so go ahead and create a new class called IndexBuffer in the same package as VertexBuffer. You can copy/paste over the member variable and constructor from VertexBuffer and make the following changes:

- Use short[] and ShortBuffer as the types.

- Use GL_ELEMENT_ARRAY_BUFFER instead of GL_ARRAY_BUFFER.

- To get the size in bytes, add the new constant BYTES_PER_SHORT to Constants with the value 2, and use that instead of BYTES_PER_FLOAT when you call glBufferData().

We'll need to use the buffer ID when we use it to draw, so let's add an accessor for it:

Heightmap/src/com/particles/android/data/IndexBuffer.java
```
public int getBufferId() {
    return bufferId;
}
```

Now that we have our supporting code in place, let's get that height map loaded in.

12.3 Loading in the Height Map

To load the height map into OpenGL, we need to load in the image data and convert it into a set of vertices, one for each pixel. Each vertex will have a position based on its position in the image and a height based on the brightness of the pixel. Once we have all of the vertices loaded in, we'll use the index buffer to group them into triangles that we can draw with OpenGL.

Generating the Vertex Data

Let's create a new class called Heightmap in the com.particles.android.objects package, adding the following code inside the class to start out:

Heightmap/src/com/particles/android/objects/Heightmap.java
```
private static final int POSITION_COMPONENT_COUNT = 3;

private final int width;
private final int height;
private final int numElements;
private final VertexBuffer vertexBuffer;
```

```
private final IndexBuffer indexBuffer;

public Heightmap(Bitmap bitmap) {
    width = bitmap.getWidth();
    height = bitmap.getHeight();

    if (width * height > 65536) {
        throw new RuntimeException("Heightmap is too large for the index buffer.");
    }
    numElements = calculateNumElements();
    vertexBuffer = new VertexBuffer(loadBitmapData(bitmap));
    indexBuffer = new IndexBuffer(createIndexData());
}
```

We pass in an Android bitmap, load the data into a vertex buffer, and create an index buffer for those vertices. Let's start adding the definition for loadBitmap-Data():

Heightmap/src/com/particles/android/objects/Heightmap.java
```
private float[] loadBitmapData(Bitmap bitmap) {
    final int[] pixels = new int[width * height];
    bitmap.getPixels(pixels, 0, width, 0, 0, width, height);
    bitmap.recycle();

    final float[] heightmapVertices =
        new float[width * height * POSITION_COMPONENT_COUNT];
    int offset = 0;
```

To efficiently read in all of the bitmap data, we first extract all of the pixels with a call to getPixels(), and then we recycle the bitmap since we won't need to keep it around. Since there will be one vertex per pixel, we create a new array for the vertices with the same width and height as the bitmap.

Let's add some code to convert the bitmap pixels into height map data:

Heightmap/src/com/particles/android/objects/Heightmap.java
```
    for (int row = 0; row < height; row++) {
        for (int col = 0; col < width; col++) {
            final float xPosition = ((float)col / (float)(width - 1)) - 0.5f;
            final float yPosition =
                (float)Color.red(pixels[(row * height) + col]) / (float)255;
            final float zPosition = ((float)row / (float)(height - 1)) - 0.5f;

            heightmapVertices[offset++] = xPosition;
            heightmapVertices[offset++] = yPosition;
            heightmapVertices[offset++] = zPosition;
        }
    }
    return heightmapVertices;
}
```

To generate each vertex of the height map, we first calculate the vertex's position; the height map will be 1 unit wide in each direction and centered at an *x-z* of (0, 0), so with these loops, the upper left corner of the bitmap will map to (-0.5, -0.5), and the lower right corner will map to (0.5, 0.5).

We assume that the image is grayscale, so we read the red component of the pixel and divide that by 255 to get the height. A pixel value of 0 will correspond to a height of 0, and a pixel value of 255 will correspond to a height of 1. Once we've calculated the position and the height, we can write out the new vertex to the array.

Before we move on, let's take a closer look at this loop. Why do we read the bitmap row by row, scanning each column from left to right? Why not read the bitmap column by column instead? The reason we read the data row by row is because that's how the bitmap is laid out sequentially in memory, and CPUs are much better at caching and moving data around when they can do it in sequence.

It's also important to note the way we are accessing the pixels. When we extracted the pixels using getPixels(), Android gave us a one-dimensional array. How then do we know where to read in the pixels? We can calculate the right place with the following formula:

pixelOffset = currentRow * height + currentColumn

Using this formula, we can use two loops to read in a one-dimensional array as if it were a two-dimensional bitmap.

Generating the Index Data

Back in the constructor, we figured out how many index elements we needed by calling calculateNumElements(), and we saved the result in numElements. Let's go ahead and create that method now:

Heightmap/src/com/particles/android/objects/Heightmap.java
```
private int calculateNumElements() {
    return (width - 1) * (height - 1) * 2 * 3;
}
```

The way this works is that for every group of 4 vertices in the height map, we'll generate 2 triangles, 3 indices for each triangle, for a total of 6 indices. We can calculate how many groups we need by multiplying (width - 1) by (height - 1), and then we just multiply that by 2 triangles per group and 3 elements per triangle to get the total element count. For example, a height map of 3 x 3 will have (3 - 1) x (3 - 1) = 2 x 2 = 4 groups. With two triangles per group and 3 elements per triangle, that's a total of 24 elements.

Let's generate the indices with the following code:

Heightmap/src/com/particles/android/objects/Heightmap.java

```
private short[] createIndexData() {
    final short[] indexData = new short[numElements];
    int offset = 0;

    for (int row = 0; row < height - 1; row++) {
        for (int col = 0; col < width - 1; col++) {
            short topLeftIndexNum = (short) (row * width + col);
            short topRightIndexNum = (short) (row * width + col + 1);
            short bottomLeftIndexNum = (short) ((row + 1) * width + col);
            short bottomRightIndexNum = (short) ((row + 1) * width + col + 1);

            // Write out two triangles.
            indexData[offset++] = topLeftIndexNum;
            indexData[offset++] = bottomLeftIndexNum;
            indexData[offset++] = topRightIndexNum;

            indexData[offset++] = topRightIndexNum;
            indexData[offset++] = bottomLeftIndexNum;
            indexData[offset++] = bottomRightIndexNum;
        }
    }

    return indexData;
}
```

This method creates an array of shorts with the required size, and then it loops through the rows and columns, creating triangles for each group of four vertices. We don't even need the actual pixel data to do this; all we need is the width and the height. We first learned about indices back in Section 11.3, *Creating a Cube*, on page 221, and this code follows the same pattern.

Something interesting happens if you try to store index values greater than 32,767: the cast to short will cause the number to *wrap around into a negative value*. However, due to two's complement, these negative numbers will have the right value when OpenGL reads them in as unsigned values (see *Converting Between Signed and Unsigned Data Types*, on page 225). As long as we don't have more than 65,536 elements to index, we'll be fine.

Tips & Gotchas

There are a few things to watch out for when using buffer objects. Technically, Android supports OpenGL ES 2 starting from Android 2.2 (Froyo), but unfortunately these bindings are broken, and vertex and index buffers are unusable from Java without writing a custom Java Native Interface (JNI) binding.

The good news is that these bindings were fixed in Android's Gingerbread release, and as of the time of this writing, only 9 percent of the market is still on Froyo, so this problem isn't as big of a deal as it used to be.

Just like with Java's ByteBuffers, using OpenGL buffer objects improperly can lead to native crashes, which can be difficult to debug. If your application suddenly disappears and you see something like "Segmentation fault" in the Android log, it's a good idea to double-check all of your calls involving the buffers, especially calls to glVertexAttribPointer().

12.4 Drawing the Height Map

Now that we have the height map loaded in, let's get it drawn to the screen. Create a new file called heightmap_vertex_shader.glsl in your /res/raw folder, and add the following code:

Heightmap/res/raw/heightmap_vertex_shader.glsl
```
uniform mat4 u_Matrix;
attribute vec3 a_Position;
varying vec3 v_Color;

void main()
{
    v_Color = mix(vec3(0.180, 0.467, 0.153),    // A dark green
                  vec3(0.660, 0.670, 0.680),    // A stony gray
                  a_Position.y);

    gl_Position = u_Matrix * vec4(a_Position, 1.0);
}
```

This vertex shader uses a new shader function, mix(), to smoothly interpolate between two different colors. We set up our height map so that the height is between 0 and 1, and we use this height as the ratio between the two colors. The height map will appear green near the bottom and gray near the top.

Let's add a matching fragment shader called heightmap_fragment_shader.glsl:

Heightmap/res/raw/heightmap_fragment_shader.glsl
```
precision mediump float;

varying vec3 v_Color;

void main()
{
    gl_FragColor = vec4(v_Color, 1.0);
}
```

To wrap this shader in Java, add a new class called HeightmapShaderProgram to com.particles.android.programs using the same pattern as the other classes in that package. Once that's done, go back to Heightmap and add the following methods to the end of the class:

Heightmap/src/com/particles/android/objects/Heightmap.java
```
public void bindData(HeightmapShaderProgram heightmapProgram) {
    vertexBuffer.setVertexAttribPointer(0,
        heightmapProgram.getPositionAttributeLocation(),
        POSITION_COMPONENT_COUNT, 0);
}

public void draw() {
    glBindBuffer(GL_ELEMENT_ARRAY_BUFFER, indexBuffer.getBufferId());
    glDrawElements(GL_TRIANGLES, numElements, GL_UNSIGNED_SHORT, 0);
    glBindBuffer(GL_ELEMENT_ARRAY_BUFFER, 0);
}
```

We'll use bindData() to tell OpenGL where to get the data when we call draw(). In draw(), we tell OpenGL to draw the data using the index buffer. This call uses a slightly different glDrawElements() than the one we used in the last chapter: like with glVertexAttribPointer(), the last parameter is changed from a Buffer reference to an int offset, which is used to tell OpenGL at which index to start reading.

As before, we also bind the buffer before use and make sure to unbind it afterward.

Adding the Height Map and New Matrices to ParticlesRenderer

With our components in place, let's head to ParticlesRenderer and glue everything together. First we'll need to add a couple of new matrices to the top of the class, so let's update the list of matrices as follows:

Heightmap/src/com/particles/android/ParticlesRenderer.java
```
private final float[] modelMatrix = new float[16];
private final float[] viewMatrix = new float[16];
private final float[] viewMatrixForSkybox = new float[16];
private final float[] projectionMatrix = new float[16];

private final float[] tempMatrix = new float[16];
private final float[] modelViewProjectionMatrix = new float[16];
```

We'll also need two new members for the height map and the height map shader program:

Heightmap/src/com/particles/android/ParticlesRenderer.java
```
private HeightmapShaderProgram heightmapProgram;
private Heightmap heightmap;
```

Initialize these in onSurfaceCreated():

```
heightmapProgram = new HeightmapShaderProgram(context);
heightmap = new Heightmap(((BitmapDrawable)context.getResources()
    .getDrawable(R.drawable.heightmap)).getBitmap());
```

We need to make a few more changes to reduce the amount of copy/paste with our matrix code. We can do this by using one matrix to represent a camera for all of our objects and a second matrix for the skybox that represents just the rotation.

Add a new method to the class called updateViewMatrices() as follows:

```
private void updateViewMatrices() {
    setIdentityM(viewMatrix, 0);
    rotateM(viewMatrix, 0, -yRotation, 1f, 0f, 0f);
    rotateM(viewMatrix, 0, -xRotation, 0f, 1f, 0f);
    System.arraycopy(viewMatrix, 0, viewMatrixForSkybox, 0, viewMatrix.length);

    // We want the translation to apply to the regular view matrix, and not
    // the skybox.
    translateM(viewMatrix, 0, 0, -1.5f, -5f);
}
```

With this code, we can use viewMatrix to apply the same rotation and translation to the height map and particles, and we can use viewMatrixForSkybox to apply the rotation to the skybox.

This follows the same idea as the matrix hierarchy we introduced back in *A Simple Matrix Hierarchy*, on page 156. Let's call this new method by adding a call to updateViewMatrices() to the end of handleTouchDrag(). We'll also need to replace the code inside onSurfaceChanged() after the call to perspectiveM() with another call to updateViewMatrices(), as follows:

```
@Override
public void onSurfaceChanged(GL10 glUnused, int width, int height) {
    glViewport(0, 0, width, height);
    MatrixHelper.perspectiveM(projectionMatrix, 45, (float) width
        / (float) height, 1f, 10f);
    updateViewMatrices();
}
```

We also need a couple of new helper methods to multiply the matrices together into a final, combined model-view projection matrix, depending on whether we're drawing the skybox or drawing something else. Add the following two methods to the class:

Heightmap/src/com/particles/android/ParticlesRenderer.java

```
private void updateMvpMatrix() {
    multiplyMM(tempMatrix, 0, viewMatrix, 0, modelMatrix, 0);
    multiplyMM(modelViewProjectionMatrix, 0, projectionMatrix, 0, tempMatrix, 0);
}
private void updateMvpMatrixForSkybox() {
    multiplyMM(tempMatrix, 0, viewMatrixForSkybox, 0, modelMatrix, 0);
    multiplyMM(modelViewProjectionMatrix, 0, projectionMatrix, 0, tempMatrix, 0);
}
```

We need to use a temporary matrix to hold the intermediate result, as these methods will mess up the matrix if we use the same matrix as both a destination and as an operand. Now we can update drawSkybox() by deleting the existing matrix code and replacing it with the following:

Heightmap/src/com/particles/android/ParticlesRenderer.java

```
setIdentityM(modelMatrix, 0);
updateMvpMatrixForSkybox();
```

For drawParticles(), replace the existing matrix code with the following:

Heightmap/src/com/particles/android/ParticlesRenderer.java

```
setIdentityM(modelMatrix, 0);
updateMvpMatrix();
```

Once that's done, we can fix our setUniforms() calls for the skybox and particles by replacing the missing viewProjectionMatrix references with modelViewProjectionMatrix. We're now taking care of the camera's rotation and pushing things into the scene with the view matrix, so we no longer need to copy/paste the matrix setup code for every object. By calling setIdentityM(modelMatrix, 0), we're resetting the model matrix to the identity matrix, which does nothing, so when we multiply all of the matrices together in updateMvpMatrix(), only the view and projection matrices will take effect.

Drawing the Height Map

With the matrix stuff out of the way, let's go ahead and draw the height map! In onDrawFrame(), add a call to drawHeightmap() just after the call to glClear(). Add the body of that method as follows:

Heightmap/src/com/particles/android/ParticlesRenderer.java

```
private void drawHeightmap() {
    setIdentityM(modelMatrix, 0);
    scaleM(modelMatrix, 0, 100f, 10f, 100f);
    updateMvpMatrix();
    heightmapProgram.useProgram();
    heightmapProgram.setUniforms(modelViewProjectionMatrix);
    heightmap.bindData(heightmapProgram);
    heightmap.draw();
}
```

This time we use the model matrix to make the height map one hundred times wider in the *x* and *z* directions and only ten times taller in the *y* direction, since we don't want the mountains to be too extreme. Wait—won't this mess up the color interpolation in our shader, since that's dependent on the vertex's *y* position? It won't, because in the shader we're reading in the vertex's position *before* we multiply it with the matrix.

We'll need to update the projection matrix to give us enough room, so in onSurfaceChanged(), change the last parameter to perspectiveM() to 100f; this will set up the projection so that we can draw stuff up to a hundred units distant before it gets clipped by the far plane.

12.5 Occluding Hidden Objects

We now have everything in place, so let's run the app to see what happens. You might be surprised to find that the terrain doesn't show up at all! Let's take a look at onDrawFrame() to see what might be going on:

Heightmap/src/com/particles/android/ParticlesRenderer.java

```
glClear(GL_COLOR_BUFFER_BIT);
drawHeightmap();
drawSkybox();
drawParticles();
```

We first draw the height map, but then we draw the skybox right after, obliterating everything that was there before. Switch the two draw calls so that the skybox is drawn first and the height map is drawn second, and see what happens.

The terrain should now show up, but you'll likely see some strange artifacts, as seen in Figure 60, *Terrain with strange artifacts*, on page 246. The reason for this is because we have the same overwriting problem with the terrain itself: different parts are being drawn over each other, with no regard as to which parts of the terrain are actually closer to the viewer. You might also notice that the particles still fall "into the earth," which doesn't make much sense.

Removing Hidden Surfaces with the Depth Buffer

Can we sort all of the triangles so that we draw things in order from back to front—that is, so that things appear as expected? This is one possible solution, but it suffers from two big problems: first, the draw order is dependent on the current viewpoint, and computing it can be complex; and second, this solution is also wasteful, as we will spend a lot of time drawing stuff that will never be seen because it will get drawn over by something closer.

Figure 60—Terrain with strange artifacts

OpenGL gives us a better solution in the form of the *depth buffer*, a special buffer that records the depth of every fragment on the screen. When this buffer is turned on, OpenGL performs a *depth test* for every fragment: if the fragment is closer than what's already there, draw it; otherwise discard it.

Let's revert the draw order in onDrawFrame() so that the height map is drawn first, and then let's turn on the depth buffer by adding a call to glEnable(GL_DEPTH_TEST) inside onSurfaceCreated(), just after the call to glClearColor(). We'll also need to update the call to glClear() in onDrawFrame() to glClear(GL_COL-OR_BUFFER_BIT | GL_DEPTH_BUFFER_BIT). This tells OpenGL to also clear the depth buffer on every new frame.

Let's give the app another run to see what we get. The terrain now works fine, and the particles no longer fall into the ground, but as we can see in the next figure, our skybox is now really messed up.

Figure 61—Problems rendering the skybox

Depth Testing

Back in Section 11.4, *Adding a Skybox Shader Program*, on page 224, we configured our skybox shader program so that the skybox would be drawn on the far plane. Now that depth testing is turned on, this causes a problem for us because by default OpenGL will only let the fragments through if they're either closer than another fragment or closer than the far plane. We probably shouldn't see any of the skybox at all, but floating point imprecision lets some of it show through.

To fix this, we can either change the skybox shader so it's drawn slightly closer, or we can change the depth test to let the fragments through. Let's edit drawSkybox() to change the depth test as follows:

```
glDepthFunc(GL_LEQUAL);
«draw»
glDepthFunc(GL_LESS);
```

By default, the depth test is set to GL_LESS, which means "let the new fragment through if it's closer than whatever's already there, or closer than the far plane." By changing this to GL_LEQUAL just for the skybox, we change the meaning to "let the new fragment through if it's closer or at the same distance as what's already there." We then reset the test back to the default so that everything else still gets drawn as expected.

The Depth Buffer and Translucent Objects

If we run the app again, the skybox should now look fine, but we still have a strange issue with the particles, as we can see in the next figure. They now get clipped by the ground, but they also seem to be occluding each other! This doesn't make sense, because we want the particles to be translucent and to blend with each other. We need a way for the particles to not block each other while still clipping them where they touch the ground.

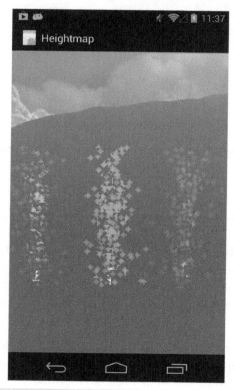

Figure 62—Problems with the depth buffer and translucent objects

In OpenGL, it's possible to disable depth updates while keeping the tests turned on. This means that the particles will be tested against the ground; however, they will not write new information into the depth buffer, so they will not block each other. This will work fine since we are drawing the particles last.

Let's turn off depth writes by updating drawParticles() as follows:

```
glDepthMask(false);
«draw»
glDepthMask(true);
```

Give the app another run; everything should now look as expected.

The Depth Buffer and the Perspective Divide

The depth buffer stores depth values *after* the perspective divide has been done, which creates a nonlinear relationship between the depth value and the distance. This has the effect of providing a lot of depth precision close to the near plane and a lot less precision further away, which can lead to artifacts. For this reason, the ratio between the perspective projection's near and far planes should not be larger than necessary for the current scene (that is, a near value of 1 and a far value of 100 is probably fine, but a near value of 0.001 and a far value of 100,000 could lead to problems).

Culling

OpenGL also provides us another easy way of increasing performance through hidden surface removal by enabling *culling*. By default, OpenGL renders all polygon surfaces as if they were two-sided. You can easily see this in effect by editing updateViewMatrices() and changing the last parameter of the call to translateM() to 15f; this should place our viewpoint right underneath the height map. If we look around, everything looks rather strange, and we'd never expect to see terrain "inside out" like Figure 63, *Underneath the height map*, on page 250.

There's no use in ever rendering the underside of the terrain, so we can cut down on draw overhead by telling OpenGL to turn off two-sided drawing. We can do this by going back to onSurfaceCreated() and adding a call to glEnable(GL_CULL_FACE). OpenGL will then look at the *winding order* of each triangle, which is the order in which we defined the vertices. If this winding order appears counterclockwise from our point of view, then the triangle will be drawn; otherwise it will be discarded.

Figure 63—Underneath the height map

I didn't point it out at the time, but we've actually been careful to define all of our objects with the correct triangle order from the expected viewpoints, so once we enable culling, it just works without any further effort on our part.

12.6 A Review

In this chapter, we learned how to load in a height map from a file and convert it into a form that OpenGL can draw using vertex buffer objects and index buffer objects. Height maps can be a great way of representing terrain, but because they are based off of two-dimensional maps, they cannot easily represent "holes" in the terrain, such as caves or arches. Height maps also have fixed resolution in all dimensions that is based on the source image's width, height, and precision per pixel.

We also covered depth testing and culling, two techniques that make it a lot easier for us to render objects properly and increase performance at the same time. When we created the skybox shader back in Section 11.4, *Adding a*

Skybox Shader Program, on page 224, we mentioned that putting the skybox on the far plane and drawing it *after* other objects would result in a performance boost. One reason this happens is because when we have the depth buffer enabled, the GPU discards non-visible fragments, saving time on drawing them into the frame. Another reason is because many mobile GPUs use tile-based rendering, allowing these GPUs to quickly discard large areas of hidden geometry.[3]

It can be a good idea to take advantage of this hardware culling and draw things like the skybox after all other opaque objects, so that the GPU will be able to see that most of the skybox is occluded by the terrain and save time by skipping those parts.

12.7 Exercises

We covered quite a few new features in this chapter, so let's take the time to explore them in more detail:

- Read up about glCullFace() and glFrontFace(). Then, as an experiment, add a call to glFrontFace(GL_CW) in onSurfaceCreated().

- Change the terrain fragment shader to render the terrain with the fragment depth as the color (Hint: You can use gl_FragCoord.z to get the current depth value in a range from 0 to 1; don't forget that this value is nonlinear).

- Add a texture to the height map. To make things more interesting, blend between two different textures, depending on the height.

- Once you have that working, add a flat plane of water to cover up the bottom.

- Change the height map implementation to use triangle strips and to degenerate triangles (you can find out how to do this with your favorite search engine, or at Learn OpenGL ES[4]). Don't worry, these degenerates aren't evil—they are actually a good way of storing a height map in a more compact and efficient form.

As a research exercise, you can also read up about voxels, an alternative to height maps that store the terrain as a 3D array. Minecraft is a famous example of these.

When you're ready, let's head to the next chapter!

---

3. http://developer.apple.com/library/ios/#documentation/3DDrawing/Conceptual/OpenGLES_ProgrammingGuide/OpenGLESPlatforms/OpenGLESPlatforms.html
4. http://www.learnopengles.com/android-lesson-eight-an-introduction-to-index-buffer-objects-ibos/

CHAPTER 13

Lighting Up the World

The simulation of light has been a major research topic in the world of computer graphics, and we can see the impacts of this research not only in the steady visual improvement of games over time but also in areas like computer-generated imagery (CGI) in movies and TV shows.

The use of lighting algorithms can make a big difference in the way a scene looks. Day can pass into night, areas can fall into shadow, and a mountain can reveal peaks, valleys, and crevices; even a 2D scene can take advantage of the properties of light for things like visual depth, explosions, and other special effects. In this chapter, we're going to learn how to use some simple lighting algorithms to add some contrast to our mountains, and then we'll darken into a night backdrop and make those particle fountains glow.

Let's go over our game plan for this chapter:

- We'll first learn how to implement diffuse reflection using a directional light source, making it appear as if the scene were lit up by the sun in the skybox, and then we'll learn how to minimize dark shadows by adding some ambient lighting.

- We'll then switch out our skybox for a darker skybox and turn down the brightness, and we'll learn how to use point lights to light up each particle fountain.

Let's get the show started by copying over the project from the previous chapter into a new project called 'Lighting'.

13.1 Simulating the Effects of Light

When we see the world around us, we are really seeing the cumulative effect of trillions upon trillions of tiny little particles called photons. These photons are emitted by energy sources like the sun; and after traveling a long distance, they will bounce off some objects and get refracted by others, until they finally strike the retinas in the backs of our eyes. Our eyes and brain take it from there and reconstruct the activity of all of these photons into the world that we can see around us.

Computer graphics have historically simulated the effects of light by either simulating the behavior of actual photons or by using shortcuts to fake that behavior. One way of simulating the behavior of the actual photons is with a *ray tracer*. A ray tracer simulates the photons by shooting rays into the scene and calculating how those rays interact with the objects in the scene. This technique is quite powerful, and it can lend itself well to really good reflections and refractions and other special effects like caustics (the patterns you see when light passes through water, for example).

Unfortunately, ray tracing is usually too expensive to use for real-time rendering. Instead, most games and apps simplify things and approximate the way that light works at a higher level, rather than simulating it directly. Simple lighting algorithms can go a long way, and there are also ways of faking reflections, refractions, and more. These techniques can use OpenGL to put most of the workload on the GPU and run blazing fast, even on a mobile phone.

Using Light in OpenGL

To add light to an OpenGL scene, we can generally organize the different light sources into the following groups:

Ambient light

> Ambient light appears to come from all directions, lighting up everything in the scene to the same extent. This approximates the type of lighting we get from large, equal sources of light, like the sky, and ambient light can also be used to fake the way that light can bounce off many objects before reaching our eyes, so shadows are usually never pitch black.

Directional lights

> Directional light appears to come from one direction, as if the light source was extremely far away. This is similar to the type of lighting we get from the sun or the moon.

Point lights

> Point lights appear to be casting their light from somewhere nearby, and the intensity of the light decreases with distance. This is good for representing close sources of light that cast their light in all directions, like a light bulb or a candle.

Spot lights

> Spot lighting is similar to point lighting, with the added restriction of being focused in a particular direction. This is the type of light we would get from a flashlight, or as the name suggests, a spot light in an enclosure.

We can also group the way that light reflects off an object into two main categories:

Diffuse reflection

> Diffuse reflection spreads out equally in all directions and is good for representing materials with an unpolished surface, like a carpet or an exterior concrete wall. These types of surfaces appear similar from many different points of view.

Specular reflection

> Specular reflection reflects more strongly in a particular direction and is good for materials that are polished or shiny, like smooth metal or a recently waxed car.

Many materials combine aspects of both; take an asphalt road surface, for example. A road generally appears the same from many directions, but when the sun is low in the sky and the conditions are right, one direction can reflect enough sun glare to the point of blinding drivers and causing a road hazard.

13.2 Implementing a Directional Light with Lambertian Reflectance

To implement diffuse reflection, we can use a simple technique known as *Lambertian reflectance*. Named after Johann Heinrich Lambert, a Swiss mathematician and astronomer who lived in the eighteenth century, Lambertian reflectance describes a surface that reflects the light hitting it in all directions, so that it appears the same from all viewpoints. Its appearance depends only on its orientation and distance from a light source.

Let's look at an example with a flat surface and a single, directional light source that does not diminish with distance, so the only thing that matters is the orientation of the surface with respect to the light. In Figure 64, *A surface directly facing a light source*, on page 256, we can see the surface facing the light source head on. At this angle, it's capturing and reflecting as much light as it can. In the subsequent figure, the surface has now been rotated 45 degrees with respect to the light source, so it's no longer able to capture and reflect as much of the light.

How much less light does the surface reflect at 45 degrees? If we measure the cross section, we'll see that it's only about 0.707 times as wide as when the surface is not rotated. This relationship follows the cosine of the angle

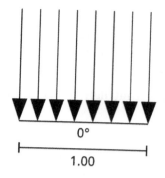

0°

1.00

Figure 64—A surface directly facing a light source

(see Figure 43, *Unit circle*, on page 148); and to figure out how much light a surface receives, all we need to do is figure out how much light it would receive if it were facing the light directly and then multiply that by the cosine of the angle.

Here's an example: if a Lambertian surface would normally reflect 5 lumens of light from a directional light source when at 0 degrees, then it will reflect (5 * cos 45°) = ~3.5 lumens of light when oriented at 45 degrees with respect to the light source. Understanding this relationship is all we need to know to understand Lambertian reflectance.

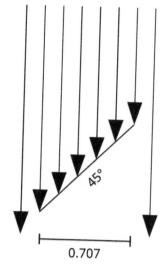

45°

0.707

Figure 65—A surface at an angle to a light source

Calculating the Orientation of the Height Map

Before we can add Lambertian reflectance to our height map, we need some way of knowing what the orientation of the surface is. Since a height map is not a flat surface, we'll need to calculate this orientation for every point on the height map. We can represent the orientation by using a *surface normal*, a special type of vector that is perpendicular to the surface and has a unit length of 1; we first learned about these back in Section 9.3, *Moving Around an Object by Dragging*, on page 177.

Since a surface normal is used for surfaces and not for points, we'll calculate the normal for each point by joining together the neighboring points to create a plane. We'll represent this plane with two vectors: one from the right point to the left point, and another from the top point to the bottom point. If we calculate the cross product of these two vectors, we'll get a vector that is perpendicular to the plane, and we can then normalize that vector to get the surface normal for the center point.[1]

Let's take a look at the following figure as an example.

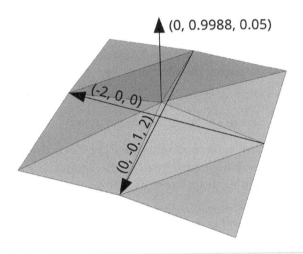

Figure 66—Generating a surface normal for a point on a height map

Let's say that each point is spaced one unit apart, with x increasing to the right and z increasing downward. The heights for the top, left, right, and bottom points are 0.2, 0.1, 0.1, and 0.1, respectively. To calculate the vector

---

1. http://en.wikipedia.org/wiki/Cross_product

going from right to left, we subtract the left point from the right point to get a vector of (-2, 0, 0), and we do the same thing with the top and bottom points to get a vector of (0, -0.1, 2). Once we have these two vectors, we calculate their cross product to get a vector of (0, 4, 0.2), and we normalize that vector to get a surface normal of (0, 0.9988, 0.05).

Why do we use a vector from right to left and not, for instance, from left to right? We want the surface normal to point upward, away from the height map, so we use the right-hand rule of a cross product to figure out which direction each vector needs to be in so that the cross product will be in the correct direction.[2]

Now that we know what to do, let's open up our Heightmap class and start making some changes to the code. First, we'll add some new constants:

Lighting/src/com/particles/android/objects/Heightmap.java
```
private static final int NORMAL_COMPONENT_COUNT = 3;
private static final int TOTAL_COMPONENT_COUNT =
    POSITION_COMPONENT_COUNT + NORMAL_COMPONENT_COUNT;
private static final int STRIDE =
    (POSITION_COMPONENT_COUNT + NORMAL_COMPONENT_COUNT) * BYTES_PER_FLOAT;
```

We'll change the vertex buffer so that it stores both the positions and the normals together, and to do this, we also need to know the total component count and the stride. Let's update the assignment to heightmapVertices in load-BitmapData() to add some space for the normals:

Lighting/src/com/particles/android/objects/Heightmap.java
```
final float[] heightmapVertices =
    new float[width * height * TOTAL_COMPONENT_COUNT];
```

This will ensure that we have enough space for both the positions and the normals. Still inside loadBitmapData(), head to the section inside the loop where we generate the position and update it as follows:

Lighting/src/com/particles/android/objects/Heightmap.java
```
final Point point = getPoint(pixels, row, col);

heightmapVertices[offset++] = point.x;
heightmapVertices[offset++] = point.y;
heightmapVertices[offset++] = point.z;
```

We've factored out the generation of the position into a separate method, which we'll add soon. Let's add some code to get the neighboring points and generate the surface normal for the current point:

---

2.   http://en.wikipedia.org/wiki/Cross_product#Definition

Lighting/src/com/particles/android/objects/Heightmap.java

```
final Point top = getPoint(pixels, row - 1, col);
final Point left = getPoint(pixels, row, col - 1);
final Point right = getPoint(pixels, row, col + 1);
final Point bottom = getPoint(pixels, row + 1, col);

final Vector rightToLeft = Geometry.vectorBetween(right, left);
final Vector topToBottom = Geometry.vectorBetween(top, bottom);
final Vector normal = rightToLeft.crossProduct(topToBottom).normalize();

heightmapVertices[offset++] = normal.x;
heightmapVertices[offset++] = normal.y;
heightmapVertices[offset++] = normal.z;
```

To generate the normal, we follow the algorithm we outlined earlier: first we get the neighboring points, then we use these points to create two vectors representing a plane, and finally we take the cross product of those two vectors and normalize that to get the surface normal. We haven't defined normalize() yet, so let's open up the Geometry class, find the definition for Vector, and add the method as follows:

Lighting/src/com/particles/android/util/Geometry.java

```
public Vector normalize() {
    return scale(1f / length());
}
```

Let's continue Heightmap by adding the missing definition for getPoint():

Lighting/src/com/particles/android/objects/Heightmap.java

```
private Point getPoint(int[] pixels, int row, int col) {
    float x = ((float)col / (float)(width - 1)) - 0.5f;
    float z = ((float)row / (float)(height - 1)) - 0.5f;

    row = clamp(row, 0, width - 1);
    col = clamp(col, 0, height - 1);

    float y = (float)Color.red(pixels[(row * height) + col]) / (float)255;

    return new Point(x, y, z);
}

private int clamp(int val, int min, int max) {
    return Math.max(min, Math.min(max, val));
}
```

This code works much the same as it did before when the code was inside the loop, but we now have clamping for the cases when a neighboring point is out of bounds. For example, when we generate the normal for (0, 0) and retrieve the points to the top and to the left, these points don't actually exist in the height map. In this case, we pretend that they do and we give them the same height as the center vertex. This way, we can still generate a surface normal for that vertex.

Let's finish up our changes and update bindData() as follows:

Lighting/src/com/particles/android/objects/Heightmap.java

```
public void bindData(HeightmapShaderProgram heightmapProgram) {
    vertexBuffer.setVertexAttribPointer(0,
        heightmapProgram.getPositionAttributeLocation(),
        POSITION_COMPONENT_COUNT, STRIDE);

    vertexBuffer.setVertexAttribPointer(
        POSITION_COMPONENT_COUNT * BYTES_PER_FLOAT,
        heightmapProgram.getNormalAttributeLocation(),
        NORMAL_COMPONENT_COUNT, STRIDE);
}
```

Since we're now storing both the position and the normal data in the same vertex buffer object, we now have to pass the stride to our setVertexAttribPointer() helper that calls glVertexAttribPointer(), so that OpenGL knows how many bytes to skip between each element. For the second call to setVertexAttribPointer(), it's very important that we also specify the starting offset for the normals in terms of bytes; otherwise OpenGL will read part of the position and part of the normal together and interpret *that* as the normal, which would look extremely weird.

Adding a Directional Light to the Shader

Now that our height map includes the normals, our next task is to update the height map shader and add support for directional lighting. Let's start off by adding a new uniform to heightmap_vertex_shader.glsl:

Lighting/res/raw/heightmap_vertex_shader.glsl

```
uniform vec3 u_VectorToLight;
```

This vector will contain a normalized vector pointing toward our directional light source. We'll also need a new attribute for the height map normals:

Lighting/res/raw/heightmap_vertex_shader.glsl

```
attribute vec3 a_Normal;
```

Now that we have that in place, let's add the following to the main body of the shader after the first assignment to v_Color:

Lighting/res/raw/heightmap_vertex_shader.glsl

```
vec3 scaledNormal = a_Normal;
scaledNormal.y *= 10.0;
scaledNormal = normalize(scaledNormal);
```

You may remember that when we draw our height map, we are currently expanding it by using scaleM() to make it ten times taller and a hundred times wider, so in other words, the height map is now ten times wider than it is tall. Scaling things in this way changes the shape of the height map, meaning that our pregenerated normals are no longer correct. To compensate for this, we scale the normal in the opposite direction, making the normal ten times taller than it is wide. After renormalizing the normal, it will now match the new geometry.

The reason this works involves some advanced math, so you'll have to take this on faith for now. Later on, we'll look at a more general way of adjusting the normals in *Adding Point Lighting to the Shader*, on page 265.

Now that we've adjusted the surface normal, let's calculate the Lambertian reflectance:

Lighting/res/raw/heightmap_vertex_shader.glsl
```
float diffuse = max(dot(scaledNormal, u_VectorToLight), 0.0);
v_Color *= diffuse;
```

To calculate the cosine of the angle between the surface and the light, we calculate the dot product of the vector to the light and the surface normal. The reason this works is because when two vectors are normalized, the dot product of those two vectors will give us the cosine of the angle between them, which is exactly what we need to calculate the Lambertian reflectance.[3]

To avoid negative results, we clamp the minimum cosine to 0 with max(), and then we apply the lighting by multiplying the current vertex's color with the cosine. The cosine will be between 0 and 1, so the final color will be somewhere between black and the original color.

Updating the Shader Wrapping Code

We now need to update our wrapper class to account for the new changes. Let's start off by adding the following new constants to ShaderProgram:

Lighting/src/com/particles/android/programs/ShaderProgram.java
```
protected static final String U_VECTOR_TO_LIGHT = "u_VectorToLight";
protected static final String A_NORMAL = "a_Normal";
```

Let's switch to HeightmapShaderProgram and add new member variables for the directional light uniform location and the normal attribute location:

---

3. http://en.wikipedia.org/wiki/Dot_product

Lighting/src/com/particles/android/programs/HeightmapShaderProgram.java
```
private final int uVectorToLightLocation;
private final int aNormalLocation;
```

Let's assign the new locations by adding the following to the end of the constructor:

Lighting/src/com/particles/android/programs/HeightmapShaderProgram.java
```
uVectorToLightLocation = glGetUniformLocation(program, U_VECTOR_TO_LIGHT);
aNormalLocation = glGetAttribLocation(program, A_NORMAL);
```

We'll need to update setUniforms() as follows so that we can update the new uniform:

Lighting/src/com/particles/android/programs/HeightmapShaderProgram.java
```
public void setUniforms(float[] matrix, Vector vectorToLight) {
    glUniformMatrix4fv(uMatrixLocation, 1, false, matrix, 0);
    glUniform3f(uVectorToLightLocation,
        vectorToLight.x, vectorToLight.y, vectorToLight.z);
}
```

Let's finish up the changes to the class with a new accessor for the normal attribute location:

Lighting/src/com/particles/android/programs/HeightmapShaderProgram.java
```
public int getNormalAttributeLocation() {
    return aNormalLocation;
}
```

With that in place, we can glue things together in the renderer class and see our new lighting in action.

Seeing Our Directional Light in Action

Let's open up ParticlesRenderer and define the actual vector to our light source:

Lighting/src/com/particles/android/ParticlesRenderer.java
```
private final Vector vectorToLight = new Vector(0.61f, 0.64f, -0.47f).normalize();
```

This vector points approximately toward the sun in the skybox. You can calculate a similar result with these steps:

1. Create a vector pointing toward (0, 0, -1), that is, pointing straight ahead.

2. Rotate this vector in the reverse direction of the scene rotation.

3. Add logging statements to print out the current direction of the vector, and then run the app and rotate the scene until the sun is centered in the middle of the screen.

We also normalize the vector so that we can pass it into the shader and use it to calculate the Lambertian reflectance. Let's pass in the vector to the shader by updating the call to heightmapProgram.setUniforms() in drawHeightmap() as follows:

Lighting/src/com/particles/android/ParticlesRenderer.java
```
heightmapProgram.setUniforms(modelViewProjectionMatrix, vectorToLight);
```

That's it! Give the app a run and see what we get; it should look similar to the following figure:

Figure 67—Our first attempt at directional lighting

We can now see the shape and form of the mountains, but you'll probably notice that the dark areas are far too dark. The problem is that we have no global illumination; in real life, light diffuses through the sky and reflects off many objects before it reaches our eyes, so shadows cast by the sun are nowhere near pitch black. We can fake this in our scene by adding an ambient light level that will apply equally to everything. Let's return to heightmap_vertex_shader.glsl and add the following code after the line that multiplies v_Color with the diffuse reflection:

Lighting/res/raw/heightmap_vertex_shader.glsl
```
float ambient = 0.2;
v_Color += ambient;
```

This will add a base level of illumination to the entire height map, so nothing appears too dark. Let's give it another shot and see what we get. As we can see in the next figure, the shadows look a lot more reasonable now.

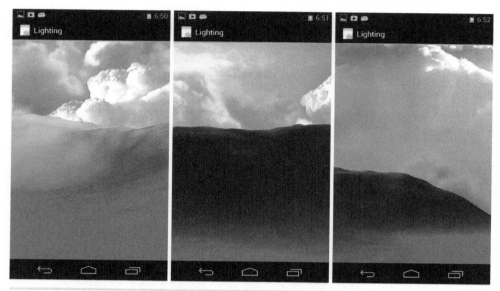

Figure 68—Adding ambient lighting

13.3 Adding Point Lights

We're now ready to add some point lights to our scene so we can make our particle fountains glow. We won't be able to see this too well with a bright backdrop, so the first thing we'll do is switch over to a night skybox. You can download the night skybox from the website and place it in your project's /res/drawable-nodpi folder.[4]

To switch to the night skybox, let's return to ParticlesRenderer and update the assignment to skyboxTexture as follows:

```
Lighting/src/com/particles/android/ParticlesRenderer.java
skyboxTexture = TextureHelper.loadCubeMap(context,
new int[] { R.drawable.night_left, R.drawable.night_right,
        R.drawable.night_bottom, R.drawable.night_top,
        R.drawable.night_front, R.drawable.night_back});
```

We can then update the vector to the light as follows:

---

4.   http://pragprog.com/book/kbogla/

Lighting/src/com/particles/android/ParticlesRenderer.java
```
private final Vector vectorToLight = new Vector(0.30f, 0.35f, -0.89f).normalize();
```

This new vector points toward the moon in the skybox. We'll also need to tone down the light strength in the shader, so let's return to heightmap_vertex_shader.glsl and add the following adjustment to the diffuse reflectance before we multiply it with v_Color:

Lighting/res/raw/heightmap_vertex_shader.glsl
```
diffuse *= 0.3;
```

We should also tone down the ambient lighting:

Lighting/res/raw/heightmap_vertex_shader.glsl
```
float ambient = 0.1;
```

If you go ahead and run the app now, you should see a night backdrop and the height map darkened to match.

Understanding Point Light Sources

Since we're sticking to diffuse reflectance with the Lambertian reflectance model, the math for our point lights will be similar to that for our directional light. However, there are a couple of key differences that we'll need to keep in mind:

- For a directional light, we just stored a vector to that light, since that vector is the same for all points in a scene. For a point light, we'll store the position instead, and we'll use that position to calculate a vector to the point light for each point in the scene.

- In real life, the brightness of a point light source tends to decrease with the square of the distance; this is known as the inverse square law.[5] We'll use the point light's position to figure out the distance for each point in the scene.

Adding Point Lighting to the Shader

To implement point lights, we'll need to make some changes to our shader, and we'll use this opportunity to take a more structured and general approach to lighting in the shader. Let's take a look at some of the most important changes:

- We'll put our positions and normals into *eye space*, a space where all positions and normals are relative to the camera's position and orientation;

---

5. http://en.wikipedia.org/wiki/Inverse-square_law

we'll do this so that we can compare distances and orientations with everything in the same coordinate space. The reason why we use eye space instead of world space is because specular lighting also depends on the position of the camera, and even though we're not using specular lighting in this chapter, it's still a good idea to learn how to use eye space so that we can use it in the future.

- To put a position into eye space, we just multiply it with the model matrix to put it into world space, and then we multiply it with the view matrix to get it into eye space. To simplify matters, we can multiply the view matrix with the model matrix to get a single matrix called the *modelview* matrix, and we use that matrix to put our positions into eye space.

- This also works for the normals if the modelview matrix only contains translations or rotations, but what if we've also scaled an object? If the scale was done equally in all directions, then we just need to renormalize the normals so that their length remains 1, but if the object was also flattened in one direction, then we have to compensate for that as well.

When we added the directional lighting, we knew exactly how much the height map was scaled by, so we were able to directly compensate for that. This is not a flexible solution, and the general way of doing this is by inverting the modelview matrix, transposing the inverted matrix, multiplying the normal with that matrix, and then normalizing the result. The reason this works involves some advanced math; if you're curious, there are a couple of great explanations linked here that go into a lot more detail.[6]

Let's begin by replacing heightmap_vertex_shader.glsl with the following contents:

Lighting/res/raw/heightmap_vertex_shader.glsl
```
uniform mat4 u_MVMatrix;
uniform mat4 u_IT_MVMatrix;
uniform mat4 u_MVPMatrix;

uniform vec3 u_VectorToLight;           // In eye space
uniform vec4 u_PointLightPositions[3];  // In eye space
uniform vec3 u_PointLightColors[3];

attribute vec4 a_Position;
attribute vec3 a_Normal;

varying vec3 v_Color;
```

---

6.   http://arcsynthesis.org/gltut/index.html and http://www.cs.uaf.edu/2007/spring/cs481/lecture/01_23_matrices.html, respectively.

```
vec3 materialColor;
vec4 eyeSpacePosition;
vec3 eyeSpaceNormal;

vec3 getAmbientLighting();
vec3 getDirectionalLighting();
vec3 getPointLighting();
```

We'll now use u_MVMatrix to represent the modelview matrix, u_IT_MVMatrix to represent the transpose of the inverse of that matrix, and u_MVPMatrix to represent the combined model view projection matrix, as we were doing with u_Matrix before.

The directional light vector remains the same as before, except that we now expect it to be in eye space. We pass in the point light positions with u_PointLightPositions, which is also in eye space, and we pass in the colors with u_PointLightColors. These last two uniforms are defined as arrays so that we can pass in multiple vectors through one uniform.

For the attributes, we now represent the position as a vec4, reducing the number of vec3 and vec4 conversions required. We don't need to change our vertex data, as OpenGL will use a default of 1 for the fourth component, but be careful: uniforms don't work the same way, and they must have all components specified.

Our varying remains the same as before; after the varying, we've added some new variables that we'll use to calculate the lighting, and we also have declarations for three new functions, which we'll define later on in the shader.

Let's continue the shader with the following code:

Lighting/res/raw/heightmap_vertex_shader.glsl
```
void main()
{
    materialColor = mix(vec3(0.180, 0.467, 0.153),     // A dark green
                        vec3(0.660, 0.670, 0.680),     // A stony gray
                        a_Position.y);
    eyeSpacePosition = u_MVMatrix * a_Position;

    // The model normals need to be adjusted as per the transpose
    // of the inverse of the modelview matrix.
    eyeSpaceNormal = normalize(vec3(u_IT_MVMatrix * vec4(a_Normal, 0.0)));

    v_Color = getAmbientLighting();
    v_Color += getDirectionalLighting();
    v_Color += getPointLighting();

    gl_Position = u_MVPMatrix * a_Position;
}
```

In the main body of the shader, we assign the material color as before, and then we calculate the current position and normal in eye space. We then calculate each type of light, adding the result color to v_Color, and then we project the position as before.

Let's continue with the following code:

Lighting/res/raw/heightmap_vertex_shader.glsl
```
vec3 getAmbientLighting()
{
    return materialColor * 0.1;
}

vec3 getDirectionalLighting()
{
    return materialColor * 0.3
        * max(dot(eyeSpaceNormal, u_VectorToLight), 0.0);
}
```

These two functions calculate the ambient and directional lighting just as we were doing before. Let's finish off the shader with the following function for point lighting:

Lighting/res/raw/heightmap_vertex_shader.glsl
```
vec3 getPointLighting()
{
    vec3 lightingSum = vec3(0.0);

    for (int i = 0; i < 3; i++) {
        vec3 toPointLight = vec3(u_PointLightPositions[i])
                          - vec3(eyeSpacePosition);
        float distance = length(toPointLight);
        toPointLight = normalize(toPointLight);

        float cosine = max(dot(eyeSpaceNormal, toPointLight), 0.0);
        lightingSum += (materialColor * u_PointLightColors[i] * 5.0 * cosine)
                       / distance;
    }

    return lightingSum;
}
```

The way this works is that we loop through each point light, calculating the lighting for each and adding the result to lightingSum. This code calculates the light level with Lambertian reflectance, just like the directional lighting did before, but there are a few important differences:

- For each point light, we calculate the vector from the current position to that light, and we also calculate the distance from the current position to that light.

- Once we have the normalized vector, we can calculate the Lambertian reflectance. We then multiply the material color with the point light color to apply that color to the current vertex. We scale the result up by 5 to make things a bit brighter, and then we multiply that by the cosine to apply the Lambertian reflectance.

- Before adding the result to lightingSum, we diminish the light intensity with distance by dividing the result from the previous step by the distance.

With this last calculation in place, our shader is now complete.

The Nonlinear Nature of Your Display

Lighting and colors can sometimes be tricky to get right in OpenGL due to a difference of opinion between OpenGL and your display. To OpenGL, colors lie on a linear spectrum, so a color value of 1.0 is twice as bright as a color value of 0.5. However, due to the nonlinear nature of many displays, the actual difference in brightness on your display could be much greater than this.

The reason things work this way is partly due to history. Once upon a time, we all used big, bulky CRT monitors as our main displays, and these monitors worked by shooting an electron beam at a phosphor screen. These phosphors tended to have an exponential response rather than a linear response, so that 1.0 was much more than twice as bright as 0.5. For compatibility and other reasons, many displays maintain similar behavior today.[7]

This nonlinear behavior can muck up our lighting, making things appear darker than they should. Normally, light falloff should be done by dividing the intensity by the distance squared, but to keep our point lights from falling off too quickly, we can remove the exponent and just divide by the distance.

Updating the Shader Wrapping Code

We now need to update our shader wrapping code to match our new shader.

Let's open up ShaderProgram and add some new constants:

---

7.   See http://stackoverflow.com/questions/6397817/color-spaces-gamma-and-image-enhancement and http://http.developer.nvidia.com/GPUGems3/gpugems3_ch24.html.

Lighting/src/com/particles/android/programs/ShaderProgram.java
```
protected static final String U_MV_MATRIX = "u_MVMatrix";
protected static final String U_IT_MV_MATRIX = "u_IT_MVMatrix";
protected static final String U_MVP_MATRIX = "u_MVPMatrix";
protected static final String U_POINT_LIGHT_POSITIONS =
    "u_PointLightPositions";
protected static final String U_POINT_LIGHT_COLORS = "u_PointLightColors";
```

We'll need to make some changes to HeightmapShaderProgram as well. Remove uMatrixLocation and the associated code, and add the following new members:

```
private final int uMVMatrixLocation;
private final int uIT_MVMatrixLocation;
private final int uMVPMatrixLocation;
private final int uPointLightPositionsLocation;
private final int uPointLightColorsLocation;
```

We'll also need to update the constructor:

```
uMVMatrixLocation = glGetUniformLocation(program, U_MV_MATRIX);
uIT_MVMatrixLocation = glGetUniformLocation(program, U_IT_MV_MATRIX);
uMVPMatrixLocation = glGetUniformLocation(program, U_MVP_MATRIX);

uPointLightPositionsLocation =
    glGetUniformLocation(program, U_POINT_LIGHT_POSITIONS);
uPointLightColorsLocation =
    glGetUniformLocation(program, U_POINT_LIGHT_COLORS);
```

To finish up the changes, let's remove the current setUniforms() and build a new one, starting with the following code:

```
public void setUniforms(float[] mvMatrix,
                        float[] it_mvMatrix,
                        float[] mvpMatrix,
                        float[] vectorToDirectionalLight,
                        float[] pointLightPositions,
                        float[] pointLightColors) {
    glUniformMatrix4fv(uMVMatrixLocation, 1, false, mvMatrix, 0);
    glUniformMatrix4fv(uIT_MVMatrixLocation, 1, false, it_mvMatrix, 0);
    glUniformMatrix4fv(uMVPMatrixLocation, 1, false, mvpMatrix, 0);
```

We now pass in several matrices, as well as the directional light and point light positions and colors. The first three lines of the method body send all of the matrices on to the shader. Let's pass in the lighting data and complete the method with the following code:

```
    glUniform3fv(uVectorToLightLocation, 1, vectorToDirectionalLight, 0);

    glUniform4fv(uPointLightPositionsLocation, 3, pointLightPositions, 0);
    glUniform3fv(uPointLightColorsLocation, 3, pointLightColors, 0);
}
```

The first line passes on the directional light vector to the shader, and the next two lines pass the point light positions and colors on to the shader as well. We had defined these last two uniforms in the shader as arrays with a length of three vectors each, so for each uniform, we call glUniform*fv() with the second parameter set to 3, which is the count. This tells OpenGL that it needs to read in three vectors from the array into the uniform.

Updating the Renderer Class

Now we just need to update ParticlesRenderer so we can define and pass in these new uniforms. First we'll need a couple of new matrices at the top of the class:

Lighting/src/com/particles/android/ParticlesRenderer.java

```
private final float[] modelViewMatrix = new float[16];
private final float[] it_modelViewMatrix = new float[16];
```

Let's update updateMvpMatrix() to set these new matrices:

```
private void updateMvpMatrix() {
    multiplyMM(modelViewMatrix, 0, viewMatrix, 0, modelMatrix, 0);
    invertM(tempMatrix, 0, modelViewMatrix, 0);
    transposeM(it_modelViewMatrix, 0, tempMatrix, 0);
    multiplyMM(
        modelViewProjectionMatrix, 0,
        projectionMatrix, 0,
        modelViewMatrix, 0);
}
```

This sets modelViewMatrix to the combined modelview matrix and it_modelViewMatrix to the transpose of the inverse of that matrix. Back at the top of the class, we'll also need to add some new members for the new lights:

```
final float[] vectorToLight = {0.30f, 0.35f, -0.89f, 0f};

private final float[] pointLightPositions = new float[]
    {-1f, 1f, 0f, 1f,
      0f, 1f, 0f, 1f,
      1f, 1f, 0f, 1f};

private final float[] pointLightColors = new float[]
    {1.00f, 0.20f, 0.02f,
     0.02f, 0.25f, 0.02f,
     0.02f, 0.20f, 1.00f};
```

The new definition for vectorToLight should replace the previous definition; you'll soon see why we need to have it stored in a plain floating-point array. We also store the positions and colors for each point light in their respective arrays, with the positions and colors roughly matching the positions and colors we gave to each particle shooter. The main differences are that each point light is raised one unit above its particle shooter, and since the terrain itself is green, the green light has been dimmed somewhat so it doesn't overpower the red light and the blue light.

Now we just need to replace the call to setUniforms() in drawHeightmap() with the following code:

Lighting/src/com/particles/android/ParticlesRenderer.java

```
// Put the light positions into eye space.
final float[] vectorToLightInEyeSpace = new float[4];
final float[] pointPositionsInEyeSpace = new float[12];
multiplyMV(vectorToLightInEyeSpace, 0, viewMatrix, 0, vectorToLight, 0);
multiplyMV(pointPositionsInEyeSpace, 0, viewMatrix, 0, pointLightPositions, 0);
multiplyMV(pointPositionsInEyeSpace, 4, viewMatrix, 0, pointLightPositions, 4);
multiplyMV(pointPositionsInEyeSpace, 8, viewMatrix, 0, pointLightPositions, 8);

heightmapProgram.setUniforms(modelViewMatrix, it_modelViewMatrix,
    modelViewProjectionMatrix, vectorToLightInEyeSpace,
    pointPositionsInEyeSpace, pointLightColors);
```

We need to put the directional light vector and point light positions in eye space, and to do this, we use Android's Matrix class to multiply them with the view matrix. The positions were already in world space, so there was no need to also multiply them with a model matrix beforehand. Once that's done, we pass all of the data into the shader with a call to heightmapProgram.setUniforms().

Let's give it a shot! If everything went well, your screen should look similar to Figure 69, *Point lights against a night backdrop*, on page 273.

13.4 A Review

We covered a lot of material in this chapter, learning all about ambient lighting, directional lights, and point lights, and we also learned how to implement diffuse reflection with Lambertian reflectance. These lighting equations can go a long way in helping us come up with games and live wallpapers that look quite neat.

The framework that we've put in place here can also be used to expand into more complicated types of lighting, such as specular reflection. As the calculations get more involved, we'll generally build on what we did before, just as point lighting built on what we did for directional lighting.

13.5 Exercises

Here are some exercises to let you explore these concepts in some more depth and detail:

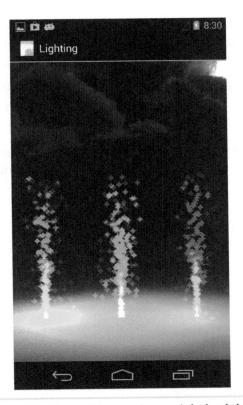

Figure 69—Point lights against a night backdrop

- Move the directional lighting calculations out of the shader and store the results in the height map vertex buffer as a single additional float per vertex, so that we only have to calculate this once.

- Adjust the lighting to make it dynamic. One way you can do this is by turning the particle shooters on and off and then adjusting the brightness of each shooter based on how many particles are still above the ground. If you're feeling particularly creative, you can even time this to a beat.

- Move the lighting calculations into the fragment shader so that the lighting is calculated for each fragment rather than for each vertex. When you pass your data to the fragment shader, keep in mind that you should only use a varying for data that can reasonably be linearly interpolated; otherwise you don't really gain anything. You can safely pass the vertex normals, but you'll need to renormalize them in the fragment shader.

We also have a couple of research exercises to follow up on what we've learned:

- See if there's a way to optimize the height map normal generation and remove redundant steps. A tool like Wolfram Alpha can help you do this automatically.[8]

- Find out about the other ways that we can tesselate and use a height map to improve the visual look of things. Here are a couple of linked resources to get you started.[9]

When you're ready, let's head to the next chapter and turn this lighting project into a live wallpaper that can run on your Android's home screen!

8. http://www.wolframalpha.com/ or http://www.flipcode.com/archives/Calculating_Vertex_Normals_for_Height_Maps.shtml.
9. http://web.eecs.umich.edu/~sugih/courses/eecs494/fall06/lectures/workshop-terrain.pdf and http://mtnphil.wordpress.com/2012/10/15/terrain-triangulation-summary/.

CHAPTER 14

Creating a Live Wallpaper

Ever since the early days of Android, users have been able to replace their device's home screen background with a *live wallpaper*, a special type of application that can draw a dynamic and animated background. These live wallpapers have proven to be quite popular, with many of them going into the millions of downloads! In this chapter, you'll learn how to implement your own live wallpaper using OpenGL and the same GLSurfaceView that we've been using to date.

Let's take a look at our live wallpaper game plan:

- We'll first learn how to wrap our lighting project from the last chapter with a live wallpaper service and a customized GLSurfaceView.

- We'll then learn how to optimize the performance and battery usage.

We'll begin by continuing the Lighting project from the previous chapter, copying it over into a new project called 'LiveWallpaper'. When we're done, our live wallpaper will look similar to Figure 70, *Our live wallpaper, running on the home screen*, on page 276.

14.1 Implementing the Live Wallpaper Service

To implement a live wallpaper, we'll use an Android service, which is a special type of application component that can be used to provide features to the rest of the system. Android provides the base live wallpaper implementation with WallpaperService, and to create a live wallpaper, all we need to do is extend this base class with our own custom implementation.[1]

---

1. http://developer.android.com/reference/android/service/wallpaper/WallpaperService.html and http://android-developers.blogspot.ca/2010/02/live-wallpapers.html, respectively.

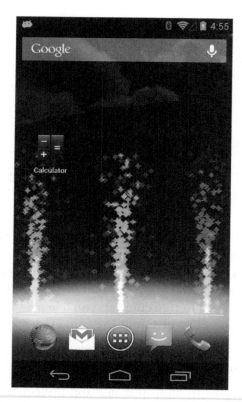

Figure 70—Our live wallpaper, running on the home screen

Extending WallpaperService

Let's start off by creating a new package called com.particles.android.wallpaper. In that new package, let's create a new class called GLWallpaperService as follows:

LiveWallpaper/src/com/particles/android/wallpaper/GLWallpaperService.java
```java
public class GLWallpaperService extends WallpaperService {
    @Override
    public Engine onCreateEngine() {
        return new GLEngine();
    }
}
```

The wallpaper service itself is very simple: there's just one method to override, onCreateEngine(), and to implement a live wallpaper, all we need to do is override that method to return a new instance of a WallpaperService.Engine. This engine will contain the actual implementation of the live wallpaper, with life cycle events that are quite similar to the ones we learned about for the Activity class back in Chapter 1, *Getting Started*, on page 1.

Extending WallpaperService.Engine

Let's add a basic implementation of the engine to GLWallpaperService as an inner class:

LiveWallpaper/src/com/particles/android/wallpaper/GLWallpaperService.java
```
public class GLEngine extends Engine {
    @Override
    public void onCreate(SurfaceHolder surfaceHolder) {
        super.onCreate(surfaceHolder);
    }

    @Override
    public void onVisibilityChanged(boolean visible) {
        super.onVisibilityChanged(visible);
    }
    @Override
    public void onDestroy() {
        super.onDestroy();
    }
}
```

These life cycle events will get called by Android as follows:

onCreate(SurfaceHolder surfaceHolder)

> When WallpaperService is created by the system, it will create its own rendering surface for the application to draw on. It will then initialize the wallpaper engine via a call to onCreate() and pass this surface in as a SurfaceHolder, which is an abstract interface to the surface.

onVisibilityChanged(boolean visible)

> This will be called whenever the live wallpaper becomes visible or hidden. The behavior is similar to the onPause() and onResume() callbacks of an Activity, and we'll need to pause rendering whenever the live wallpaper is hidden and resume rendering when it becomes visible again.

onDestroy()

> This is called when the live wallpaper is destroyed. Like with other Android components, it's always possible that the system doesn't call onDestroy() when the process is killed.

For our live wallpaper to behave properly, we just need to implement these life cycle callbacks and handle them in much the same way as we do in ParticlesActivity.

Let's start out with onCreate() and initialize OpenGL in the same way that we currently do in ParticlesActivity; let's add two new member variables to GLEngine and update onCreate() as follows:

LiveWallpaper/src/com/particles/android/wallpaper/GLWallpaperService.java
```java
private WallpaperGLSurfaceView glSurfaceView;
private boolean rendererSet;

@Override
public void onCreate(SurfaceHolder surfaceHolder) {
    super.onCreate(surfaceHolder);
    glSurfaceView = new WallpaperGLSurfaceView(GLWallpaperService.this);

    // Check if the system supports OpenGL ES 2.0.
    ActivityManager activityManager =
        (ActivityManager) getSystemService(Context.ACTIVITY_SERVICE);
    ConfigurationInfo configurationInfo = activityManager
        .getDeviceConfigurationInfo();

    final boolean supportsEs2 =
        configurationInfo.reqGlEsVersion >= 0x20000
            // Check for emulator.
            || (Build.VERSION.SDK_INT >= Build.VERSION_CODES.ICE_CREAM_SANDWICH_MR1
             && (Build.FINGERPRINT.startsWith("generic")
              || Build.FINGERPRINT.startsWith("unknown")
              || Build.MODEL.contains("google_sdk")
              || Build.MODEL.contains("Emulator")
              || Build.MODEL.contains("Android SDK built for x86")));

    final ParticlesRenderer particlesRenderer =
        new ParticlesRenderer(GLWallpaperService.this);

    if (supportsEs2) {
        glSurfaceView.setEGLContextClientVersion(2);
        glSurfaceView.setRenderer(particlesRenderer);
        rendererSet = true;
    } else {
        Toast.makeText(GLWallpaperService.this,
            "This device does not support OpenGL ES 2.0.",
            Toast.LENGTH_LONG).show();
        return;
    }
}
```

This is more or less the same OpenGL initialization code that we've been using in every chapter; the main difference is that we're using this inside of a live wallpaper service rather than in an activity, and since GLSurfaceView is primarily meant to work with activities, we'll need to create a customized version with a few minor changes.

Creating a Custom GLSurfaceView

Let's add a customized GLSurfaceView to GLEngine as an inner class:

LiveWallpaper/src/com/particles/android/wallpaper/GLWallpaperService.java

```java
class WallpaperGLSurfaceView extends GLSurfaceView {
    WallpaperGLSurfaceView(Context context) {
        super(context);
    }
    @Override
    public SurfaceHolder getHolder() {
        return getSurfaceHolder();
    }
    public void onWallpaperDestroy() {
        super.onDetachedFromWindow();
    }
}
```

Normally, a GLSurfaceView is added to an activity's view hierarchy and renders to a surface within that activity. Since a live wallpaper does things somewhat differently, we need to change the behavior. The GLSurfaceView will call getHolder() to get access to its surface within the activity, so we just need to override getHolder() to return the live wallpaper's rendering surface instead; we do this by calling [WallpaperService.Engine].getSurfaceHolder().

We also need to change the way we clean up a GLSurfaceView. A GLSurfaceView normally cleans itself up when it's detached from the window, and it normally finds out about this when the activity's view hierarchy calls onDetachedFromWindow(). Since we won't be adding the GLSurfaceView to an activity, we create a new method called onWallpaperDestroy(), and we'll call this when the wallpaper is destroyed so that the GLSurfaceView knows that it's time to clean up.

Completing the Wallpaper Engine

Now that we have our custom GLSurfaceView in place, let's finish up the rest of the wallpaper engine:

```java
@Override
public void onVisibilityChanged(boolean visible) {
    super.onVisibilityChanged(visible);
    if (rendererSet) {
        if (visible) {
            glSurfaceView.onResume();
        } else {
            glSurfaceView.onPause();
        }
    }
}
@Override
public void onDestroy() {
    super.onDestroy();
    glSurfaceView.onWallpaperDestroy();
}
```

We pause and resume the GLSurfaceView based on whether the live wallpaper is visible or not, and we clean things up in the onDestroy(). Now that we have that in place, our live wallpaper service is ready for testing.

Adding an XML Descriptor

Now we need to add an XML file that will describe our live wallpaper to Android. To do this, let's create a new folder called xml in the /res folder, and inside that new folder, create a new file called wallpaper.xml with the following contents:

LiveWallpaper/res/xml/wallpaper.xml
```
<?xml version="1.0" encoding="utf-8"?>
<wallpaper xmlns:android="http://schemas.android.com/apk/res/android"
    android:thumbnail="@drawable/ic_wallpaper" />
```

This XML file gives Android additional info about our live wallpaper, such as what icon should be displayed in the list of live wallpapers. The ic_wallpaper drawable can be downloaded from this book's website and placed in /res/drawable-xhdpi.[2]

Updating the Android Manifest and Excluding from Unsupported Devices

We just need to make a couple of changes to AndroidManifest.xml, and then we'll be able to test out our new live wallpaper! Open up AndroidManifest.xml and add the following after <uses-sdk>:

LiveWallpaper/AndroidManifest.xml
```
<uses-feature android:name="android.software.live_wallpaper" />
<uses-feature android:glEsVersion="0x00020000" android:required="true" />
```

These tags let Android know that this application contains a live wallpaper and that it also requires OpenGL ES 2.0 or greater. App stores like Google Play use these tags to filter search results and to hide applications from unsupported devices.

We also need to add a reference to the live wallpaper service. Let's add the following inside the <application> tag, after the <activity> tag:

LiveWallpaper/AndroidManifest.xml
```
<service
    android:name=".wallpaper.GLWallpaperService"
    android:label="@string/app_name"
    android:permission="android.permission.BIND_WALLPAPER" >
    <intent-filter>
        <action android:name="android.service.wallpaper.WallpaperService" />
```

---

2. http://pragprog.com/book/kbogla/

```
    </intent-filter>
    <meta-data
        android:name="android.service.wallpaper"
        android:resource="@xml/wallpaper" />
</service>
```

When our application is installed on a device, this <service> tag and its contents tell Android that GLWallpaperService is a live wallpaper service, and that it can retrieve additional info about that service from /res/xml/wallpaper.xml. Once an application has been released to the market, the android:name= of the <service> should not be changed because changing it will cause the live wallpaper to be reset when the app is upgraded.[3]

Trying Out the New Live Wallpaper

Now that we've completed the implementation, let's build and run the app and see things in action. When we run the application from Eclipse, our activity opens by default. We want to check out the live wallpaper instead, so let's follow these steps to add our new live wallpaper to the home screen:

1. First head to your device's home screen, and then press and hold an empty part of the screen until a menu appears.

2. Select 'Live Wallpapers', and then select our live wallpaper from the list that appears.

3. Select 'Set wallpaper'. You should then see the live wallpaper appear on your home screen, as we saw in Figure 70, *Our live wallpaper, running on the home screen*, on page 276.

Figure 71, *Steps to add a live wallpaper*, on page 282 shows the sequence of these steps.

Try switching between home screens, go to the app drawer (the list of all of your installed applications), and then head back to the home screen and see what happens! What do you notice about the performance and the behavior?

Scrolling the Background Along with the Home Screen

The first thing you might have noticed is that the live wallpaper doesn't move when we swipe back and forth between different pages on the home screen. We can implement this by implementing the onOffsetsChanged() method in GLEngine as follows:[4]

---

3. http://android-developers.blogspot.ca/2011/06/things-that-cannot-change.html

4. http://developer.android.com/reference/android/service/wallpaper/WallpaperService.Engine.html#onOff-setsChanged(float, float, float, float, int, int)

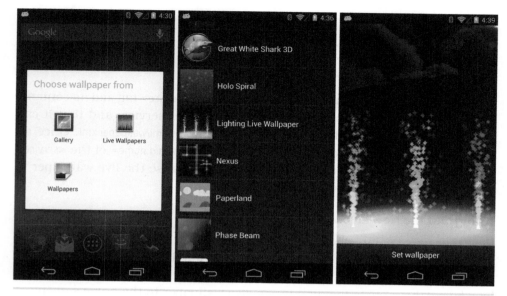

Figure 71—Steps to add a live wallpaper

LiveWallpaper/src/com/particles/android/wallpaper/GLWallpaperService.java
```java
@Override
public void onOffsetsChanged(final float xOffset, final float yOffset,
    float xOffsetStep, float yOffsetStep, int xPixelOffset, int yPixelOffset) {
    glSurfaceView.queueEvent(new Runnable() {
        @Override
        public void run() {
            particlesRenderer.handleOffsetsChanged(xOffset, yOffset);
        }
    });
}
```

When the user scrolls the home screen, onOffsetsChanged() will be called with *x* and *y* offsets, each between 0 and 1. We'll pass these offsets on to the renderer, and in the renderer, we'll call handleOffsetsChanged() and use these offsets to move the scene. This method hasn't been implemented yet, so we'll do that soon.

First, pull out particlesRenderer from onCreate() into a member variable of GLEngine so that we can access it from onOffsetsChanged(). Once that's done, let's switch to ParticlesRenderer and add a couple of new member variables to hold the offsets:

LiveWallpaper/src/com/particles/android/ParticlesRenderer.java
```java
private float xOffset, yOffset;
```

Let's add the implementation for handleOffsetsChanged():

LiveWallpaper/src/com/particles/android/ParticlesRenderer.java

```
public void handleOffsetsChanged(float xOffset, float yOffset) {
    // Offsets range from 0 to 1.
    this.xOffset = (xOffset - 0.5f) * 2.5f;
    this.yOffset = (yOffset - 0.5f) * 2.5f;
    updateViewMatrices();
}
```

When handleOffsetsChanged() gets called, we'll adjust the offsets so that they range from -2.5 to +2.5 instead of 0 to 1, so that we'll scroll from around the left particle fountain to around the right particle fountain. Let's use these offsets to update the view matrix by adjusting the call to translateM() inside of update-ViewMatrices(), as follows:

LiveWallpaper/src/com/particles/android/ParticlesRenderer.java

```
translateM(viewMatrix, 0, 0 - xOffset, -1.5f - yOffset, -5f);
```

We can think of translateM() as moving the entire scene from side to side, so when the user moves left on the home screen, we want our viewpoint to move left as well, which means that we want the entire scene to move *right*. We do that here by subtracting xOffset and yOffset from the x and y parts of the translateM() call.

Give the live wallpaper another shot, and try switching between different home screens. You should now see the background and the particle fountains move as well.

14.2 Playing Nicely with the Rest of the System

Users tend to have fairly high expectations of a live wallpaper—not only does it need to look great on their home screen, but it also needs to be frugal with the device's resources. People tend to get pretty upset if a live wallpaper drains half of their battery in an hour or if it lags their device. They also expect a live wallpaper to stop consuming the battery when it gets sent to the background and quickly start back up when they return to the home screen.

Limiting the Frame Rate

By default, Android will ask OpenGL to render the frames in line with the display refresh rate, usually at around 60 frames per second. This can chew through battery power pretty quickly, so to reduce the impact on the battery and on system performance, we can add a frame rate limiter to render fewer frames per second and consume less battery. Let's return to ParticlesRenderer and add a new member variable to the top of the class:

LiveWallpaper/src/com/particles/android/ParticlesRenderer.java
```java
private long frameStartTimeMs;
```

This variable will store the elapsed time in milliseconds between each frame. Let's modify the beginning of onDrawFrame() as follows:

LiveWallpaper/src/com/particles/android/ParticlesRenderer.java
```java
@Override
public void onDrawFrame(GL10 glUnused) {
    limitFrameRate(24);
```

Each time we render a new frame, we'll call limitFrameRate() to limit the frame rate to 24 frames per second. Let's add the definition for this new method:

LiveWallpaper/src/com/particles/android/ParticlesRenderer.java
```java
private void limitFrameRate(int framesPerSecond) {
    long elapsedFrameTimeMs = SystemClock.elapsedRealtime() - frameStartTimeMs;
    long expectedFrameTimeMs = 1000 / framesPerSecond;
    long timeToSleepMs = expectedFrameTimeMs - elapsedFrameTimeMs;

    if (timeToSleepMs > 0) {
        SystemClock.sleep(timeToSleepMs);
    }
    frameStartTimeMs = SystemClock.elapsedRealtime();
}
```

When we call this method, we first calculate how much time has elapsed since the last frame was rendered, and then we calculate how much time we have left before we need to render the next frame. We then pause the thread for that length of time so that we slow things down to the requested frame rate.

For example, let's say that normally a frame renders in 20 milliseconds, which is 50 frames per second, and we want to slow each frame down to 40 milliseconds, or 25 frames per second. When we call limitFrameRate(25) from onDrawFrame(), we'll find that elapsedFrameTimeMs is around 20 milliseconds, and since we want to slow things down to 25 frames per second, we'll have an expectedFrameTimeMs of 40 milliseconds. Once we subtract the elapsed frame time from the expected frame time, we'll have a timeToSleepMs of 20 milliseconds, and then we'll call SystemClock.sleep(timeToSleepMs) to sleep until it's time to draw the next frame.

To log the actual frame rate, let's add a constant and two more member variables to the class:

LiveWallpaper/src/com/particles/android/ParticlesRenderer.java
```java
private static final String TAG = "ParticlesRenderer";
private long startTimeMs;
private int frameCount;
```

We'll log the frame rate by calling a new method called logFrameRate() from the beginning of onDrawFrame(), just after the call to limitFrameRate():

LiveWallpaper/src/com/particles/android/ParticlesRenderer.java

```
@Override
public void onDrawFrame(GL10 glUnused) {
    limitFrameRate(24);
    logFrameRate();
```

Now we just need to add in the definition for logFrameRate():

LiveWallpaper/src/com/particles/android/ParticlesRenderer.java

```
private void logFrameRate() {
    if (LoggerConfig.ON) {
        long elapsedRealtimeMs = SystemClock.elapsedRealtime();
        double elapsedSeconds = (elapsedRealtimeMs - startTimeMs) / 1000.0;

        if (elapsedSeconds >= 1.0) {
            Log.v(TAG, frameCount / elapsedSeconds + "fps");
            startTimeMs = SystemClock.elapsedRealtime();
            frameCount = 0;
        }
        frameCount++;
    }
}
```

This method will measure and log the frame count for each elapsed second. Try it out and see what frame rate you end up with.

Preserving the EGL Context

You may have noticed that when we move away from the home screen and return to it later, the scene is reloaded and the particles reinitialized, often with a noticeable delay. This happens because when we pause the GLSurfaceView, it releases all of the OpenGL resources by default, and when we resume it later, our surface is recreated and onSurfaceCreated() is called again, requiring us to reload all of the data.

Behind the scenes, GLSurfaceView is actually using an API called the EGL Native Platform Graphics Interface.[5] When we initialize OpenGL by using a GLSurfaceView, an EGL context is created, and all of the textures, buffers, and other resources that OpenGL might use are linked to this context. These contexts are a limited resource on older devices, so our GLSurfaceView will normally release the context and flush all of OpenGL's resources whenever we ask it to pause.

---

5. http://www.khronos.org/egl

Many newer devices can afford to keep multiple contexts around, and starting with Android 3.0 Honeycomb, we can preserve the EGL context by calling GLSurfaceView.setPreserveEGLContextOnPause(true). If the context can be preserved, then our live wallpaper will be able to resume immediately without having to reload all of the OpenGL data.

Let's update the onCreate() method of GLWallpaperService.GLEngine by adding the following code just after the call to glSurfaceView.setEGLContextClientVersion():

LiveWallpaper/src/com/particles/android/wallpaper/GLWallpaperService.java
```
if (Build.VERSION.SDK_INT >= Build.VERSION_CODES.HONEYCOMB) {
    glSurfaceView.setPreserveEGLContextOnPause(true);
}
```

This code first checks that the current version of Android is Honeycomb or later, and then we ask the GLSurfaceView to preserve the EGL context on pause. Even if this code might run on an earlier version of Android, we don't need to use Java reflection to make the method call as long as we wrap the code with a version check.

Give the live wallpaper another shot, and try switching to the app drawer and then returning to the home screen. You should now find that the wallpaper resumes much more quickly and the particles don't get reset.

14.3 A Review

Congratulations on completing another project and on creating your first live wallpaper! We learned how to put our particle scene onto the home screen, and we also took a look at how to reduce resource and battery usage by reducing the frame rate while keeping things efficient by holding onto the EGL context between pauses and resumes.

As we built up this project, we also covered many core aspects of OpenGL, such as how to use vertex and index buffers, how to do hidden surface removal with a depth buffer, and how to add effects by using blending and lighting techniques. You won't always need to use all of these techniques, and indeed, many of the most popular games on the Android market get away with using simple and cute 2D graphics. However, now that you have these techniques at hand, you have a base from which you can learn more, as well as the flexibility and tools to bring your artistic visions to life.

14.4 Exercises

We've covered a lot of the basics of live wallpapers in this chapter, but there's still a lot of low-hanging fruit left for us to pick. Let's start off with the following exercises:

- To optimize performance, let's change the way we initialize the particle system and reduce the total particle count from 10,000 to something a lot lower. Once that's done, let's optimize things further by removing particles that fall below the terrain. One way you can do this is by swapping each particle to be removed with the last good active particle in the array.

  When you make these changes, try updating the behavior so that the particle system doesn't get reset if onSurfaceCreated() is called a second time.

- Android live wallpapers support an additional settings activity, which can be configured by adding an android:settingsActivity= attribute to the <wallpaper> tag in /res/xml/wallpaper.xml. Add a settings screen with an easy way of altering the live wallpaper's frame rendering rate per second.[6]

- New to Android 4.2 Jelly Bean, Android also supports Daydreams, interactive screen savers that take over when the device is idle and charging. Try implementing the same OpenGL scene as a Daydream.[7]

Another way of implementing a live wallpaper with OpenGL is by reimplementing much of GLSurfaceView rather than by subclassing it. You can learn more about this approach and implement it by following the linked resources.[8]

When you're ready, let's head over to the next chapter and take the next step.

---

6. http://www.learnopengles.com/how-to-use-opengl-es-2-in-an-android-live-wallpaper/

7. http://android-developers.blogspot.ca/2012/12/daydream-interactive-screen-savers.html

8. http://www.rbgrn.net/content/354-glsurfaceview-adapted-3d-live-wallpapers, https://github.com/GLWallpaperService/GLWallpaperService/blob/master/GLWallpaperService/src/net/rbgrn/android/glwallpaperservice/GLWallpaperService.java, and http://www.learnopengles.com/how-to-use-opengl-es-2-in-an-android-live-wallpaper/.

CHAPTER 15

Taking the Next Step

We've finally made it to the last chapter! To start off, we'll take a look at a couple of ways of expanding our reach beyond Android alone. We'll go over a couple of cross-platform frameworks and approaches that can help out with this, and we'll evaluate the pros and cons of each approach.

We'll also take some time to review some of the more advanced areas of OpenGL that go beyond what we've learned in this book, including multitexturing, anisotropic filtering, and antialiasing (AA), as well as techniques that can be particularly useful in 2D games and applications, such as billboarding and texture atlasing. We'll also take a quick look at what's coming down the pipeline in OpenGL ES 3.0.

As we review the material, you can also follow a sample implementation of some of these techniques by downloading this book's code files and importing the project in the TakingTheNextStep folder.[1]

15.1 Looking Toward Other Platforms

If you're thinking about moving beyond Android some day and expanding your reach, then you'll definitely want to give some thought to portability and cross-platform code. OpenGL ES 2 is well supported on many major platforms, including iOS and the Web via WebGL; however, these other platforms are often built around other programming languages. On iOS, Objective C is the primary development language, and on the Web, JavaScript is the primary development language.

Since rewriting code for each platform tends to take more resources, cross-platform development can have a lot of appeal. On one end of the spectrum, you have proprietary environments that use the same language on all

---

1. http://pragprog.com/book/kbogla/

platforms and abstract everything away from you; on the other end of the spectrum, you can do everything yourself and build up your own framework. Occupying the middle ground are open source frameworks such as libgdx (created by Mario Zechner) and Cocos2d-x (founded by Zhe Wang), which allow you to support multiple platforms without rewriting too much of the code.[2]

When thinking about cross-platform development, there are a couple of important points to keep in mind: first, you want to make sure that it doesn't take more work than just maintaining a separate code base for each platform; and second, you also want to avoid falling into the trap of tailoring everything to the lowest common denominator, leading to a bad experience on all platforms.

We'll take a quick look at how you can use either libgdx or Cocos2d-x as a framework for your code and the pros and cons of each approach.

Building upon Java by Using Libgdx

Libgdx is a popular open source game development library that uses Java and supports both OpenGL ES 1 and 2. In addition to great support for Android, it even supports other platforms by including a different back end for each platform and a translation layer to translate the Java code. It does this for the Web by using Google Web Toolkit to compile Java into JavaScript, and it does this for iOS by using a tool called ikvmc to compile Java into .NET intermediate language, which can then be turned into an iOS binary by using a .NET compiler such as Xamarin.iOS.

By using Java as the main programming language, you can avoid manual memory management, stack and heap corruption, undefined behavior, and other related issues that can come up when using another programming language such as C or C++. On the other hand, it will be more difficult to control the performance when garbage collection and multiple translation layers are involved.

Building on C and C++ by Using Cocos2d-x

Instead of using Java, you can also use C or C++ with compilers available for almost all platforms. Cocos2d-x is a popular game development framework that uses C++ and OpenGL ES 2 to target Android, iOS, and other platforms with a minimum of abstractions and translation layers; as the name hints, Cocos2d-x is also optimized for 2D games. Since C and C++ compile directly

---

2. https://code.google.com/p/libgdx/ and http://www.cocos2d-x.org/, respectively.

to machine code, this approach is often popular with game developers looking for the best performance and control (Java also has decent performance, but the Dalvik VM is not as good as desktop JVMs at producing fast JIT code).

One of the main downsides of this approach is that Android's support for C and C++ is definitely not as good as it is for Java, and then you're also opening up Pandora's box of stack and heap corruption, undefined behavior, and other subtle errors that can destabilize the program, though recent versions of GCC and Clang do have a lot of great diagnostics to help out with this. For now, C and C++ are also more difficult to port to the Web, though this may not always be the case: Google is helping to bring native languages to the Web with Native Client, and there are even compilers out there that can compile C++ into JavaScript, which can then run in a browser.

15.2 Learning About More Advanced Techniques

Now that we've made it this far, let's take some time to go over a few of the more advanced ways of rendering things in OpenGL.

Multitexturing

Back in Chapter 7, *Adding Detail with Textures*, on page 115, we learned that we can easily apply a texture by specifying a set of texture coordinates and by using a texture unit to pass in the actual texture. OpenGL ES 2.0 actually provides support for multiple texture units, with most GPUs supporting at least two of them. This can be used to blend between two textures to apply various effects. In the sample project, we use multitexturing to draw the terrain with a blend between a grassy texture at low elevations and a stony texture at higher elevations.

Anisotropic Filtering

In the same chapter, we also learned that OpenGL supports a few texture filtering modes, including nearest-neighbor and bilinear without mipmaps, and bilinear and trilinear with mipmaps. Enabling mipmapping increases both the performance and the quality, but one problem with standard mipmapping is that it's optimized for rendering textures head on rather than at an angle. If we look at the ground in the sample project, we can see that it gets excessively smeared with distance. We could always turn off mipmapping, but that both lowers performance and makes the far areas of the scene very jumpy and noisy.

We can often improve on the quality of textures at an angle by using *anisotropic filtering*, a type of texture filtering that takes the viewing angle into account. In the following figure, you can see an example of trilinear filtering versus 15x anisotropic filtering, the maximum supported on a Nexus 7's Tegra 3. With anisotropic filtering, textures at an oblique viewing angle can look much better with a lot less smearing; the trade-off is that performance may be reduced. Higher levels of anisotropic filtering will filter more oblique surfaces with improved quality.

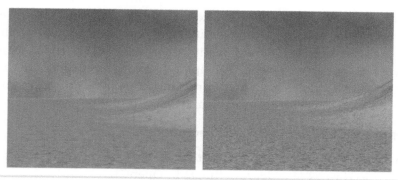

Figure 72—Trilinear filtering versus 15x anistotropic filtering

OpenGL leaves the actual implementation up to the hardware, and not all GPUs will support anisotropic filtering. In the sample project, you'll see how to check for support as well as how to enable the maximum amount of anisotropic filtering if it's supported.

Antialiasing

Antialiasing is a rendering technique that is used to reduce aliasing, which often manifests itself in the form of "jaggies" along the edges of triangles in a 3D scene.[3] There are many different ways of antialiasing a scene, and each method comes with its own pros and cons.

In the old days, applications would often antialias a scene by simply rendering the same scene several times in a row, with a slightly different perspective projection for each render. The antialias would be applied by blending these renders together. In OpenGL ES, some GPUs can antialias through OpenGL itself by using *multisample antialiasing*, and some NVIDIA chipsets also support *coverage antialiasing*. In the following figure, you can see an example of regular rendering versus NVIDIA's coverage antialiasing using the 2x coverage mode.

---

3.   http://en.wikipedia.org/wiki/Aliasing

Figure 73—Regular rendering versus NVIDIA's 2x coverage antialiasing

With the high resolutions and small pixels prevalent on mobile devices, antialiasing is not as important as it used to be on the desktop. Also, antialiasing can consume a lot of additional resources for a small gain in image quality. However, it can make sense in some applications, and in the sample project, we've adapted code from Google's Game Developers Conference (GDC) 2011 demo (a great sample of different OpenGL ES 2 techniques) to show you how to enable antialiasing in your own projects (Figure 74, *A slightly modified GDC 11 demo*, on page 294).[4]

Billboarding and Other 2D Techniques

In Chapter 10, *Spicing Things Up with Particles*, on page 191, we learned how to render particles as 2D textures by using point sprites. *Billboarding* is another way of rendering a 2D sprite in a 3D scene, and the way that it works is by drawing a rectangular quad of two triangles, rendering a texture on this quad with transparent areas, and orienting this quad so that it always faces the camera no matter which direction it's facing. This can work well for the same sort of things that we'd use point sprites for, with the advantage of there being no point size limit.

For some other things, like grass, a better technique is to use the same 2D quads, but instead of changing their orientation so that they always face the camera, we instead keep their orientation fixed, and we use several of them together and position them in ways so that they overlap each other. This can be seen to great effect in games like Assassin's Creed 3 when traveling in the forested areas. This technique can be a little heavy for today's mobile phones and tablets, but as devices like the Ouya (an Android-based game console) take off, we can expect to see these sorts of techniques used more and more often.

---

4.   https://code.google.com/p/gdc2011-android-opengl/

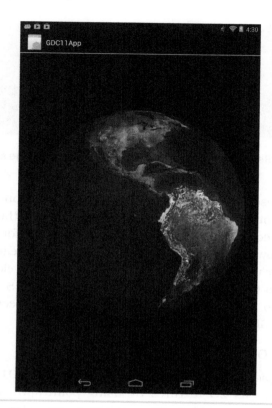

Figure 74—A slightly modified GDC 11 demo

Using a Texture Atlas

Switching textures can be expensive, so why not put a bunch of different textures together into one giant texture and then use different parts of this texture for different objects? This giant texture is known as a *texture atlas*, and using one can lead to a performance boost for certain types of games, especially 2D sprite-based and tile-based games. Using a texture atlas can also boost performance for in-game custom font rendering.

Texture atlases do have a few downsides: mipmaps can blend together data from adjacent subtextures, and sometimes fitting all of the textures together in the texture atlas can be a pain. There are tools that can help out with this, and libgdx, one of the cross-platform frameworks that we talked about back in *Building upon Java by Using Libgdx*, on page 290, has one of these tools built in.[5]

---

5.   https://code.google.com/p/libgdx/wiki/TexturePacker

Introducing OpenGL ES 3.0

In August 2012, the Khronos Group announced the release of the OpenGL ES 3.0 specification, an iterative improvement building on OpenGL ES 2.0. The new specification hasn't had time to roll out and doesn't appear on Android's device dashboard at the moment, but sooner or later, devices will start supporting 3.0. The following are some of the new features that we can expect:[6]

- The texturing has been greatly improved, with support for many new texture types and features. High quality ETC2/EAC texture compression is now built in as a standard feature, and cube maps are now guaranteed to be seamless.[7]

- The rendering pipeline now supports multiple rendering targets as well as advanced features such as occlusion queries and instanced rendering.

- The specification includes an expanded set of required texture and buffer formats, reducing the differences between different implementations.

These new features improve the capabilities of OpenGL ES 2, bringing in some advanced capabilities and making it easier for developers to port code from desktop OpenGL. Your device may even currently support some of these features (such as seamless cube mapping), either by default or as an OpenGL extension.

15.3 Sharing Your Artistic Vision with the World

There's a lot more that we haven't covered. There are all kinds of advanced effects that can be done through the power of OpenGL ES 2, such as specular lighting, fog, reflections, shadows, and various post-processing effects like high dynamic range lighting and depth of field.

We don't currently see too many of these more advanced effects in the mobile world, in part because most of the GPUs out there aren't yet powerful enough, and also in part because they can be overkill for your typical side scroller or 3D running game. This will change over time, as we see Android increasingly used in other areas such as game consoles and also as the phones and tablets themselves become more and more powerful. OpenGL ES 2 brings a lot of power to the table, and we've only scratched the surface of what's truly possible.

---

6. http://www.khronos.org/news/press/khronos-releases-opengl-es-3.0-specification
7. http://en.wikipedia.org/wiki/Ericsson_Texture_Compression#ETC2_and_EAC

We've now reached the end of our adventure together. OpenGL ES 2 is a powerful graphics library with a lot of potential, and you now have the tools to draw on some of that potential. As you continue the journey on your own, stay adventurous, stay curious, and share your artistic vision with the world.

The Matrix Math Behind the Projections

There are two main types of projections in OpenGL: orthographic and perspective. Both projections are used for transforming coordinates from a virtual world space into normalized device coordinates ranging from -1 to 1 on each axis. The projection defines what will be visible and how big it will appear.

Before we continue, you might want to give Section 5.3, *Linear Algebra 101*, on page 83, another read.

A1.1 The Math Behind Orthographic Projections

We'll start off with orthographic projections, as they're easier to understand. An orthographic projection maps part of our 3D world onto the screen, and it does so in a way such that everything appears the same size, no matter how near or far it is. For this reason, this type of projection is great for doing 2D games and art.

Creating an Identity Orthographic Projection

The following is a basic definition of an orthographic projection matrix:

$$
\begin{bmatrix}
\dfrac{2}{\text{right}-\text{left}} & 0 & 0 & -\dfrac{\text{right}+\text{left}}{\text{right}-\text{left}} \\
0 & \dfrac{2}{\text{top}-\text{bottom}} & 0 & -\dfrac{\text{top}+\text{bottom}}{\text{top}-\text{bottom}} \\
0 & 0 & \dfrac{-2}{\text{far}-\text{near}} & -\dfrac{\text{far}+\text{near}}{\text{far}-\text{near}} \\
0 & 0 & 0 & 1
\end{bmatrix}
$$

Given this matrix, all coordinates between left and right, bottom and top, and near and far will be mapped into normalized device coordinates, and anything within this range will be visible on the screen.

Let's take a look at this in action: for our first example, we'll create an identity orthographic projection. Let's build the matrix by passing in -1 for left, bottom, and near, and +1 for right, top, and far. A basic substitution would give us the following matrix:

$$\begin{bmatrix} \dfrac{2}{1--1} & 0 & 0 & -\dfrac{1+-1}{1--1} \\ 0 & \dfrac{2}{1--1} & 0 & -\dfrac{1+-1}{1--1} \\ 0 & 0 & \dfrac{-2}{1--1} & -\dfrac{1+-1}{1--1} \\ 0 & 0 & 0 & 1 \end{bmatrix}$$

Simplifying the negations gives us the following:

$$\begin{bmatrix} \dfrac{2}{1+1} & 0 & 0 & -\dfrac{1-1}{1+1} \\ 0 & \dfrac{2}{1+1} & 0 & -\dfrac{1-1}{1+1} \\ 0 & 0 & \dfrac{-2}{1+1} & -\dfrac{1-1}{1+1} \\ 0 & 0 & 0 & 1 \end{bmatrix}$$

The next step is to add and subtract the terms together:

$$\begin{bmatrix} \dfrac{2}{2} & 0 & 0 & -\dfrac{0}{2} \\ 0 & \dfrac{2}{2} & 0 & -\dfrac{0}{2} \\ 0 & 0 & \dfrac{-2}{2} & -\dfrac{0}{2} \\ 0 & 0 & 0 & 1 \end{bmatrix}$$

Finally, we evaluate the fractions and end up with the final matrix:

$$\begin{bmatrix} 1 & 0 & 0 & 0 \\ 0 & 1 & 0 & 0 \\ 0 & 0 & -1 & 0 \\ 0 & 0 & 0 & 1 \end{bmatrix}$$

It looks almost exactly like the identity matrix! This happens because normalized device coordinates range from -1 to 1 on each axis, so when we also pass in -1 and 1 as our ranges, we are essentially asking for an orthographic projection that leaves its coordinates unchanged, just like an identity matrix. The main difference is that the z-axis is inverted. This is entirely due to convention, as explained in *Left-Handed and Right-Handed Coordinate Systems*, on page 88.

Creating a Regular Orthographic Projection

For our next example, let's create an orthographic projection that will actually do something. What if we don't like negative numbers and we want to specify all of our coordinates in the range [0, 1] instead of [-1, 1]? This means that left, bottom, and near will be 0, and right, top, and far will be 1.

When we call orthoM(), we are saying that we want a matrix that will map [0, 1] onto the range [-1, 1] for the x, y, and z components. Here's what the initial matrix would look like:

$$\begin{bmatrix} \dfrac{2}{1-0} & 0 & 0 & -\dfrac{1+0}{1-0} \\ 0 & \dfrac{2}{1-0} & 0 & -\dfrac{1+0}{1-0} \\ 0 & 0 & \dfrac{-2}{1-0} & -\dfrac{1+0}{1-0} \\ 0 & 0 & 0 & 1 \end{bmatrix}$$

We won't go through all of the simplification steps this time. Let's just look at the final result:

$$\begin{bmatrix} 2 & 0 & 0 & -1 \\ 0 & 2 & 0 & -1 \\ 0 & 0 & -2 & -1 \\ 0 & 0 & 0 & 1 \end{bmatrix}$$

To "prove" that this matrix will indeed transform a coordinate in the range [0, 1] to the range [-1, 1] (remembering the special inversion of the z-axis), let's try it out with a few different vectors. First we'll start with a vector at the minimum range, with all components at 0:

$$\begin{bmatrix} 2 & 0 & 0 & -1 \\ 0 & 2 & 0 & -1 \\ 0 & 0 & -2 & -1 \\ 0 & 0 & 0 & 1 \end{bmatrix} \begin{bmatrix} 0 \\ 0 \\ 0 \\ 1 \end{bmatrix} = \begin{bmatrix} -1 \\ -1 \\ -1 \\ 1 \end{bmatrix}$$

As expected, everything maps to -1 in normalized device coordinates. Now we'll try a vector in the middle:

$$\begin{bmatrix} 2 & 0 & 0 & -1 \\ 0 & 2 & 0 & -1 \\ 0 & 0 & -2 & -1 \\ 0 & 0 & 0 & 1 \end{bmatrix} \begin{bmatrix} 0.5 \\ 0.5 \\ -0.5 \\ 1 \end{bmatrix} = \begin{bmatrix} 0 \\ 0 \\ 0 \\ 1 \end{bmatrix}$$

The result is also in the middle in normalized device coordinates, with x, y, and z all set to zero. Now let's try a vector at the maximum range of 1:

$$\begin{bmatrix} 2 & 0 & 0 & -1 \\ 0 & 2 & 0 & -1 \\ 0 & 0 & -2 & -1 \\ 0 & 0 & 0 & 1 \end{bmatrix} \begin{bmatrix} 1 \\ 1 \\ -1 \\ 1 \end{bmatrix} = \begin{bmatrix} 1 \\ 1 \\ 1 \\ 1 \end{bmatrix}$$

This time, everything is also at the maximum range in normalized device coordinates.

Note that before multiplying it with the matrix, we specified a negative z in the vector instead of a positive z; even though we specified *near* as 0 and *far* as 1, we actually have to pass in a range from 0 to -1. This is just us adjusting for the inverted z-axis, as described in *Left-Handed and Right-Handed Coordinate Systems*, on page 88.

A1.2 The Math Behind Perspective Projections

Perspective projections work somewhat differently. They also map part of the virtual world onto the screen, but they do so by using perspective: the further away something is, the smaller it will appear on the screen. The projection matrix can't do this by itself, so it uses a fourth component, w, in conjunction with the perspective divide. You can read more in *Perspective Division*, on page 97.

The following is a very basic perspective projection matrix. This matrix assumes a right-handed coordinate space (see *Left-Handed and Right-Handed Coordinate Systems*, on page 88), with the near plane beginning at a *z* of -1. As a quick exercise, see if you can guess where the far end lies, remembering that OpenGL will divide each component by *w*:

$$
\begin{bmatrix}
1 & 0 & 0 & 0 \\
0 & 1 & 0 & 0 \\
0 & 0 & -1 & -2 \\
0 & 0 & -1 & 0
\end{bmatrix}
$$

Let's take a look at what's happening in this matrix:

- The first two rows of this matrix simply copy over the *x* and *y* components without modifying them.

- The third row of this matrix copies over the *z* component, inverting it at the same time. The -2 in the fourth column will be multiplied with a vertex's *w*, which defaults to 1, so this row of the matrix ends up setting the final *z* to *-1z - 2*. For example, a *z* of -1 will be set to -1, a *z* of -2 will be set to 0, a *z* of -3 will be set to 1, and so on.

  Why do we use -2 and not some other number? With a -1 in the third column, a -2 in the fourth column is simply the number that will map the near plane of the frustum to the near plane in normalized device coordinates (-1 will map to -1); and since the same *z* of -1 will create a *w* of 1, the *z* value will remain -1 after the perspective divide.

  As another exercise, the mathematically inclined may wish to derive a formal proof of this. Songho.ca has an excellent write-up on how these values can be derived.[1] However, a formal proof is not required to understand how to use a projection matrix.

- The fourth row sets the final *w* to the negative *z*. Once OpenGL does the perspective divide, this will have the effect of shrinking objects that are further away.

Let's see what happens when we multiply this matrix with a point on the near end of the frustum:

---

1. http://www.songho.ca/opengl/gl_projectionmatrix.html

$$\begin{bmatrix} 1 & 0 & 0 & 0 \\ 0 & 1 & 0 & 0 \\ 0 & 0 & -1 & -2 \\ 0 & 0 & -1 & 0 \end{bmatrix} \begin{bmatrix} -1 \\ -1 \\ -1 \\ 1 \end{bmatrix} = \begin{bmatrix} -1 \\ -1 \\ -1 \\ 1 \end{bmatrix}$$

With a z of -1, the result has a z of -1 and a w of 1. Let's take a look at two more points, each further away than the previous one:

$$\begin{bmatrix} 1 & 0 & 0 & 0 \\ 0 & 1 & 0 & 0 \\ 0 & 0 & -1 & -2 \\ 0 & 0 & -1 & 0 \end{bmatrix} \begin{bmatrix} -1 \\ -1 \\ -2 \\ 1 \end{bmatrix} = \begin{bmatrix} -1 \\ -1 \\ 0 \\ 2 \end{bmatrix}$$

$$\begin{bmatrix} 1 & 0 & 0 & 0 \\ 0 & 1 & 0 & 0 \\ 0 & 0 & -1 & -2 \\ 0 & 0 & -1 & 0 \end{bmatrix} \begin{bmatrix} -1 \\ -1 \\ -3 \\ 1 \end{bmatrix} = \begin{bmatrix} -1 \\ -1 \\ 1 \\ 3 \end{bmatrix}$$

As the point gets further away, both z and w get larger and larger.

Dividing by W

We've explored the first part of the magic of perspective projection: defining a matrix that will create a w value that increases as distance increases. There's another step remaining, however: the perspective divide. After OpenGL divides each component by w, we'll end up with the following results:

$$\begin{bmatrix} -1 \\ -1 \\ -1 \\ 1 \end{bmatrix} = \begin{bmatrix} -1/1 \\ -1/1 \\ -1/1 \end{bmatrix} = \begin{bmatrix} -1 \\ -1 \\ -1 \end{bmatrix}$$

$$\begin{bmatrix} -1 \\ -1 \\ 0 \\ 2 \end{bmatrix} = \begin{bmatrix} -1/2 \\ -1/2 \\ 0/2 \end{bmatrix} = \begin{bmatrix} -0.5 \\ -0.5 \\ 0 \end{bmatrix}$$

$$\begin{bmatrix} -1 \\ -1 \\ 1 \\ 3 \end{bmatrix} = \begin{bmatrix} -1/3 \\ -1/3 \\ 1/3 \end{bmatrix} = \begin{bmatrix} -0.3\bar{3} \\ -0.3\bar{3} \\ 0.3\bar{3} \end{bmatrix}$$

Let's try this out with some points that are even further away. The following is a point at a z of -100:

$$\begin{bmatrix} 1 & 0 & 0 & 0 \\ 0 & 1 & 0 & 0 \\ 0 & 0 & -1 & -2 \\ 0 & 0 & -1 & 0 \end{bmatrix} \begin{bmatrix} -1 \\ -1 \\ -100 \\ 1 \end{bmatrix} = \begin{bmatrix} -1 \\ -1 \\ 98 \\ 100 \end{bmatrix} = \begin{bmatrix} -1/100 \\ -1/100 \\ 98/100 \end{bmatrix} = \begin{bmatrix} -0.01 \\ -0.01 \\ 0.98 \end{bmatrix}$$

Here is a point at a z of -10,000:

$$\begin{bmatrix} 1 & 0 & 0 & 0 \\ 0 & 1 & 0 & 0 \\ 0 & 0 & -1 & -2 \\ 0 & 0 & -1 & 0 \end{bmatrix} \begin{bmatrix} -1 \\ -1 \\ -10000 \\ 1 \end{bmatrix} = \begin{bmatrix} -1 \\ -1 \\ 9998 \\ 10000 \end{bmatrix} = \begin{bmatrix} -1/10000 \\ -1/10000 \\ 9998/10000 \end{bmatrix} = \begin{bmatrix} -0.0001 \\ -0.0001 \\ 0.9998 \end{bmatrix}$$

With this type of projection matrix, the far end of the frustum actually lies at infinity. Eric Lengyel refers to this as an "infinite projection matrix."[2] No matter how far away the z, it will approach but not quite match the far plane of 1 in normalized device coordinates within the limits of the hardware's precision.

You might also have noticed that after OpenGL divides everything by w, the relationship between our input z and our output z is no longer linear. Going from an input z of -1 to -2 increases the output z from -1 to 0, but going from an input z of -10,000 to -20,000 only has a very small effect on the output z. This nonlinear relationship has important implications when it comes to rendering objects at different distances in our scene, which we cover in more detail in *Removing Hidden Surfaces with the Depth Buffer*, on page 245.

2. http://www.terathon.com/gdc07_lengyel.pdf.

Debugging

As we develop our OpenGL applications, sooner or later we'll run into a strange issue that needs to be debugged. Maybe our objects don't get rendered as we expected, or maybe our app crashes with a segmentation fault.[1] In this appendix, you'll be introduced to a few different ways of troubleshooting these issues, as well as to some of the common pitfalls to watch out for.

A2.1 Debugging with glGetError

With OpenGL, one of the first ways to troubleshoot a problem is by checking if we made a call or passed in an argument that OpenGL didn't like. We can do this by calling glGetError() to get the state of OpenGL's error flags. Here are some of the most common error codes:

GL_INVALID_ENUM

> We passed in a value to a function that doesn't accept that value. For example, maybe we passed in GL_FLOAT to glEnable() or something else that doesn't make sense for that function.

GL_INVALID_VALUE

> One of the numeric arguments we passed in to a function was out of range.

GL_INVALID_OPERATION

> We tried to perform an invalid operation for the given OpenGL state.

In addition to glGetError(), we also have more specific ways of looking for an error, such as the methods we learned about back in *Retrieving the Shader Info Log*, on page 42. To catch the errors close to where they occur, it's a good idea to call glGetError() often. Since more than one error flag can be recorded

---

1. http://en.wikipedia.org/wiki/Segmentation_fault

at a time, the OpenGL manual also recommends calling it in a loop until it returns GL_NO_ERROR.

Let's test this out with an example. Open up one of the projects from this book and add a call to glEnable(GL_TEXTURE_2D) at the beginning of onSurfaceCreated(). After the call to glEnable(), add another call to glGetError() and check the return value. When you run the program, you should see that glGetError() returns GL_INVALID_ENUM, since GL_TEXTURE_2D is not one of the constants accepted by glEnable() on OpenGL ES 2.0.

With OpenGL ES 1, we could ask our GLSurfaceView to wrap *every* call to OpenGL by giving us a wrapped interface in our renderer callback methods. Unfortunately, this doesn't work with OpenGL ES 2, since we're calling static methods directly on the GLES20 class. One way we can work around this is by creating our own wrapper class that wraps each OpenGL function and loops through glGetError() after each one. If we use that class and an OpenGL error occurs, we'll know about it pretty close to the source of that error.

A2.2 Using Tracer for OpenGL ES

Starting with Android 4.1, OpenGL applications can also be debugged with the Tracer for OpenGL ES tool.[2] This tool can capture the stream of OpenGL commands sent for each frame rendered, their execution time, and the OpenGL state for each frame. You can run the tracer by following these steps:

- Switch to the tracer perspective in Eclipse by selecting Window→Open Perspective→Other and then select Tracer for OpenGL ES.

- Click the trace capture button in the toolbar; it looks like the following image:

- A trace options window will appear, as seen in the following figure. Select the device or emulator instance to debug (keeping in mind that trace results will be more accurate and relevant on a device), enter the package name and the activity to launch, and then enter the destination for the trace file.

---

2. http://developer.android.com/tools/help/gltracer.html and http://www.teamblubee.com/2012/09/22/android-openggl-and-slow-rendering/.

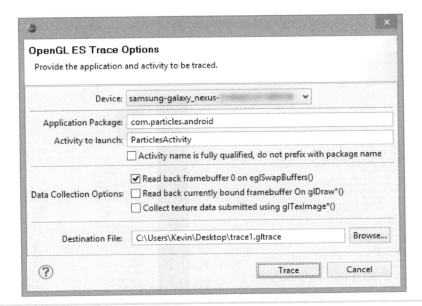

Figure 75—OpenGL ES trace options

Next you'll see a window with the trace in progress. Once you're done tracing, select Stop Tracing. You'll then see a detailed window appear with all of the trace information, as seen in Figure 76, *OpenGL ES trace results*, on page 308.

The trace results contain a frame selector to see all of the information for a given frame. Once a frame is selected, you'll be able to see a lot of details for that frame, including the list of OpenGL calls, the time each call took, a snapshot of the frame, the total time for each different type of OpenGL call, and the current OpenGL state. You may want to take the execution times with a grain of salt, as I've noticed that they can sometimes be greatly understated.

In addition to the OpenGL tracer that comes with the Android SDK, many GPU vendors also provide their own tools; for example, NVIDIA provides PerfHUD ES for Tegra GPUs,[3] and PowerVR provides PVRTrace for PowerVR GPUs.[4] These tools can often dive even deeper; for example, PerfHUD ES gives you detailed shader compilation info and lets you edit and recompile shaders in real time, and it even shows you how each frame gets drawn, step by step.[5]

---

3.   https://developer.nvidia.com/nvidia-perfhud-es

4.   http://www.imgtec.com/powervr/insider/pvrtrace.asp

5.   http://www.curious-creature.org/2012/12/01/android-performance-case-study/

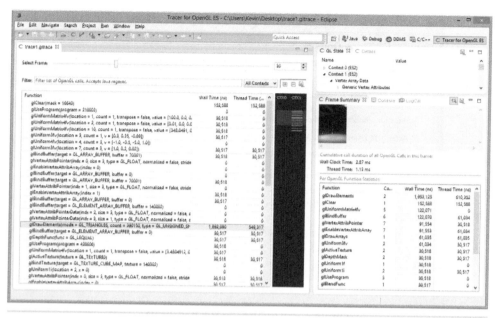

Figure 76—OpenGL ES trace results

     Joe asks:

Why Doesn't the Tracer Work for Me?

The tracer should work so long as your device is running Android 4.1 or later; however, if you have a Nexus device running Android 4.2.2, then unfortunately you may be running into a regression that breaks the tracer. If this happens to you, check out the linked bug reports, because the issue might be fixed by the time you read this.[a]

For now you can also work around this problem by downgrading your device to Android 4.1. To do this, you'll need to download a stock factory image for your Nexus device from the Google Developers website,[b] and then you'll need to follow a guide to flash your device with the stock factory image; the guide linked here should work for your Nexus device.[c] Please keep in mind that flashing a device isn't for the faint of heart, as you could void your warranty or turn your device into an expensive paperweight if something goes wrong.

a.   https://code.google.com/p/android/issues/detail?id=52446 and https://code.google.com/p/android/issues/detail?id=53426.

b.   https://developers.google.com/android/nexus/images

c.   http://forums.androidcentral.com/nexus-4-rooting-roms-hacks/223923-guide-nexus-4-factory-image-restore.html

A2.3 Pitfalls to Watch Out For

Sometimes the problem isn't obvious: glGetError() doesn't return anything unusual, and the traces appear fine. Other times, the app might blow up with a segmentation fault at an unexpected place, robbing us of the chance to put in a breakpoint and figure out what's going on. When these problems occur, we have to fall back to standard debugging techniques and narrow things down until we find the problem.[6]

One of the easiest methods to get wrong is glVertexAttribPointer() (see *Associating an Array of Vertex Data with an Attribute*, on page 49 for a refresher), and getting it wrong will often lead to strange display issues and segmentation faults. As an example, let's say that we have a vertex array for an object with a position attribute, a color attribute, and a normal attribute, with three floats per attribute, or nine floats in all. To bind to each attribute, we add the following code:

```
private static final int POSITION_COUNT = 3;
private static final int COLOR_COUNT = 3;
private static final int NORMAL_COUNT = 3;
private static final int STRIDE = POSITION_COUNT + COLOR_COUNT + NORMAL_COUNT;
```

≪body≫

```
floatBuffer.position(0);
glVertexAttribPointer(positionAttributeLocation, POSITION_COUNT,
        GL_FLOAT, true, STRIDE, floatBuffer);

floatBuffer.position(POSITION_COUNT);
glVertexAttribPointer(colorAttributeLocation, COLOR_COUNT,
        GL_FLOAT, false, STRIDE, floatBuffer);

floatBuffer.position(COLOR_COUNT);
glVertexAttribPointer(normalAttributeLocation, NORMAL_COUNT,
        GL_SHORT, false, STRIDE, floatBuffer);
```

Can you spot the bugs? Here are a couple:

- We forgot to specify the stride in terms of bytes.

- When we set the float buffer starting position for the normals, we're mistakenly setting it to COLOR_COUNT, which is 3. What we really want to be doing is setting it to POSITION_COUNT + COLOR_COUNT, since the normals start at the sixth float.

---

6. http://blog.regehr.org/archives/849

What else do you see? There are many other places where this can also go wrong; for example, we could call floatBuffer.position(COLOR_COUNT * BYTES_PER_FLOAT), which wouldn't make sense since the argument there should be in terms of floats, not bytes. It also doesn't make sense to pass in GL_SHORT when we meant to pass in GL_FLOAT. When something goes wrong, one of the first things you should check is your calls to glVertexAttribPointer().

Here are some other ideas for tackling a few of the more common pitfalls that you may run across:

- Check that your shaders compile and that there are no warning or error messages in the shader log. Sometimes even if a shader compiles fine, the calculations might be incorrect or useless. You can narrow down the problem by simplifying the shader and replacing calculations with hard-coded values and then giving the app another run to see how things look.

  Another way of debugging a shader is by checking for a condition and then drawing the fragment one color if the condition is true and another color if the condition is false.

- It's also easy to forget to unbind from an OpenGL object or to reset a particular state. For example, if adding a call to glBindBuffer(GL_ARRAY_BUFFER, 0) fixes the problem, then you probably forgot to unbind from a vertex buffer object. You can then work backward from there and find the place where that call is supposed to go.

- If an object doesn't display, sometimes you can figure out what's going on by disabling depth testing or culling. If it shows up, then the problem might be its position in the scene, or it might be the way that culling is configured or the object's triangle winding order (see *Culling*, on page 249).

- Some GPUs won't display a texture if its dimensions are not a power of two (see Section 7.1, *Understanding Textures*, on page 116). Sometimes the textures might also turn completely black or white if you use an image format that has an alpha channel for transparency and your shader code doesn't take that into account.

It's always possible that there's a bug with the driver or GPU itself, so sometimes it also helps to compare between different devices or between the device and the emulator. With consistent searching and narrowing down on the problem, the culprit can usually be found and fixed.

Bibliography

[AGH05]   Ken Arnold, James Gosling, and David Holmes. *The Java Programming Language*. Prentice Hall, Englewood Cliffs, NJ, 4th, 2005.

[Blo08]   Joshua Bloch. *Effective Java*. Addison-Wesley, Reading, MA, 2008.

[Bur10]   Ed Burnette. *Hello, Android: Introducing Google's Mobile Development Platform, Third Edition*. The Pragmatic Bookshelf, Raleigh, NC and Dallas, TX, 2010.

[Eck06]   Bruce Eckel. *Thinking in Java*. Prentice Hall, Englewood Cliffs, NJ, Fourth, 2006.

[Zec12]   Mario Zechner. *Beginning Android Games*. Apress, New York City, NY, 2012.

Index

More Android Programming

Learn more about Android as a programmer and a power user.

Google's Android is shaking up the mobile market in a big way. With Android, you can write programs that run on any compatible cell phone or tablet in the world. It's a mobile platform you can't afford not to learn, and this book gets you started. *Hello, Android* has been updated to Android 2.3.3, with revised code throughout to reflect this updated version. That means that the book is now up-to-date for tablets such as the Kindle Fire. All examples were tested for forwards and backwards compatibility on a variety of devices and versions of Android from 1.5 to 4.0. (Note: the Kindle Fire does not support home screen widgets or wallpaper, so those samples couldn't be tested on the Fire.)

Ed Burnette
(280 pages) ISBN: 9781934356562. $34.95
http://pragprog.com/book/eband3

Become an Android power user and get the most out of your Android phone or tablet! You'll find out how to take advantage of this completely open, tinker-friendly platform and personalize your phone or tablet's look and feel—even if you have no programming experience. You'll customize your phone's home screen and apps, and then create a series of tasks that automate your device in unique and interesting ways, from creating your own talking clock to having Android sound an alert when approaching a specific geographic location. It's something that only the open nature of the Android operating system can offer.

Mike Riley
(220 pages) ISBN: 9781937785543. $36
http://pragprog.com/book/mrand

Android Games

You can develop for Android using Lua and Processing in addition to Java. Come see what you're missing.

Develop cross-platform mobile games with Corona using the Lua programming language! Corona is experiencing explosive growth among mobile game developers, and this book gets you up to speed on how to use this versatile platform. You'll use the Corona SDK to simplify game programming and take a fun, no-nonsense approach to write and add must-have gameplay features. You'll find out how to create all the gaming necessities: menus, sprites, movement, perspective and sound effects, levels, loading and saving, and game physics. Along the way, you'll learn about Corona's API functions and build three common kinds of mobile games from scratch that can run on the iPhone, iPad, Kindle Fire, Nook Color, and all other Android smartphones and tablets.

Silvia Domenech
(220 pages) ISBN: 9781937785574. $36
http://pragprog.com/book/sdcorona

Create mobile apps for Android phones and tablets faster and more easily than you ever imagined. Use "Processing," the free, award-winning, graphics-savvy language and development environment, to work with the touchscreens, hardware sensors, cameras, network transceivers, and other devices and software in the latest Android phones and tablets.

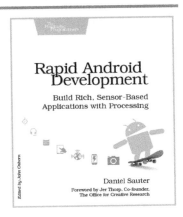

Daniel Sauter
(300 pages) ISBN: 9781937785062. $35
http://pragprog.com/book/dsproc

Welcome to the New Web

You need a better JavaScript and better recipes that professional web developers use every day. Start here.

CoffeeScript is JavaScript done right. It provides all of JavaScript's functionality wrapped in a cleaner, more succinct syntax. In the first book on this exciting new language, CoffeeScript guru Trevor Burnham shows you how to hold onto all the power and flexibility of JavaScript while writing clearer, cleaner, and safer code.

Trevor Burnham
(160 pages) ISBN: 9781934356784. $29
http://pragprog.com/book/tbcoffee

Modern web development takes more than just HTML and CSS with a little JavaScript mixed in. Clients want more responsive sites with faster interfaces that work on multiple devices, and you need the latest tools and techniques to make that happen. This book gives you more than 40 concise, tried-and-true solutions to today's web development problems, and introduces new workflows that will expand your skillset.

Brian P. Hogan, Chris Warren, Mike Weber, Chris Johnson, Aaron Godin
(344 pages) ISBN: 9781934356838. $35
http://pragprog.com/book/wbdev

Seven Databases, Seven Languages

There's so much new to learn with the latest crop of NoSQL databases. And instead of learning a language a year, how about seven?

Data is getting bigger and more complex by the day, and so are your choices in handling it. From traditional RDBMS to newer NoSQL approaches, *Seven Databases in Seven Weeks* takes you on a tour of some of the hottest open source databases today. In the tradition of Bruce A. Tate's *Seven Languages in Seven Weeks*, this book goes beyond a basic tutorial to explore the essential concepts at the core of each technology.

Eric Redmond and Jim Wilson
(330 pages) ISBN: 9781934356920. $35
http://pragprog.com/book/rwdata

You should learn a programming language every year, as recommended by *The Pragmatic Programmer*. But if one per year is good, how about *Seven Languages in Seven Weeks*? In this book you'll get a hands-on tour of Clojure, Haskell, Io, Prolog, Scala, Erlang, and Ruby. Whether or not your favorite language is on that list, you'll broaden your perspective of programming by examining these languages side-by-side. You'll learn something new from each, and best of all, you'll learn how to learn a language quickly.

Bruce A. Tate
(328 pages) ISBN: 9781934356593. $34.95
http://pragprog.com/book/btlang

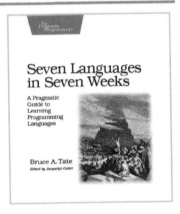

The Pragmatic Bookshelf

The Pragmatic Bookshelf features books written by developers for developers. The titles continue the well-known Pragmatic Programmer style and continue to garner awards and rave reviews. As development gets more and more difficult, the Pragmatic Programmers will be there with more titles and products to help you stay on top of your game.

Visit Us Online

This Book's Home Page
http://pragprog.com/book/kbogla
Source code from this book, errata, and other resources. Come give us feedback, too!

Register for Updates
http://pragprog.com/updates
Be notified when updates and new books become available.

Join the Community
http://pragprog.com/community
Read our weblogs, join our online discussions, participate in our mailing list, interact with our wiki, and benefit from the experience of other Pragmatic Programmers.

New and Noteworthy
http://pragprog.com/news
Check out the latest pragmatic developments, new titles and other offerings.

Save on the eBook

Save on the eBook versions of this title. Owning the paper version of this book entitles you to purchase the electronic versions at a terrific discount.

PDFs are great for carrying around on your laptop—they are hyperlinked, have color, and are fully searchable. Most titles are also available for the iPhone and iPod touch, Amazon Kindle, and other popular e-book readers.

Buy now at *http://pragprog.com/coupon*

Contact Us

Online Orders:	*http://pragprog.com/catalog*
Customer Service:	*support@pragprog.com*
International Rights:	*translations@pragprog.com*
Academic Use:	*academic@pragprog.com*
Write for Us:	*http://pragprog.com/write-for-us*
Or Call:	+1 800-699-7764

CPSIA information can be obtained at www.ICGtesting.com
Printed in the USA
LVOW021733240613

339997LV00003B/10/P

9 781937 785345